More Praise for

Zen Questions

"Taigen Leighton is one of the West's most important Zen scholar-priests and one of our foremost exponents of bringing out into the world the insights we find on the meditation cushion. This book contains some enormously important reflections on the nature of the Zen practice of just sitting, through a close reflection on the great master Dōgen, the Sufi poet Rumi, as well as Bob Dylan, Mary Oliver, and the American Zen original Gary Snyder. Perhaps even more importantly, Leighton offers a number of reflections and pointers for finding our way amid the messiness of life. This is an incredibly valuable book, useful for anyone who wishes to integrate their heart-work with work in the world."
—James Ishmael Ford, author of *Zen Master WHO?*

"Unique and scintillating. I highly recommend this book to anyone who cherishes the illumination of wisdom both ancient and modern."
—Lewis Richmond, author of *Work as a Spiritual Practice*

"This book comes as a welcome reminder that my own questioning is my completeness. I become whole simply by asking: What does it mean to be a human being? Giant thanks for this book that brings me the simplicity of zazen and a sense of deep engagement with the struggle for social and environmental justice—all woven together in Taigen Leighton's big-hearted expression."
—Susan Moon, author of *Not Turning Away*

ZEN QUESTIONS:

Zazen, Dōgen, and the Spirit of Creative Inquiry

by Taigen Dan Leighton

WISDOM PUBLICATIONS • BOSTON

Wisdom Publications
199 Elm Street
Somerville MA 02144 USA
www.wisdompubs.org

Library of Congress Cataloging-in-Publication Data

Leighton, Taigen Daniel
Zen questions : zazen, Dōgen, and the spirit of creative inquiry / by Taigen Dan Leighton.
   p. cm.
Includes bibliographical references.
ISBN 0-86171-645-0 (pbk. : alk. paper)
1. Meditation—Zen Buddhism. 2. Dogen, 1200–1253. I. Title.
BQ9288.L47 2011
294.3'4435—dc23
                         2011022682

ISBN 9780861716456
eBook ISBN 9780861717088

15 14 13 12 11
5 4 3 2 1

Cover design by Phil Pascuzzo. Interior design by Gopa&Ted2. Set in Scala Pro 10/15.

Wisdom Publications' books are printed on acid-free paper and meet the guidelines
for permanence and durability of the Production Guidelines for Book Longevity of the
Council on Library Resources.

Printed in the United States of America.

This book was produced with environmental mindfulness. We have
elected to print this title on 30% PCW recycled paper. As a result,
we have saved the following resources: 22 trees, 8 million BTUs
of energy, 2,180 lbs. of greenhouse gases, 9,832 gallons of water, and 624 lbs. of solid
waste. For more information, please visit our website, www.wisdompubs.org. This paper
is also FSC® certified. For more information, please visit www.fscus.org.

This book is for Naomi

Contents

Preface

Z EN IS ABOUT QUESTIONING. Zen continuously questions. Zen questioning does not necessarily involve finding answers, but it does involve finding a space in which to sustain questioning, being willing to remain present and upright in the middle of questions. To persevere in Zen practice requires faith, but not a fundamentalist, literalist faith that merely believes in some easily digestible dogma or totally relies on some external being to provide answers and tell us how to live. Zen faith is alive, with the willingness and readiness to persist in questioning. Of course at times insights and responses appear, sometimes more frequently as we settle into the open spaciousness of meditation. But if the answers are worthy they allow more questions, or they help foster readiness for the new questions offered by the world, by life, and by our own insights. This book offers questions, and provokes more questions, and hopefully may encourage the willingness to question, thereby supporting more creative, open awareness.

In the title *Zen Questions*, the second word is a verb, at least as much as a noun. Actually, from the Buddhist context all words—and all beings—are verbs, in dynamic activity. But provisionally in our language we need to utilize words as nouns or adjectives, even at the risk of producing deadened objects. Indeed, Zen questions; it questions our world, our experience, and reality itself. I remember the old bumper sticker, which I still see sometimes, "Question Authority." Certainly received authorities, whether cultural, spiritual, or the authority of corporations or governmental institutions, need and deserve to be questioned. This is certainly congenial with the traditional questioning in Zen practice and literature. But in the phrase "Question Authority" I also hear "questioning" as an adjective describing a type of authority. True authority and integrity derive from the willingness to be questioned and to continue the activity of questioning. Much of Zen lore consists of questioning of the venerable old masters by their students. Indeed, questioning creates genuine authority.

The material in this book is based on my articles and Dharma talks from the time span 1994 to 2010. This book also encompasses the scope of my own life-interests and of my Dharma teaching, beginning with the practice of zazen, or Zen meditation. I received my first formal zazen instruction on the Upper West Side of Manhattan when I was twenty-four, from a Japanese Sōtō Zen priest. It immediately felt like home, and I have been enjoying everyday zazen practice since, leading over many years to becoming a Sōtō Zen priest and transmitted Dharma teacher myself. That first evening of instruction, Rev. Kandō Nakajima also spoke about Eihei Dōgen, the thirteenth-century founder of Japanese Sōtō Zen. Dōgen's insightful writings have become instrumental in the introduction of Buddhism to the West and have remained my touchstone along with meditation practice. Their inspiring quality led to my studying Japanese and Chinese and eventually working on collaborative translations of many of Dōgen's profound, provocative, and deeply nourishing writings. This book provides an opportunity to offer some of my own commentaries on writings from Dōgen that I helped translate.

My study of Dōgen's writings reflects my general appreciation of literary and other creative expression. I see such expression as the natural extension of meditative awareness. This book includes, sporadically throughout and focused in one of its sections, commentary on some of the varied writers who inspire me. Especially I mention the singer-songwriter Bob Dylan, whose songs through his long career I confess to rather uncritically valuing and whose wisdom has often been a helpful guide.

In addition to practicing Zen Buddhism and Dōgen study, I have intermittently engaged in social activism, stretching back to organizing against the Vietnam War in high school and now with concerns for our environment. My interest in social justice and peace has always seemed to me deeply in accord with, and a responsibility arising from, Buddhist studies and bodhisattva practice and their implications for compassionate response to our suffering world. The last section of this book offers Buddhist-influenced perspectives on several current world issues.

The chapters in the first of the five sections of this book, "The World of Zazen," deal with the essential physical practice of zazen. Although this term is commonly translated, as I do herein, as "meditation," or literally "sitting meditation," zazen is not a meditation program with a process of stages of development or accomplishment. Rather, zazen is the physical realm for enacting and expressing the fundamental insight and kindness of buddha nature, the omnipresent capacity for awakened awareness. Zazen is the posture and attitude in which we actually meet the totality of our true life. As expressed above, and developed in the first chapter, Zen is a practice of questioning, an attitude of sustained inquiry. This practice and the awareness it involves does lead to transformation in various ways, even if these never match the outcomes we might seek. Zazen is also a ritual act performed in the religious context of the bodhisattva path, concerned with realizing interconnectedness and supporting the communal aim of reciprocal awakening. Zazen is thus a kind of performance art, a mode of expression that supports and mutually informs all of the other particular creative activities in our lives and offers us an entryway into true repose and joy.

I am extremely grateful that I have had the opportunity to work on many translations from the brilliant founder of Japanese Sōtō Zen, Eihei Dōgen (1200–1253). In the second and third sections of this book I offer commentaries on Dōgen and some of his works, although he is also mentioned at times in the other sections. Commencing with my "Reflections on Translating Dōgen," the second section includes comments on a few specific essays from one of Dōgen's two masterworks, Shōbōgenzō (The True Dharma Eye Treasury), composed in its longest form of ninety-five essays expansively and poetically elaborating on Zen themes, images, and koans. I discuss Dōgen's view of enlightenment and delusion in his celebrated essay "Genjōkōan." Then I discuss works I have translated, including Dōgen's account of the awesome work of active buddhas and the awakened expression of dream as our life. Lastly I consider startling aspects of Dōgen's writing on monastic practice and standards, curiously relevant to contemporary Zen lay practice.

In the third section I discuss six specific selections from the other major work by Dōgen, *Eihei Kōroku*, which I translated with Shohaku Okumura as *Dōgen's Extensive Record*. This massive work includes a number of elements, but its bulk is the usually short formal talks, or Dharma hall discourses, mostly from the second of his two decades of teaching, after he had departed the Japanese capital of Kyoto for the remote mountains near the north coast. Although brief and formal, these talks are paradoxically more revealing of Dōgen's own personality, sense of humor, and his training of the monk successors who went on in the next few generations to widely spread Dōgen's tradition in the countryside, such that Sōtō Zen became the second largest branch of Japanese Buddhism. Most Zen teaching, including almost all of Dōgen's writing, is occasional, not presented as timeless principles, but addressed to particular people at specific times and places, and this is especially evident in *Eihei Kōroku*. My commentaries herein also are edited from talks given to specific audiences. Many of Dōgen's talks and several of the six I discuss herein consist of his commentaries on the traditional koan literature. Dōgen achieved extraordinary mastery of this koan material, and he was instrumental in introducing this literature to Japan. He also developed his own mode of teaching with koans, which are often associated in modern times exclusively with the contrasting Rinzai approach to koans. These talks from *Eihei Kōroku* further illuminate the dynamics of Zen training and the unfolding of its expression.

The fourth section, "Zen Expressions," honors the creativity of Zen awareness and practice, and the fact that most Zen teaching is not discursive but rather poetic and imaginative. In China, Chan (pronounced *Zen* in Japanese) developed through the influence of Chinese and Daoist culture to convey Buddhist teaching using nature images and poetry as a primary mode, along with the colloquial dialogues used as koans. Zen employs imagery, metaphor, and the arts to intimately convey awakening teaching, beyond the conventional logic and rational, philosophical discourse used by many spiritual traditions, including much of Buddhism. This section consists of discussions of writings that express Zen reality from several of my favorite poets, the first three not at all formally "Buddhist." I start with the thirteenth-century Sufi poet Rumi, who addresses fundamental Zen questioning, providing useful perspective and language about the complexities of love. I discuss from the lens of Zen Mind the sublime song "Visions of Johanna" by the brilliant American Dharma bard, Bob Dylan. Nature poet Mary Oliver addresses many contexts of Zen questioning in her works, including what Buddha really wished for us. Finally, American Zen pioneer Gary Snyder in his *Practice of the Wild* has presented an illuminating image for practice through the dynamics of wilderness, including our environment, our language, and our minds.

In the final, fifth section of this book, "American Zen Engagement," I shift to reflect on the relevance of Zen awareness and practical engagement to contemporary societal concerns. Zen is a living tradition, enacted as appropriate here and now. Zen is firmly rooted in the way of the bodhisattvas, the awakening beings dedicated to relieving suffering and to universal liberation. Bodhisattva practice reveals that awakening can never be a private, self-centered matter, as in reality all beings are intricately interconnected. If Buddhism were only about finding personal inner peace it would not have survived for twenty-five hundred years, and it would not deserve to survive today in the West.

Zen Buddhist values apply in three realms: First, bringing awareness to the complexity and suffering of this body and mind on our own seat. Second, when we return from formal practice to everyday activities, we express our meditative awareness and caring with friends, family, and coworkers, all the many beings we personally encounter. And third, we explore how to express buddha heart to respond to the challenges and troubles of our society and culture. The fifth section of this book includes consideration of the mutually supportive relationship of the American democratic ideal of freedom with Buddhist universal liberation, referencing the many enduring insights and problematic career of Thomas Jefferson. Also considered are the deep conflict between consumerism and Zen, and Buddhist teachings about temporality and environmental awareness that may be informative to contemporary problems of climate damage and energy systems. Finally, I consider the importance of the ancient Buddhist teaching of right livelihood to our current societal challenges.

From this summary of the five sections of this book, it is apparent that I discuss a diverse range of topics herein. Furthermore, these essays are collected and edited from an assortment of contexts and to some extent still express a variety of my voices as well as interests. I thereby welcome the reader to dive in to this collection anywhere and skip to any essay that may spark your interest, rather than feeling obliged to read the whole in sequence.

I have attempted to maintain consistency of capitalization and in diacriticals for Sanskrit and Japanese terms throughout this work, including changing these when they vary in quoted texts. *Dharma* is generally capitalized when referring to truth or the teaching of buddhas, but lowercase *dharmas* is used when referring to the elements of reality, as in the Abhidharma system. *Buddha* is capitalized when referring to Śākyamuni or other specific buddhas but generally lowercase when referring to "the many buddhas" or to "the principle of awakening as buddha."

ACKNOWLEDGMENTS

The essays herein are based on, then revised and expanded from, selected published articles and transcriptions of my Dharma talks ranging from 1994 to 2010. From 1994 until I moved to Chicago in the beginning of 2007, I taught at the Mountain Source Sangha in the San Francisco Bay Area, which included small groups in San Rafael, San Francisco, and at Bolinas, where I gave Dharma talks at monthly sittings, a couple of which are adapted for chapters in this book. During this period I also gave periodic Sunday morning Dharma talks at Green Gulch Farm Zen Center near

Muir Beach in Marin County, part of the San Francisco Zen Center where I received most of my Zen training. Four chapters based on these Green Gulch talks are included here. The Bolinas and Green Gulch talks were all transcribed by Liz Tuomi of Bolinas. I am very grateful to Liz not only for these transcriptions, but for all her help with Mountain Source Sangha.

I started teaching at Ancient Dragon Zen Gate in Chicago in 2004, although I also was guest teacher at many Dharma centers around the United States throughout the period until I relocated to Chicago in January 2007. Ten of the chapters of this book are based on Dharma talks given at Ancient Dragon. I am very grateful to Jennifer Obst for transcribing all of these and the talk on the "Awesome Presence of Active Buddhas" given at the Clouds in Water Zen group in St. Paul Minnesota, in 2007. The latter chapter also includes some material from a talk given at Udumbara Sangha in Evanston, Illinois, in 2004, also kindly transcribed by Liz Tuomi. Thanks also to Jack Cram of Clouds in Water for transcribing my talk on "Genjōkōan" given there in 2006. The sources for each chapter are itemized at the end of the book.

I am very grateful to all the sangha members from both Mountain Source Sangha in the Bay Area and Ancient Dragon Zen Gate in Chicago, who participated in these Dharma talks as active listeners. Thanks also to Kevin Iverson, the website manager at Ancient Dragon Zen Gate, who has made the original versions of these materials available on the Ancient Dragon website. Thanks to Alan Senauke for helpful suggestions after reading an early version. I thank also all the people at Wisdom Publications who have made this book available, and especially Josh Bartok for his great assistance in focusing and clarifying this material.

Thanks to the many teachers in America and some in Japan who have helped inform my sense of how to convey this delightful Zen practice and teaching. Especially I thank my ordination and Dharma transmission teacher, Tenshin Reb Anderson, Senior Dharma Teacher and former Abbot of the San Francisco Zen Center, for his tireless patience and kindness.

PART 1

The World of Zazen

Zazen as Inquiry

THE PRACTICE OF GENTLE ATTENTION

IN THE SŌTŌ ZEN TRADITION, and in the style of the Suzuki Roshi lineage in which I trained, meditation is pretty gentle, settling in, just sitting. We try to find a way of practice that is sustainable if not necessarily comfortable, at least a restful and compassionate space in which to sit. In our practice we emphasize some sense of connecting with this space of zazen every day. Our zazen is just gentle upright sitting, not an athletic, competitive event, as if whomever could sit in the most difficult position for the longest without moving was the most enlightened. But at the same time, gentle, steady sitting should not be dull and listless. Despite the emphasis on not acquiring anything, this is not just idly passing time. Zazen is a question, an inquiry. Even when sitting quietly, gently, at the core of our sitting is the activity of questioning.

What are we doing in zazen? Each of us have some question that somewhere back there was behind our wanting to engage in this Buddhist meditation. What question has led you to face the wall in zazen, what is this? There is a question that we each have to explore.

The point of this practice of questioning, however, is not to discover an answer. We sit upright, centered, with ease and restfulness. And yet there is some problem, some question, something we are looking into. How do we practice with question? There is not just one way to do this, because we each have our own version of this question. But we must recognize that there is a question. How do we live this life? How do we take care of this world, face the problems that we each have in our life, the problems that we share together?

This practice of sitting involves facing the questions, learning about questioning, deepening our question, and allowing questions to arise.

THE QUESTION IN YOUR NERVES

Such questioning is clarified in Bob Dylan's line "A question in your nerves is lit, Yet you know there is no answer fit, To satisfy, insure you not to quit, To keep it in your mind and not forget, That it is not he or she or them or it, That you belong to."[1] The first part, "A question in your nerves is lit," is just the fact that you are present, willing to engage in facing yourself in upright sitting. There is a question beyond your conscious questions. There is a question in your nerves, in your bones, in your marrow. But we do not need to be agitated and upset about getting the answer to that question. The point is to stay present with such questioning. Dylan says, "You know there is no answer fit." The answer may not be so important. Be willing to live upright and present in this body and mind, just as yourself, not trying to become somebody else, in this world and life with all its problems, willing to face that question. Insights that may arise are part of the questioning process. But you need not receive some answer that you can write down and put on the wall so that all is settled. We learn to connect with this place of facing the questions in our nerves, lit on fire. It may not satisfy you, but you can keep the question in your mind, rather than some answer, and not forget. Practice is a way of relating and dancing with this questioning.

One expression of this questioning in the Zen tradition is koan study. In Zen this is the formal practice of working with a particular traditional story or saying. How do you stay present with these questions? Concerning these traditional stories or dialogues, the Japanese Sōtō Zen founder, Eihei Dōgen, often says, "Do you completely understand this? Please study this completely. Please thoroughly penetrate this question."

THREE THOUSAND WORLDS AMID EVERYDAY LIFE

We also have questions that arise in our own hearts, in our own body and mind, occurring via family, relationships, and the people around us. Dōgen calls the questions that arise from our own struggle to find our center, from our own problems with being this person, *genjōkōan*, the koan as it manifests in our life. What is this appearing in front of me? As we sit in meditation, thoughts, feelings, our whole world appears before us, not just the wall or the floor. Being present, upright and gently aware in a settled posture, we can look at: What is this that thus comes? How is it that this, just this, is here in front of me? What is it? How do I engage it? The point is just staying present in relationship to that question or to the further questions that come up from it. Our way of responding and actually working with these questions is not about an answer. Yet something may arise, not based on our limited human consciousness. This arises from a deeper place that we connect with when we are sitting upright, willing to settle into this space and find our own way of sustaining this space. We can face our life in a way that is deeper than our limited human ideas about who we are and what the world is.

One traditional Buddhist teaching from the Japanese Tendai school is that in each moment or in each thought are three thousand worlds. The Zen approach to questioning involves these three thousand worlds in each thought. Every thought we have, if we tried to track it, is connected to so many aspects of our life, including things that we do not even know are in our life, that truly, in each moment of thought are three thousand worlds. Of course, three thousand may mean three hundred thousand or three hundred million.

COMPLETE CHILD-LIKE QUESTIONING

Each of those three thousand worlds is a question. How can we face and include three thousand worlds? One useful teaching about questions appears in a poem by Wallace Stevens called "Questions are Remarks."

In the weed of summer comes this green sprout why.
The sun aches and ails and then returns halloo
Upon the horizon amid adult enfintillages.

Its fire fails to pierce the vision that beholds it,
Fails to destroy the antique acceptances,
Except that the grandson sees it as it is,

Peter the voyant, who says, "Mother what is that"—
The object that rises with so much rhetoric,
But not for him. His question is complete.

It is the question of what he is capable
It is the extreme, the expert aetat. 2.
    [expert at being about age two]
He will never ride the red horse she describes.

His question is complete because it contains
His utmost statement. It is his own array,
His own pageant and procession and display,

As far as nothingness permits…Hear him.
He does not say, "Mother, my mother, who are you,"
The way the drowsy, infant, old men do.[2]

Stevens illustrates how questions can be statements, or remarks. In the weed of summer, in the middle of our life, "comes this green sprout why" voiced by a child. Questions arise, moment by moment. The grandson sees the returning sun as it is. This spirit of questioning that is our zazen is like the questioning of a two-year-old, or a four- or six-year-old sometimes. Such elemental questioning comes from a place deeper than our ideas of who we are. It is just "this green sprout why." Sitting moment after moment we do not necessarily articulate this questioning at the core of our sitting. In the middle of our sitting are spaces where there may not be so many thoughts, just calm settling. We need that space to sustain questioning. But even in the middle of the absence of questioning there is this question in our nerves that's lit.

Sometimes the world brings the questioning to us very intently. Someone gets sick. You lose a loved one, or your house burns down. War is declared, or breaks out undeclared. And yet there is this basic question, even before the sun arises, just "this green sprout why."

About his grandson, who sees the sun and says, "Mother what is that?" Wallace Stevens says, "His question is complete." We do not need an answer to our question. To be present in the middle of question is itself complete. What brings me back to zazen every day is this possibility of the taste of wholeness. It is actually all right for things to be the way they are. And yet that sense of completeness, of wholeness, of it being okay to be this person in this world, has to do with this complete question, this "green sprout why."

Wallace Stevens goes on, "It is the question of what he is capable." The child's question is complete because it contains his utmost statement. In Zen koan work a statement may be a question, and a question can be a statement. The phrases in the old Zen stories are sometimes utterances expressing this complete questioning as utmost statements. Stevens says about his grandson, "it is his own array, his own pageant and procession and display." Zazen can be an expression, a performance art. That too is a questioning. How do we express our question, the question in our life, in our world, through our zazen? That does not just refer to sitting, finding your inner balance as you wait for the bell to ring. This space of upright questioning permeates and performs in the rest of our life. "It is his own array, his own pageant and procession and display, as far as nothingness permits . . . Hear him."

IMAGINATION QUESTIONS

Near the end of "A Vision of the Last Judgment," William Blake champions creative imagination, asking whether the sun is merely "a round disk of fire" in the sky, like a golden coin. Instead he proclaims the radiant sun a wondrous event, complete with a "Heavenly host crying 'Holy, Holy, Holy'" in celebration.[3] Blake encourages us to fully engage our imagination in questioning of reality. Blake calls forth the visionary exalted sun as miraculous. All of life comes from the sun. And yet if you tried to stand on the sun, you would burn up. The call to imagination is part of Zen's Mahāyāna legacy as well with the envisioning of bodhisattvas, awakening beings. Creative vision, sometimes childlike, enhances our ability to explore and question the reality around us.

Settling in to the dynamic quality of zazen as question and inquiry requires willingness to be present for this question. Each question is three thousand questions, and a good question provides more questions. Answers do come sometimes, but they bring more questions as well. Can we live in the middle of impermanence and uncertainty? Can we live in the middle of a life that is a question? As we build our life and try to stabilize and care for our situation, we do our best to make it all work. But still, we do not know what will happen. Everything could disappear in a flash. This question is complete. It is our own array. And it must be all right to live in a life of impermanence, because that is where we are, and abide.

HOW CAN YOU BECOME A BUDDHA?

Dōgen's comments on an old Zen story help clarify the realm of questioning in zazen. The story concerns two old Chinese teachers, Mazu Daoyi (709–788; Jpn.: Baso Dōitsu) and his teacher Nanyue Huairang (677–744; Jpn.: Nangaku Ejō). Mazu was a great Zen teacher who later had 139 enlightened disciples according to some accounts. But this story occurred when he was a young monk. Mazu was sitting zazen and his teacher Nanyue asked, "What are you trying to do sitting in meditation?" Mazu replied, "I'm trying to become a buddha." Hearing that, Nanyue picked up a tile, sat down, and started polishing it. Finally Mazu noticed him and asked, "Teacher, what are you doing?" Nanyue said, "I'm polishing this tile to make it into a mirror." When Mazu perplexedly asked, "How could you make a mirror from polishing a tile?" Nanyue responded, "How can you make a buddha from sitting zazen?"[4]

Alan Watts told this story as an excuse for not needing to engage in sitting meditation. But Dōgen gives it a different spin. He says, yes, you should polish a tile to make a mirror. And you should meditate aiming to become Buddha, even though in his early writing, "Fukanzazengi" (Universal Recommendations for Zazen), Dōgen says, "Have no designs on becoming buddha."[5]

Dōgen in his comment on polishing a tile is concerned with the basic question, "What is buddha?" This question implies: How do I live this life? How can I be aware? How can I be wise, compassionate, and kind? How can I get beyond all of my human pettiness and greed, anger, and delusion? This question arises somewhere amid the three thousand questions in each thought moment.

Dōgen's commentary to the beginning of the story has to do with this fundamental questioning in zazen. In response to Nanyue asking Mazu what he was aiming or figuring to do in zazen, Dōgen says, "We should quietly ponder and penetrate this question." What are we up to in zazen? Is there an aim beyond the framework of zazen itself that has not yet been accomplished? Another possibility would be to not aim at anything at all. That might be the way to be buddha. These are each real questions. Dōgen offers a whole series of them. Then he says, "Just in the moment of sitting zazen, what kind of aim, intention, or design is being actualized? We should diligently inquire, in detail." This sitting is questioning, closely investigating. This questioning may include our usual mode of figuring something out. But it goes deeper. This question pulses within your nerves, not about mere answers.

THE CARVED DRAGON'S QUESTION

Dōgen adds, "Do not get stuck in loving a carved dragon. We should go forward and love the real dragon." This refers to a story recorded in Han dynasty China (roughly 200 B.C.E. to 200 C.E.) about a man who loved carvings and paintings of dragons, whose whole house was filled with images of dragons. One time a dragon was flying overhead, and he heard about this man who really liked dragons. He thought, "I will go and visit him, he'll be very happy." So the dragon flew down and stuck his head in the window. But the man screamed in terror. Dōgen suggests not getting stuck in loving carved dragons but loving the real dragon. When you sit in the middle of question, you never know what is going to come up and stick its head in your window. This is another way of discussing this buddha toward which Dōgen recommends we aim.

Dōgen says, "You should study that both the carved dragon and the real dragon have the power of forming clouds and rain." Even the carved dragon has great power. Some people actually imagine that their practice is not real but just a picture of zazen. But even that carved dragon has tremendous power. Dōgen says, "Neither value the remote nor disparage what is remote. Be accustomed and intimate with the remote. Neither disparage what is close, nor value the close. Be accustomed and intimate with the close." Whether it seems far away or close, whatever our idea of buddha is, examine it. Be intimate with its closeness and its remoteness. Dōgen says, "Do not take the eyes lightly nor attach too much weight to the eyes. Do not put too much weight to the ear nor take the ears too lightly. [Keep] the ears and eyes sharp and clear." Thus we sit with eyes open, gazing at the wall or the floor. We sit with ears open, willing to hear the sounds of the suffering of the world, of the people wandering by outside, and of our own questioning and uncertainty.

BUDDHA'S AIM

In response to his teacher's question, "What are you aiming at when you sit zazen?" Mazu said, "I'm aiming at becoming buddha." Dōgen questions that statement:

> We should clarify and penetrate these words. What does becoming buddha mean? Does becoming buddha mean that we are enabled to become buddha by Buddha? Does becoming buddha mean that we make Buddha into a buddha? Does becoming buddha mean the manifestation of one face or two faces of buddha?

Is aiming at becoming buddha dropping off body and mind? Or
is it aiming at becoming buddha dropped off?

One could spend a lifetime on each of these questions. All three thousand questions are there in your sitting, somewhere in the question you have about your own life.

Dōgen says, "Aiming at becoming buddha, does he mean that even though there are ten thousand methods (or Dharma gates) to becoming buddha, becoming buddha continues to be entangled with this aiming?" Even though there are ten thousand ways in which each of us is this "green sprout why," or this green sprout buddha, it continues to be entangled with our aiming and designing. Where are we going to sit in relationship to the question? How are we going to be present in the middle of just looking at "what is this?" How am I going to respond to this particular situation? When we are willing to be here, completely, we sit in wholeness and wonder, "What am I up to?" We cannot avoid those three thousand worlds and this "green sprout why." And yet, going back to Wallace Stevens, the question is complete because it contains our utmost statement. It is our own array, our own pageant, and procession, and display.

THE FAITH OF THE COLORADO RIVER

Zen questioning is a very gentle questioning. It is the kind of questioning that the Colorado River asks the Grand Canyon over centuries and centuries. It is gentle but persistent. Can we stop all the wars our country wages? That is one question, but there are so many other questions behind that. How do we live together with peace and justice? How do we take care of the world of our own family and relations and workplace, as well as our nation, with peace and justice? How do we sit zazen with peace and justice for our own body and mind? All of those questions are present in each of them. There is not one right answer for all of us. It is not even about getting answers, but it does concern how we express the question. My way of expressing it and yours and others' are all going to be different, and they may change tomorrow. But if we are present in the middle of this question, then we can proceed. And if we are afraid, that is all right; that is just another question.

Speaking of questions, the element of faith arises. One description of faith involves letting go of our resistance to receiving. Facing the question, we also face our own resistance to that question. Our practice is not necessarily the removal of the resistance, but first just recognizing resistance. Indeed, questioning is faith. There is no faith without questioning. Faith that is allergic to questioning is just fundamentalist blind dogma. But faith-questioning is how we sit upright. This is not necessarily about releasing the reluctance or resistance but about being right there in the middle of the reluctance. Our reluctance is this question about whether I can be here, in the middle of question. Can I be willing to be the question I am? Can I really let that green sprout come forth? Faith to doubt or question means being willing to be a question ourselves. Sometimes the people who are most weird or odd, who are walking questions, may be the most inspiring. Those people allow us the opportunity to see our own reluctance to question, so they can inspire faith.

Facing our reluctance is the practice of upright questioning. We aim to be the question we are.

Zazen Mind and Transformative Function

BREATHING OUR POSTURE

ZAZEN MIND and its transformative function depend on posture and breathing. For zazen we emphasize upright posture, as this posture becomes a way in which we learn an attitude that goes beyond the formal meditation hall practice. Thus we find our deep inner balance, not leaning left or right, not leaning forward or holding back. We try to find the center, a dynamic place that always is shifting. To find uprightness that is relaxed and not tense is subtle; it takes a while to find our seat in this practice.

Breathing is always happening, but attention to this inhalation, then this exhalation, is a way of knitting together the whole of our zazen awareness. When we inhale we are actually breathing with our whole body, oxygen goes through all of our arteries, throughout the body. Feeling breath as part of our posture and being aware of breath is very helpful, not just in the formal zazen itself, but also as the awareness of zazen becomes part of our everyday activity. Breath provides excellent guidance to "re-mind" our zazen mind and body.

The practice is available to us always, and we can do it anywhere anytime—yet many people try to sit on their own and find it difficult. Practically speaking, to have a sangha place where we experience and join others in zazen helps, and also to have a Dharma context where we are exposed to this teaching tradition may be necessary as a container in which to actually take on the practice.

PRACTICE WITH THE SIXTH AND EIGHTH CONSCIOUSNESS

Mind in zazen and how it functions is a huge topic. Indian Buddhism and the Zen tradition in China and Japan include many teachings about mind. One Indian Buddhist teaching about mind, particularly helpful in practice, concerns the "six consciousnesses." Our usual idea about our mind and thought processes is fairly limited, but the zazen experience opens up different aspects of mind. The Heart Sutra refers to these six consciousnesses. First is eye consciousness, very important to human beings, as we are very visually oriented. When there is an eye object, a shape or a color, and an eye organ, the capacity to see, then visual awareness arises. This is part of our consciousness as we sit facing the wall, even as not so much is apparently happening.

Visual awareness is one aspect of consciousness, along with sound consciousness, which is recommended as a helpful meditation object. We can settle in meditation hearing the traffic and other sounds around us. We also experience nose or smell consciousness, and tongue or taste consciousness, and physical consciousness. The tactile is very important in zazen, in which we feel our body in a new way, feeling the pressure of the cushion on our bottom, feeling the tension in our knees or our back or our shoulders, feeling the effort of holding our hands in the cosmic mudra, and feeling breath as part of our posture. Physical consciousness is subtle.

But the sixth consciousness is foreign to our usual ideas about mind. The sixth is mind consciousness. Thoughts happen as we sit, they pass by, and we can be aware of these thoughts as sense scenery just as for sounds, colors, or a shape on a wall. We are used to thinking that we can control our thoughts. One of the first things we realize in zazen is that many thoughts arise, the tapes are rolling, and that this aspect of consciousness is not under our control. We can notice that we have been thinking about something and not aware of our breath or posture. The twentieth-century Japanese Sōtō master Uchiyama Roshi said that as we sit, our stomach continues to secrete digestive juices, and in the same way, our brain continues to secrete thoughts.[6] In this approach to thought and consciousness we need not identify with those thoughts. Our usual practice instruction is to just let thoughts arise, not trying to push them away, but not doing anything with them either. Thoughts arise and we let them go, just as we let the sound of vehicles pass by. But of course, thoughts are more complicated, because our consciousness is deeply patterned based on certain kinds of thoughts and ways of thinking. The Indian Yogācāra Buddhist system, a branch of Indian bodhisattva philosophy, describes in detail how we get caught in this sixth consciousness.[7]

The point of talking about this in the context of zazen practice is to provide a framework for just sitting, for being present with thoughts, allowing thoughts to come, and go, not doing anything with them while at the same time seeing when you are caught up in some thought—and again letting thoughts go, and appear again.

Thoughts returning persistently may sometimes relate to the Yogācāra eighth consciousness. But first, the seventh consciousness in Yogācāra teaching is the faculty of separating ourselves from our experience. Humans naturally believe that there is some subject smelling or tasting or feeling or thinking. We think there exists some self and some other "out there." This is the fundamental problem, that we separate ourselves from others and the world, the wall, and our own breathing. This is what humans do, and we need to be aware and know that we each are not the only one doing so. Human beings get caught in a strange form of alienation from our world.

The consciousness that we usually think of is about discrimination, making distinctions. We discern and separate this from that. Buddhist practice is not about getting rid of such consciousness but about seeing through our discriminations and not being caught by them. Getting rid of thinking is not the point; the point is settling into a deeper awareness that may include but is not limited by discriminations. The Yogācāra teaching describes an eighth consciousness where patterns of thinking are stored, both positive and negative. We have the capacity to support the positive, and yet all our thought patterns are stored in the eighth consciousness. Our own experience, what happens during the day, and all thought objects that occur appear out of this storehouse from many lifetimes of conscious-ness. Even without taking literally the notion of many lifetimes, we can still see this metaphoric storehouse simply as the thoughts created and accumulated from our years of living. All these many thoughts are con-nected to other thoughts. As we sit, naturally these thoughts arise. As we become intimate with these thought patterns, and aware of their positive and negative effects, we may be able to increasingly disengage from nega-tive patterns and support helpful tendencies.

THE BACKGROUND BEYOND THINKING

An old story from the Zen tradition about mind in zazen is perhaps a little simpler than the Yogācāra system. The Zen master Yaoshan Weiyan (745–828; Jpn.: Yakusan Igen) was sitting very upright and still and a stu-dent asked him, "What are you thinking of, sitting there so steadfastly?" Yaoshan said, "I am thinking of not thinking," or another way of translat-ing it is, "I am thinking of that which does not think."

This student was very good, and so we remember this dialogue. He said, "How do you do that? How do you think of not thinking?" Or maybe, "How is thinking of that which does not think?" Yaoshan responded using a different negative. He said, "Beyond thinking." It has also been translated as "Nonthinking."[8]

This concerns foreground and background. We are used to thinking about the thoughts that are floating around in our sixth consciousness. We have been trained as human beings to have an ego; this is not only a problem in our culture, and it is not necessarily a bad thing. We need to be able to get through the day, pay the rent, take care of our lives. Buddhist practice is not about getting rid of the ego, it is about not getting caught by it and instead seeing this background that Yaoshan refers to as "beyond thinking."

In terms of foreground and background, we do not exactly shift from the foreground to the background; it is more a kind of access between them, a link created. The background maybe can only be expressed in the fore-ground, but we begin to find more access to the background, or perhaps it has more access to us. Foreground and background have many layers, but a connection with this deeper awareness becomes available. When we intellectualize about the background and make up stories about it, that only becomes more of the foreground. But this background can emerge in each fresh breath.

Zazen offers this actual experience of a deeper awareness. It cannot exactly be called thinking, but it is a kind of awareness, a kind of consciousness. We could call it "beyond thinking," thinking that goes beyond our usual thinking, thinking of the beyond, or thinking that is beyond any thinking that does not go beyond. It is a kind of thinking, but not thinking that cuts things up into little pieces. This awareness puts things together into wholeness and allows a deeper wholeness to emerge.

A guest shows up from beyond creation, or maybe from deep within creation. We do not know from where. One of the usual ways of minding mind is figuring out mind, and we have difficulty not trying to do that. But the background awareness is about just being with, and allowing something to emerge, from our belly, or from between our shoulders, or from the end of an exhalation, or from somewhere we do not know. We become open to the unknown, and we need not fear that. We start to develop a very intimate and deep relationship with something we all share but with which each of us has our own particular relationship.

Very naturally as we sit in zazen, thoughts, sounds, and sensations are present, all of the first six consciousnesses. Some versions of the Yogācāra suggest seeing clearly how the eighth consciousness is guiding the six consciousnesses. But our practice is just to watch the whole thing, to be present and aware from this deeper place that allows the thinking but is not caught by it. Sometimes this is called Mind with a capital M, but calling it anything is part of sixth consciousness, part of discriminating consciousness. Call it anything you want; if you want a name, "beyond thinking" works. The point is to settle into the experience of just being present on our cushion, allowing ourselves to be here, studying how it is that we are present with the details of our physical posture, and really enjoying and engaging how it is to inhale and exhale.

CREATIVE TRANSFORMATION BEYOND WORDS

Allowing these sensations to be present, in ways that we may not even recognize, we start to connect with this experience of a deeper awareness, the background of all the sensations. You may wonder what the point of this might be. Again, this is not about getting rid of the first six consciousnesses, nor losing your faculty for discriminative thinking. Zazen's transformational function needs to be expressed through the bodhisattva precepts and values, and thus we need to use our abilities to taste and smell and sense in all kinds of ways, as well as to discriminate and discern. But words do not get to it, because words take things apart. It is difficult to talk about—and yet even people who recently began zazen practice each have experienced this. You may not be able to say anything about it or recognize it. But somehow, being present and accepting this deeper background awareness not caught by conventional thinking provides a great resource, opening to wider possibilities.

Zazen is a form of creative expression that fosters creative energy. Zazen is a mode of creative expression because it allows this "beyond thinking" to inform our everyday activities. New possibilities can appear, right in the lamentations of the particular life you are living, with your work, your family, and your friends, right in the specific context of the world we create together. As we are willing to settle into a regular practice of zazen, we develop a capacity to allow our lives to be informed by this beyond thinking, this deeper awareness. Again, this is not trying to achieve something called "beyond thinking." Yaoshan said, "I think of not thinking." He did not say, "I don't think."

This awareness itself *is* transformative. It is not that through zazen eventually there will be some transformation. That would be our habitual, acquisitive way of thinking, which arises because of how we have been conditioned by culture and language and family dynamics. Habitual patterns lead to thinking that if you do zazen now, then eventually, later on, you will achieve this transformation. But actually, the transformative function is happening in each moment of awareness.

How does this transformation develop? Zazen includes the craft of letting go. This practice of letting go opens up a deeper kind of awareness, and unfolds through our practice and experience. Sometimes it opens up suddenly and dramatically, and sometimes not. This transformative function does not operate according to some program or formula about awareness or transformative function. It appears in each breath, in each moment of awareness, right in this present awareness.

Yet even this amount of talking about the transformative function is a little excessive. The transformative function is already present in your zazen before you hear about it. Awareness itself does the buddha work. This is not only awareness of thinking but your awareness of hearing, your openness to seeing the wall in front of you, whether the wall is white plaster or red brick, or even if you imagine the world beyond that wall. As you sit, what is this?

This awareness requires you just to show up and be present. And then to continue to show up and be present, with each inhalation, with each exhalation, to pay attention. This is not some particular kind of attention, like a military yell, "Attention!" That might help, at times, to salute the buddha nature in your zazen, but what is most effective is steady, gentle, persistent, generous attention to what is happening, in yet another period of sitting upright on your cushion, with eyes, ears, nose, body open. This transformative function works over time, but also within each breath there is a kind of opening of capacity, or increased tolerance, both in body and mind, for the manifestation of this body right now.

ZAZEN AND COMFORT

As for discomfort in zazen, trying to just sit through excruciating pain is not necessary or helpful. However, it is vital to sometimes go beyond your idea of your comfort zone in zazen, to be willing to feel a little discomfort in your knee, or your shoulder, or lower back, or in your heart. Pay attention and bring your awareness to your body; awareness is not just mental but happens physically as well as in your mind. Bringing awareness to the details of your posture, there is an opening or capacity, a letting go of some idea of how your body should be, and a willingness to tolerate some further level of discomfort. This is exactly the transformative function in your body. This is a yogic practice to become more flexible physically as well as mentally.

In your mind as well, thoughts come and go, the brain continues to secrete thoughts, as we settle and breathe and bring awareness to our thoughts, without trying to crush or control them. Without needing to jump in and float down the stream of thought, whenever we do, just return and sit by the side of the stream, and pay attention. This awareness applied to the mind, and its thought stream, also develops capacity or tolerance. We are able to tolerate a greater level of confusion, a wider capacity to be present in the background awareness along with the various thoughts. We might have thoughts that we do not like, or we may notice patterns of thinking that are uncomfortable, or for which we feel ashamed or berate or blame ourselves. With this awareness and transformative function we can simply be present and accept this aspect of being human. We may develop a steadiness, a greater tolerance and openness to how it is to be this body and this mind. Of course they are not separate, although we strangely think of them as separate.

Awareness is transformative in developing openness, readiness, and willingness to be present and show up in our physical and mental sensations, to just sit with what is happening and notice all these thoughts, not trying to push away or manipulate them. Each moment with each breath includes this openness, capacity, and tolerance. Period after period of sitting, we continue to develop the craft of showing up and paying attention to our life, we start to have a steadiness and a confidence in the practice itself, that the buddhas are supporting us, that the grasses and trees and tiles and walls are supporting us, and vice versa. We are connected to each other and to many beings in the world, to all people we have sat with together and to all the people we may have been present with in other ways, and to all the people who allow and support us in many ways to show up this day. Each moment allows this creative energy, this life force, this dynamic possibility that is part of our awareness when we pay attention.

EXTENDING THE CRAFT OF ZAZEN

Awareness is transformative and this transformative quality also supports our awareness. Zazen is a mode of creative expression. How we conduct ourselves in the meditation hall is our way of expressing buddha mudra, a buddha's posture, on our cushions. This practice helps find the creative energy in our whole life.

Appreciate your creative activities as you move around during your busy life in the world. You may be a musician, gardener, or parent, or perform obviously creative work with some product, like music, pictures, or poetry, but all kinds of activities can be creative. Notice your life interests, whatever they are. You might like reading mystery stories, or going for walks, or cooking, or washing the dishes. Attend to what interests you and what you enjoy doing, and feel how that resonates with your zazen. In the middle of your zazen, you need not think about those activities, but they might naturally appear anyway as part of your thought stream as you sit. That too may help connect to the deeper creative energy we touch in zazen.

In each breath, in each inhalation and exhalation, a kind of raw, tender freshness is available. Each breath is new, yet each also depends on every single previous breath you have ever breathed. And each inhalation and exhalation you take now is absolutely necessary to every inhalation and exhalation you will ever take. Our life is alive right now. This fact is very easy to ignore. A lot of our culture and its entertainments encourage us to run away from the reality of the aliveness of our life. But the raw, open uniqueness of each breath particularly arrives when you pay attention to your life and your daily activities. We all have chores that we think we need to perform. But it is possible to enjoy washing the dishes, or taking out the garbage? Pay attention to that enjoyment in your creative activities in the world, including the details. Whatever it is you do, can you feel this creative energy?

As your capacity and tolerance for this transformative creativity opens, you might let go of some activities, and you might not be as interested in some things as before. You are alive, and change, and sometimes that is necessary. Keep turning this awareness and transformative function to that to which you give interest and attention. Notice how what you find interesting and enjoy is related to your zazen and might feed your zazen. That does not mean thinking *about* them, but your practice of listening to or making music, or of going for walks, cooking or gardening, or whatever your attention is engaged in, has something to do with the awareness of zazen mind and this transformative function in the middle of awareness. You need not run away from the person sitting on your cushion. Enjoy showing up in the activities of your life and see how they unfold and deepen.

The craft of practice includes just re-minding yourself of this mind during the course of the day and the course of your life, just as you do in the middle of a period of zazen. Mindfully inhaling and exhaling is very helpful; really developing in your body enjoyment and appreciation of your breathing. In the middle of your week in some challenging or frustrating activity, you might just remember to breathe.

FACING HABITS

In our zazen and our lives off the cushion, we must also face the fact of karmic entanglements, with our addictive patterns, habits of grasping and of feeling frustrated, fearful, lonely, or confused; this is all part of what it is to be human. Our reactions from those can cause problems and prevent us from settling more deeply into this source of creative energy. Part of our practice is facing such karmic entanglements. You do not have to turn away. Be who you are, and be kind to yourself. We learn compassion for the world by being helpful to ourselves, willing to breathe into those sticky places too, willing to look at our dark side and apply this awareness and transformative function. Of course we cannot suddenly let go of our addictions or change our stubborn habit patterns, even when we see them clearly. As Bob Dylan sang while "stuck inside of" Mobile, "Here I sit so patiently, Waiting to find out what price, You have to pay to get out of Going through all these things twice."[9] I say to Bob, "Only twice? You must be kidding." Well Dylan is a genius; most of us must go through these things many, many times.

As we pay attention to all the patterns we need to see through, settling and developing our capacity, we can learn to be with our thought streams and our habit patterns and to let go of their hold. But usually we cannot simply fix or change them. Some of them are going to be there in subtler and subtler ways for our whole life, or for lifetimes to come, but still, we need not be caught and react to habit patterns. When we do react, how do we then forgive ourselves and just bring awareness, show up and be present, and not run away from these habit patterns? Breathe and enjoy your breathing and your life, enjoy whatever it is you find engaging, interesting, enlivening. See the awareness and transformative function in all of those activities.

And then zazen will be with you always.

Please enjoy your sitting.

Hongzhi, Dōgen, and the Background of Shikan Taza

OBJECTLESS MEDITATION

O NE WAY to categorize the meditation practice of *shikan taza*, or "just sitting," is as an objectless meditation. This is a definition in terms of what it is *not*. One just sits, not concentrating on any particular object of awareness, unlike most traditional meditation practices, Buddhist and non-Buddhist, that involve intent focus on a particular object. Such objects traditionally have included colored disks, candle flames, various aspects of breath, incantations, ambient sound, physical sensations or postures, spiritual figures, mandalas including geometric arrangements of such figures or of symbols representing them, and teaching stories or key phrases from such stories. Some of these concentration practices are in the background of the shikan taza practice tradition, and some have been included with shikan taza in its actual lived experience by practitioners.

But objectless meditation focuses on clear, nonjudgmental, panoramic attention to all of the myriad arising phenomena in the present experience. Such objectless meditation is a potential universally available to conscious beings, and it has been expressed at various times in history. This just sitting is not a meditation technique or practice, or indeed any thing at all. "Just sitting" is a verb rather than a noun, the dynamic activity of being fully present.

THE CHINESE SŌTŌ BACKGROUND BEFORE HONGZHI

The specific practice experience of shikan taza was first articulated in the Sōtō (Ch.: Caodong) Zen lineage by the Chinese master Hongzhi Zhengjue

(1091–1157; Jpn.: Wanshi Shōgaku) and further elaborated by the Japanese Sōtō founder Eihei Dōgen in the thirteenth century. But prior to their expressions of this experience, there are hints of this practice in some of the earlier teachers of the tradition. The founding teachers of this lineage run from Shitou Xiqian (700–790; Jpn.: Sekitō Kisen), two generations after the Chinese Sixth Ancestor, through three generations to Dongshan Liangjie (807–869; Jpn.: Tōzan Ryokai), the usually recognized founder of the Caodong, or Sōtō, lineage in China. I will briefly mention a couple of these early practice intimations in their Sōtō lineage context before discussing the expressions of Hongzhi and Dōgen.

Shitou is most noted for his teaching poem "Sandōkai" (Harmony of Difference and Sameness), still frequently chanted in Sōtō Zen. "Sandōkai" presents the fundamental dialectic between the polarity of the universal ultimate and the phenomenal particulars. This dialectic, derived by Shitou from Chinese Huayan thought based on the "Flower Ornament" (Avataṃsaka) Sutra combined with some use of Daoist imagery, became the philosophical background of Sōtō, as expressed by Dongshan in the five ranks teachings, and later elucidated by various Sōtō thinkers.[10]

Shitou wrote another teaching poem, "Soanka" (Song of the Grass Hut), which presents more of a practice model for how to develop the space that fosters just sitting. Therein Shitou says, "Just sitting with head covered all things are at rest. Thus this mountain monk does not understand at all."[11] He is modeling a praxis not involved in the effort to gain some understanding or insight. Just sitting is the subtle activity of allowing all things to be completely at rest just as they are.

In "Song of the Grass Hut" Shitou also says, "Turn around the light to shine within, then just return.... Let go of hundreds of years and relax completely. Open your hands and walk, innocent." Probably few have seen the purpose of Zen practice as relaxing completely, especially when caught up in encouragements to acquire some special exalted experience or spiritual state. But Shitou is recommending practice that expresses just letting go, physically as in awareness, whether in sitting or everyday conduct, reminiscent of what Dōgen would later call "dropping body and mind." According to Shitou, the fundamental orientation of turning within is simply in order to "just return" to the world and to our original quality. Letting go of conditioning while steeped in completely relaxed awareness, one may be able to act more effectively, innocent of grasping and attachments. The context of this just sitting suggested by Shitou is the possibility of aware and responsive presence that is simple, open-hearted, and straightforward. "Song of the Grass Hut" concludes, "If you want to know the undying person in the hut, don't separate from this skin bag here and now." This is not a practice of reaching some altered, higher state, or becoming a more exalted person, but simply of fully realizing the reality of this mind and body, this skin bag here and now.

Another story about Shitou more directly expresses the quality of practice as nonattainment, a practice without objective. A student asked Shitou, "What is the essential meaning of Buddha Dharma?" and Shitou replied, "Not attaining, not knowing." Nothing needs to be understood or acquired. When the student followed up, "Beyond that, is there any other pivotal point?" Shitou stated, "The wide sky does not obstruct the white clouds drifting."[12] In the spaciousness of this awareness no forms need be grasped or rejected as objectives.

When teaching about zazen, Dōgen regularly quotes a saying by Shitou's successor, Yaoshan Weiyan (745–828; Jpn.: Yakusan Igen). As discussed more fully in the previous chapter, a monk asked Yaoshan what he thought of while sitting so still and steadfastly. Yaoshan replied that he thought of not-thinking, or that he thought of that which does not think. When the monk asked how Yaoshan did that, he responded, "Beyond thinking," or "Nonthinking." This is a state of awareness that can include both cognition and the absence of thought and is not caught up in either. Dōgen calls this "The essential art of zazen."[13] And this story obviously provides background for Dōgen's view of zazen. These early accounts indicate the context for Caodong/Sōtō practitioners "just sitting" well before Hongzhi and Dōgen.[14]

HONGZHI'S SERENE ILLUMINATION

Hongzhi, easily the most prominent Sōtō teacher in the twelfth century, was a literary giant, a highly prolific, elegant, and evocative writer who comprehensively articulated this meditation practice for the first time. Hongzhi does not use the actual term "just sitting," which Dōgen quotes instead from his own Sōtō lineage teacher Tiantong Rujing (1163–1228; Jpn.: Tendō Nyojō). But Tiantong Monastery, where Dōgen studied with Rujing in 1227, was the same temple where Hongzhi had been abbot for almost thirty years up to his death in 1157. Dōgen refers to Hongzhi as an "ancient buddha," and frequently quotes him, especially from his poetic writings on meditative experience. Clearly the meditative awareness that Hongzhi writes about was closely related to Dōgen's meditation, although Dōgen further developed its dynamic orientation in his own writings about just sitting.

Hongzhi's meditation teaching is usually referred to as "silent (or serene) illumination," although Hongzhi actually uses this term only a few times in his voluminous writings. In his long poem "Silent Illumination," Hongzhi emphasizes the necessity for balance between serenity and illumination, which echoes the traditional Buddhist meditation practice of śamatha-vipaśyana, or stopping and insight. This balance was recalled as *zhiguan* in the Chinese Tiantai meditation system expounded by the great Chinese Buddhist synthesizer Zhiyi (538–597). Hongzhi emphasizes the necessity for active insight as well as calm in "Silent Illumination" when he says, "If illumination neglects serenity then aggressiveness appears.... If serenity neglects illumination, murkiness leads to wasted Dharma."[15] Hongzhi's meditation values the balancing of both stopping or settling the mind and its actively illuminating functioning.

In his prose writings, Hongzhi frequently uses nature metaphors to express the natural simplicity of the lived experience of silent illumination or just sitting. (I am generally using these terms interchangeably, except when discussing differences in their usages by Hongzhi or Dōgen.) An example of Hongzhi's nature writing is this:

A person of the Way fundamentally does not dwell anywhere. The white clouds are fascinated with the green mountain's foundation. The bright moon cherishes being carried along with the flowing water. The clouds part and the mountains appear. The moon sets and the water is cool. Each bit of autumn contains vast interpenetration without bounds.[16]

Hongzhi here highlights the ease of this awareness and its function. Like the flow of water and clouds, the mind can move smoothly to flow in harmony with its environment. "Accord and respond without laboring and accomplish without hindrance. Everywhere turn around freely, not following conditions, not falling into classifications."[17]

In many places, Hongzhi provides specific instructions about how to manage one's sense perceptions so as to allow the vital presence of just sitting. "Respond unencumbered to each speck of dust without becoming its partner. The subtlety of seeing and hearing transcends mere colors and sounds."[18] Again he suggests, "Casually mount the sounds and straddle the colors while you transcend listening and surpass watching."[19] This does not indicate a presence that is oblivious to the surrounding sense world. But while the practitioner remains aware, sense phenomena do not need to become objects of attachment, or be objectified at all.

Another aspect of Hongzhi's practice is that it is objectless, not only in terms of letting go of concentration objects, but also objectless in the sense of avoiding any specific, limited goals or objectives. As Hongzhi says at the end of "Silent Illumination," "Transmit it to all directions without desiring to gain credit."[20] This serene illumination, or just sitting, is not a technique, or a means to some resulting higher state of consciousness, or any particular state of being. Just sitting, one simply meets the immediate present. Desiring some flashy experience, or anything more or other than "this," is mere worldly vanity and craving. Again invoking empty nature, Hongzhi says, "Fully appreciate the emptiness of all dharmas. Then all minds are free and all dusts evaporate in the original brilliance shining everywhere.... Clear and desireless, the wind in the pines and the moon in the water are content in their elements."[21]

THE TRAP OF PASSIVITY

This nonseeking quality of Hongzhi's meditation eventually helped make it controversial. The leading contemporary teacher in the much more prominent Linji lineage (Jpn.: Rinzai) was Dahui Zonggao (1089–1163; Jpn.: Daie Sōkō). A popular historical stereotype is that Dahui and Hongzhi were rivals, debating over Hongzhi's silent illumination meditation as opposed to Dahui's koan introspection meditation. Historians have now established that Hongzhi and Dahui were actually friends, or at least had high mutual esteem, and sent students to each other. There was no such debate, at least until future generations of their successors, although Dahui did severely critique silent illumination practice as being quietistic and damaging to Zen. Dahui clearly was not criticizing Hongzhi himself but rather some of his followers, and possibly Hongzhi's Dharma brother Changlu Qingliao (1089–1151; Jpn.: Chōryo Seiryō), from whom Dōgen's lineage descends.[22]

Dahui's criticism of silent illumination was partly valid, based on the legitimate danger of practitioners misunderstanding this approach as quietistic or passive. Dahui's critique was echoed centuries later by Japanese Rinzai critics of just sitting, such as Hakuin in the eighteenth century. Just sitting can indeed sometimes degenerate into dull attachment to inner bliss states, with no responsiveness to the suffering of the surrounding world. Hongzhi clarifies that this is not the intention of his practice, for example when he says, "In wonder return to the journey, avail yourself of the path and walk ahead.... With the hundred grass tips in the busy marketplace graciously share yourself."[23] The meditation advocated by both Hongzhi and Dōgen is firmly rooted in the bodhisattva path and its liberative purpose of assisting and awakening beings. Mere idle indulgence in peacefulness and bliss is not the point. The other aspect of Dahui's criticism related to his own advocacy of meditation focusing on koans as meditation objects, explicitly aimed at generating flashy opening experiences. Such experiences may occur in just sitting practice as well, but generally have been less valued in the Sōtō tradition. The purpose of Buddhist practice is universal awakening, not dramatic experiences of opening any more than passive states of serenity. But contrary to another erroneous stereotype, use of koans has been widespread in Sōtō teaching as well as Rinzai.

Hongzhi himself created two collections of koans with his comments, one of which was the basis for the important anthology *Book of Serenity* (Jpn.: Shōyōroku). Dōgen also created koan collections, and (ironically, considering his reputation as champion of just sitting meditation) far more of his voluminous writing, including most of the essays of his masterwork *Shōbōgenzō*, is devoted to commentary on koans than to discussion of meditation. Dōgen was actually instrumental in introducing the koan literature to Japan, and his writings demonstrate a truly amazing mastery of the depths and breadth of the range of that literature in China. Steven Heine's modern work *Dōgen and the Kōan Tradition* clearly demonstrates how Dōgen actually developed koan practice in new expansive modes that differed from Dahui's concentrated approach.[21] Although Hongzhi and Dōgen, and most of the traditional Sōtō tradition, did not develop a formal koan meditation curriculum as did Dahui, Hakuin, and much of the Rinzai tradition, the koan stories have remained a prominent context for Sōtō teaching. Conversely, just sitting has often been part of Rinzai practice, such that some Sōtō monks in the nineteenth and early twentieth centuries went to Rinzai masters for training in just sitting.

THE SAMĀDHI OF SELF-FULFILLMENT AND AWAKENED SPACE

Although a great deal of Dōgen's writing focuses on commentary on koans and sutras, and on monastic practice expressions, the practice of just sitting is clearly crucial in the background throughout his teaching career. Dōgen builds on the descriptions of Hongzhi to emphasize the dynamic function of just sitting.

In one of his first essays, "Bendōwa" (Talk on Wholehearted Practice of the Way), written in 1231 a few years after his return from training in

China, Dōgen describes this meditation as the samādhi of self-fulfillment (or enjoyment) and elaborates the inner meaning of this practice. Just sitting is simply expressed as concentration on the self in its most delightful wholeness, in total inclusive interconnection with all of phenomena. Dōgen makes remarkably radical claims for this simple experience. "When one displays the buddha mudra with one's whole body and mind, sitting upright in this samādhi for even a short time, everything in the entire Dharma world becomes buddha mudra, and all space in the universe completely becomes enlightenment."[25] Proclaiming that when one just sits all of space itself becomes enlightenment is an inconceivable statement, deeply challenging our usual sense of the nature of reality, whether we take Dōgen's words literally or metaphorically. Dōgen places this activity of just sitting far beyond our usual sense of personal self or agency. He goes on to say that "Even if only one person sits for a short time, because this zazen is one with all existence and completely permeates all times, it performs everlasting buddha guidance" throughout space and time. At least in Dōgen's faith in the spiritual or "theological" implications of the activity of just sitting, this is clearly a dynamically liberating practice, not mere blissful serenity, with striking potential environmental and societal implications.

Through his writings, Dōgen gives ample indication as to how to engage this just sitting. In another noted early writing, "Genjōkōan" (Actualizing the Fundamental Point), from 1233, Dōgen gives a clear description of the existential stance of just sitting: "To carry yourself forward and experience myriad things is delusion. That myriad things come forth and experience themselves is awakening."[26] That we are conditioned to project our own conceptions onto the world as a dead object-screen is the cause of suffering. When all of phenomena (including what we usually think of as "ours") join in mutual self-experience and expression, the awakened awareness that Hongzhi described through nature metaphors is present, doing buddha's work, as Dōgen says.

SUSTAINING DROPPED OFF BODY AND MIND

Some modern Dōgen scholars have emphasized the shift in his later teaching to the importance of strict monastic practice and supposedly away from the universal applicability of shikan taza practice. In 1243 Dōgen moved his community far from the capital of Kyoto to the snowy north coast mountains, where he established his monastery, Eiheiji. His teaching thereafter, until his death in 1253, was mostly in the form of brief talks to his monks, presented in *Eihei Kōroku* (*Dōgen's Extensive Record*). These are focused on training a core of dedicated monks to preserve his practice tradition, a mission he fulfilled with extraordinary success. But through his later work as well as the early, instructions and encouragements to just sit appear regularly.

In 1251 Dōgen was still proclaiming:

> The family style of all buddhas and ancestors is to engage the way in zazen. My late teacher Tiantong [Rujing] said, "Cross-legged sitting is the Dharma of ancient buddhas.... In just sitting it is finally accomplished."... We should engage the way in zazen as if extinguishing flames from our heads. Buddhas and ancestors, generation after generation, face to face transmit the primacy of zazen.[27]

In 1249 he exhorted his monks, "We should know that zazen is the decorous activity of practice after realization. Realization is simply just sitting zazen.... Brothers on this mountain, you should straightforwardly, single-mindedly focus on zazen."[28] For Dōgen, all of enlightenment is fully expressed in the ongoing practice of just sitting. That same year, he gave a straightforward instruction for just sitting:

> Great assembly, do you want to hear the reality of just sitting, which is the Zen practice that is dropping off body and mind?

> After a pause [Dōgen] said: Mind cannot objectify it; thinking cannot describe it. Just step back and carry on, and avoid offending anyone you face. At the ancient dock, the wind and moon are cold and clear. At night the boat floats peacefully in the land of lapis lazuli.[29]

The concluding two sentences of this talk are quoted from a poem by Hongzhi, further revealing the continuity of their practice teachings.

Dōgen also frequently describes this just sitting as "dropping away body and mind," *shinjin datsuraku* in Japanese, a phrase traditionally associated with Dōgen's awakening in China.[30] For Dōgen this "dropping off body and mind" is the true nature both of just sitting and of complete enlightenment; it is the ultimate letting go of self, directly meeting the cold, clear wind and moon. After turning within while just sitting, it is carried on in all activity and throughout ongoing engagement with the world. Although just sitting now has been maintained for 750 years since Dōgen, the teachings of Hongzhi and Dōgen remain as primary guideposts to its practice.

Zazen as Enactment Ritual

ZEN BEYOND TECHNIQUES

B UDDHIST MEDITATION has commonly been considered an instrumental technique aimed at obtaining a heightened mental or spiritual
state, or even as a method for inducing some dramatic "enlightenment"
experience. But in some branches of the Zen tradition, zazen is seen not as
a means to attaining some result but as a ritual enactment and expression
of awakened awareness. This alternate, historically significant approach
to Zen meditation and practice has been as a ceremonial, ritual expression whose transformative quality is not based on stages of attainment or
meditative prowess.

The Zen ritual enactment approach is most apparent and developed
in writings about zazen by the Japanese Sōtō Zen founder Eihei Dōgen.
This chapter will explore his ritual instructions for meditation practice,
especially in his monastic regulations for the monks' hall in *Eihei Shingi*,
then relevant teachings about meditation in a selection from Dōgen's two
massive masterworks, his extended essays in *Shōbōgenzō*, and his direct
teachings to his monks in short formal talks in *Eihei Kōroku*. Following
these, a sampling of other Zen sources with analogous approaches are
described.

ZAZEN AS TANTRA

Before focusing on Zen teachings, we may briefly note that such enactment
practice is usually associated with the Vajrayāna branch of Buddhism, in
which practitioners are initiated into ritual practices of identification with

specific buddha or bodhisattva figures. Although Vajrayāna is often considered the province of Tibetan Buddhism, increasing attention is being given to the crucial role of the Japanese forms of Vajrayāna (*mikkyō* in Sino-Japanese).[31] In the Heian period (794–1185) this *mikkyō*, also known as "esoteric" or tantric practice, was prevalent not only in Shingon (True Word), the main Japanese Vajrayāna school, but also in the comprehensive Tendai school in which were first trained not only Japanese Zen founders like Dōgen and Eisai (1141–1215) but also Pure Land founders Hōnen (1133–1212) and Shinran (1173–1262), as well as Nichiren (1222–1282). Thanks to this *mikkyō* heritage that permeated all of medieval Japanese Buddhism, in many inexplicit ways *mikkyō* or tantric practice might be seen as underlying all subsequent forms of Japanese Buddhism. Further studies exploring direct and indirect influences of *mikkyō* on Japanese Zen promise to be especially informative.

For Dōgen and others, Zen shares with the Vajrayāna tradition the heart of spiritual activity and praxis as the enactment of buddha awareness and physical presence, rather than aiming at developing a perfected, formulated understanding. In the context of Tibetan Buddhism, Robert Thurman speaks of the main thrust of Vajrayāna practice as physical rather than solely mental. "When we think of the goal of Buddhism as enlightenment, we think of it mainly as an attainment of some kind of higher understanding. But buddhahood is a physical transformation as much as a mental transcendence."[32]

The Japanese Vajrayāna teacher Kūkai (774–835), the founder of Shingon, emphasized the effects of teachings over their literal meaning. As explicated by Thomas Kasulis, "Kūkai was more interested in the teachings' *aims* than in their content, or perhaps better stated, he saw the aims as inseparable from their content. He saw no sharp distinction between theory and practice." The understanding of a teaching was not privileged independently from its practical effects. "The truth of a statement depends not on the status of its referent, but on how it affects us."[33] For Kūkai, physical postures, utterances, and mental imagery are expressions of ultimate reality, and by intentionally engaging in them, practitioners are led to realization of that reality. The performance of the ritual practice helps effect an expressive realization deeper than mere cognition.

THE PHYSICAL EXPRESSION OF PRACTICE-REALIZATION

Both the Vajrayāna and Zen emphasis on fully expressed performance of reality reflects the valuing of actual bodhisattvic workings and the realization of a teaching's enactment over theoretical dictums or attainments. In his early 1231 writing on the meaning of meditation, "Bendōwa," now considered part of Shōbōgenzō, Dōgen directly emphasizes the priority of the actualization of practice expression over doctrinal theory. "Buddhist practitioners should know not to argue about the superiority or inferiority of teachings and not to discriminate between superficial or profound Dharma, but should only know whether the practice is genuine or false."[34] This priority of a teaching's actual performance is reflected, for example, in the somewhat later Japanese Sōtō Zen prescription, "Dignified manner is Buddha Dharma; decorum is the essential teaching."[35] The point is to enact the meaning of the teachings in actualized practice, and the whole praxis, including meditation, may thus be viewed as ritual, ceremonial expressions of the teaching, rather than as means to discover and attain some understanding of it. Therefore, the strong emphasis in much of this approach to Zen training is the mindful and dedicated expression of meditative awareness in everyday activities.

In perhaps his most foundational essay on zazen, "Fukanzazengi," Dōgen gives detailed postural instructions for sitting meditation, largely patterned after Chinese Chan meditation manuals. The earliest version of this essay, no longer extant, is from 1227, written shortly after Dōgen's return to Japan from four years of studies in China. Later revisions are from 1233 and 1242, the latter cited here from his Eihei Kōroku.[36] This essay was aimed at a general audience of laypeople but still describes the practice in ritual terms. Dōgen specifies in detail preparation of the meditation space, suggesting a quiet room, and also grounding of the mental space, including to put aside involvements and affairs and not to think in terms of good or bad. He adds, "Have no designs on becoming a buddha," emphasizing the noninstrumental but rather the ritual nature of this activity. He describes postural arrangements, including details of full-lotus and half-lotus leg positions, how to hold the hand position, and physical guides for upright alignment, such as ears in line above shoulders and nose above navel. All these are provided so that the practitioner can "settle into steady, immovable sitting."

After the procedural descriptions, which were patterned closely after the Chan sources, Dōgen comments, "The zazen I speak of is not [learning] meditation practice. It is simply the Dharma gate of peace and bliss, the practice-realization of totally culminated awakening." Here Dōgen clarifies that the zazen praxis he espouses is not one of the traditional meditation programs that one can study and learn, step-by step. "Meditation" is a translation for Zen in Japanese, Chan in Chinese, or Dhyāna in Sanskrit, which can be understood in terms of the four stages of the technical *dhyāna* practices (often translated as "trances"), which predate the historical Buddha in India. But in China this term was used generally to refer to a variety of meditation curricula, the sense indicated here by Dōgen. He goes on to clarify that his zazen praxis bears no relationship to mental acuity: "Make no distinction between the dull and the sharp witted." Then he adds, "If you concentrate your effort single-mindedly, that in itself is wholeheartedly engaging the way. Practice-realization is naturally undefiled." In many of his writings, Dōgen emphasizes the oneness of "practice-realization," that meditation practice is not a means toward some future realization or enlightenment but is its inseparable expression.

The ritual context of Dōgen's zazen is highlighted at the beginning of his essay "Bendōhō" (The Model for Engaging the Way), a manual for the proper procedures for practice in the monks' hall, within which the monks sit zazen, take meals, and sleep, each at their assigned places. This is the traditional mode of Chan practice in China, which Dōgen established at Eiheiji, the monastery he founded after moving in 1243 from the capital of Kyoto to the remote mountains of Echizen (now Fukui), and which remains one of the two headquarter temples of Sōtō Zen. "Bendōhō" is one of the essays in *Eihei Shingi* (*Dōgen's Pure Standards for the Zen Community*), the seventeenth-century collection of all of Dōgen's writings in Chinese about monastic standards and regulations. "Bendōhō" follows in this text after the more celebrated essay "Tenzokyōkun" (Instructions for the Chief Cook), which propounds the appropriate attitudes and responsibility of the tenzo, as well as rituals and procedures to be followed in preparing food in the monastery kitchen.

In "Bendōhō," Dōgen states that all monks should sit zazen together, "when the assembly is sitting," and stop together when it is time for all to lie down for the night. He states that "Standing out has no benefit; being different from others is not our conduct."[37] Clearly Dōgen sees zazen as a communal ritual rather than an individual spiritual exercise. Commencing with the evening schedule, Dōgen imparts the proper ritual conduct for daily activities in the monks' hall throughout the day, including comprehensive ritual procedures for such activities as serving tea, teeth brushing, face cleaning, and using the toilet (in the lavatory located in back of the monks' hall). He speaks of zazen as one of such ritual activities and describes in detail the manner and route with which the abbot should enter the hall to lead the assembly's evening zazen. Later, after describing less formal early morning sitting, Dōgen gives further instructions for zazen that copy in many particulars the detailed postural instructions in "Fukanzazengi." It is clear in context that though Dōgen considers zazen the core ritual, it is still simply one of the many ritual activities in the everyday life of the monks' hall.

THE PRACTICE AND TRAINING OF BUDDHAS

One of the *Shōbōgenzō* essays that focuses on zazen practice is the 1242 "Zazenshin" (The Acupuncture Needle, or Point, of Zazen). In it Dōgen says, "For studying the way, the established [means of] investigation is pursuit of the way in seated meditation. The essential point that marks this [investigation] is [the understanding] that there is a practice of a buddha that does not seek to make a buddha. Since the practice of a buddha is not to make a buddha, it is the realization of the *kōan*."[38] Here, as in many places in his writings, Dōgen emphasizes as the "essential point" that zazen specifically and practice generally is not about seeking some future buddhahood. Rather, it is already the practice of buddhas, realizing with awakened awareness what is crucial in this present situation.

Dōgen declares, "There is a principle that seated meditation does not await making a buddha; there is nothing obscure about the essential message that making a buddha is not connected with seated meditation." For Dōgen zazen is adamantly not merely a means to achieve buddhahood. After commenting in detail on this, Dōgen adds, "It is the seated buddha that buddha after buddha and patriarch after patriarch have taken as their essential activity. Those who are buddhas and patriarchs have employed this essential activity, ... for it is the essential function." Although it is not an instrumental activity for gaining awakening, zazen is still the fundamental activity of buddhas for Dōgen.

"Zazenshin" concludes with Dōgen commenting on and writing his own version of a poem about the function of zazen by Chinese master Hongzhi Zhengjue (1091–1157; Jpn.: Wanshi Shōgaku), the most important Sōtō (Ch.: Caodong) teacher in the century before Dōgen, and who was a primary source and inspiration for Dōgen. The relevant point in Dōgen's discussion is that both verses begin with the proposition that zazen is "the essential function of all the buddhas." Dōgen comments that "the essential function that is realized [by buddhas] is seated meditation." Again, he sees zazen as the expression and function of buddhas, rather than buddhahood being a function, or consequence, of zazen.

Along with the playful, elaborate essays in Dōgen's *Shōbōgenzō*, noted for their poetic wordplay and intricate philosophical expressions, Dōgen's other major and massive work is *Eihei Kōroku*. The first seven of the ten volumes of *Eihei Kōroku* consist of usually brief *jōdō* (literally "ascending the hall"), which I call Dharma hall discourses. These short, formal talks are given traditionally in the Dharma hall with the monks standing. Except for the first volume of *Eihei Kōroku* from prior to his departure from Kyoto in 1243, the Dharma hall discourses in *Eihei Kōroku* are our primary source for Dōgen's mature teaching at Eiheiji, after he had finished writing the vast majority of the longer essays included in *Shōbōgenzō*. These talks to his cadre of disciples at Eiheiji reveal his personality qualities and style of training. This training apparently was effective, as Dōgen's seven major disciples present at Eiheiji, together with their disciples over the next few generations, managed to spread his Sōtō lineage and teaching widely in the Japanese countryside.[39]

In a great many of the *jōdō*, Dōgen discusses zazen as a ritual activity for enactment of buddha awareness. For example, in Dharma hall discourse 319 from 1249, just before celebrating the institution of the first Japanese monks' hall at Eiheiji, Dōgen says, "We should know that zazen is the decorous activity of practice after realization. Realization is simply just sitting zazen."[40] Dōgen again emphasizes that his zazen is not an activity prior to realization of enlightenment but its natural expression, comparable to the ongoing daily meditation by Śākyamuni Buddha after his awakening to buddhahood.

However, this ritual zazen expressing realization is not a pointless or dull, routinized activity, inertly enshrining some prior experience. In Dharma hall discourse 449 from 1251, Dōgen says, "What is called zazen is to sit, cutting through the smoke and clouds without seeking merit. Just become unified, never reaching the end.... Already such, how can we penetrate it?"[41] Behind these zazen instructions and encouragements to actively enact awareness in practice is a strong attitude of persistent inquiry that permeates Dōgen's teachings and his challenges to his disciples. Dōgen's zazen can be seen as a ritualized mode of silent inquiry, and this attitude of inquiry is reinforced in many of his mentions of zazen.

The ninth day of the ninth month was the traditional date in the Chan monastic schedule when the relaxed summer schedule ended and increased zazen practice began. Although Dōgen did not follow the relaxed schedule in his training set-up, he did honor the traditional date for renewed zazen with talks encouraging revitalized practice.[42] Dōgen's Dharma hall discourse 523 from 1252 is the last such talk given on that date to encourage zazen. In that talk he says, "Body and mind that is dropped off is steadfast and immovable. Although the sitting cushions are old, they show new impressions." Here he refers to the importance of sustaining zazen as a practice ritual and its renewal with fresh impressions (on cushions as well as minds), ritually celebrated on this occasion.

In Dharma hall discourse 531, his very last *jōdō* in 1252, during which he was succumbing to the illness that would take his life in the following year, Dōgen says in a verse, "A flower blooming on a monk's staff has merit. Smiling on our sitting cushions, there's nothing lacking."[43] In this, one of his very last teachings, he describes zazen as a joyful event that celebrates the full expression and blossoming of awakening.

THE ONENESS OF PRACTICE AND REALIZATION

Dōgen proclaims his important teaching of the unity of practice and realization (*shushō-ittō*) clearly in his early 1231 writing "Bendōwa." In response to one of the questions posed, Dōgen states:

> In Buddha Dharma, practice and enlightenment are one and the same. Because it is the practice of enlightenment, a beginner's wholehearted practice of the Way is exactly the totality of original enlightenment. For this reason, in conveying the essential attitude for practice, it is taught not to wait for enlightenment outside practice.... Since it is already the enlightenment of practice, enlightenment is endless; since it is the practice of enlightenment, practice is beginningless.[44]

For Dōgen, true practice of Buddha Dharma can only be a response to some present awareness of enlightenment or realization. And enlightenment is not realized, or meaningful, unless it is engaged in practice. Because of this unity Dōgen urges all to engage in zazen.

This expounding of awakening need not be offered only through verbal Dharma talks. It may also be fully expounded and enacted simply through the physical, ritual expression of upright sitting, of zazen. Moreover, for Dōgen the awakening of buddhas is expounded by buddhas listening to the teaching equally with those who give the teaching. Toward the end of "Gyōbutsu Īgi" (The Awesome Presence of Active Buddhas), Dōgen describes buddhas listening to as well as speaking Dharma. "Do not regard the capacity to expound the Dharma as superior, and the capacity to listen to the Dharma as inferior. If those who speak are venerable, those who listen are venerable as well."[45] The ritual enactment of a Dharma talk is performed by the listeners as well as by the speaker. Dōgen clarifies, "Know that it is equally difficult to listen to and accept this sutra. Expounding and listening are not a matter of superior and inferior.... As the fruit of buddhahood is already present, they do not listen to Dharma to achieve buddhahood; as indicated, they are already buddhas." As with zazen itself, for Dōgen the ritual of listening to the teaching is not undertaken as a means to the goal of awakening or understanding, but simply as an enactment of the buddhahood already present.

Some of Dōgen's *Jōdo* (Dharma hall discourses) in his *Eihei Kōroku* pose a further analogy to his approach to zazen as an enactment ritual. He uses his own expounding of the Dharma as an enactment ritual rather than as a mere technique to communicate philosophical doctrines or practice instructions. This mode of enactment ritual represents a primary aspect of Dōgen's Zen expression. For example, in Dharma hall discourse 70, given in 1241, Dōgen proclaims:

> As this mountain monk [Dōgen] today gives a Dharma hall discourse, all buddhas in the three times also today give a Dharma hall discourse. The ancestral teachers in all generations also today give a Dharma hall discourse.... Already together having given a Dharma hall discourse, what Dharma has been expounded? No other Dharma is expressed; but this very Dharma is expressed. What is this Dharma?... It is upheld within the monks' hall; it is upheld within the Buddha hall.[46]

Dōgen never states the content of the Dharma hall discourse, except to say that he is giving it, together with all buddhas and ancestors, and that it is upheld in the ritual activity of the monks in the monks' hall and Buddha hall. This is a ritual discourse that celebrates the ritual itself and its enactment, beyond any other content signified by the ritual. As such, it provides a mirror to the ritual enactment of zazen that Dōgen proclaims as itself the essential realization or enlightenment.

All Zen ritual activity, at least ideally, does have some impact, or liberative effect, for the participants. On the other hand, attachment to the mere procedural forms of ritual, in which the forms are followed in a routinized, rote manner, is traditionally considered a hindrance to practice. Nonattachment or not clinging is a primary feature of Dōgen's practice-realization. Such clinging would be to neglect rather than to protect and care for practice-realization. Practice marked by pursuit or attainment of enlightenment can become a form of spiritual materialism or greed. Radical nonattachment may fully demonstrate appreciation and enactment of the meaning of practice-realization. Dōgen's zazen celebrates and enacts Buddha's practice of inquiry, rather than some practice of acquisition, and takes refuge in the actuality of Buddha's practice, rather than aspiring to some external imagined ideal.

RITUAL ENACTMENT MEDITATION IN CHINESE CHAN

This approach to zazen as a ritual of enactment, clearly articulated throughout Dōgen's writings, is not unique to Dōgen. As discussed at the beginning of this chapter, in Japanese Zen it may derive partly from the significant influence throughout Japanese Buddhism of mikkyō, in which the practitioner identifies with and takes refuge in a particular buddha or bodhisattva. The bulk of the Chinese Chan koan or encounter dialogue literature does not deal directly with meditation as a ritual. But in Chinese Chan we indeed can see intimations of this practice approach of zazen as an enactment ritual.

The first chapter describes how the eighth-century Chan master Nanyue used a rock and tile to demonstrate to his student Mazu that zazen is not about "becoming a buddha." When Mazu later became a prominent Chan teacher, he taught that "This very mind is buddha." Although not directly about ritual zazen, this implies an enactment rather than attainment approach to practice. And Mazu's disciple Damei Fachang (752–839; Jpn.: Daibai Hōjō), whom Mazu and Dōgen both praised, spent thirty years on his mountain practicing zazen based on this teaching.[47]

Another prominent disciple of Mazu, Nanquan Puyuan (748–834; Jpn.: Nansen Fugan) was asked about the way by his student, the renowned adept Zhaozhou Congshen (778–897; Jpn.: Joshu Jushin). Nanquan responded that "Ordinary mind is the Way."[48] When asked by Zhaozhou how to approach this, as if it were something to be attained, Nanquan replied, "If you try to direct yourself toward it, you will move away from it." Again, this implies an enactment approach to practice, rather than seeking some attainment, which Nanquan clarifies as counterproductive. Nanquan continues, "When you reach the true Way beyond doubt, it is vast and open as space."

A major predecessor for Dōgen's teachings on meditation is the important twelfth-century Caodong (Sōtō) master Hongzhi Zhengjue, a prolific writer discussed in the previous chapter. Hongzhi's meditation teaching, sometimes referred to as silent or serene illumination, was a model for Dōgen's zazen as enactment of awakening. One sample of Hongzhi's clear, evocative articulation of his meditative praxis is:

> The practice of true reality is simply to sit serenely in silent introspection. When you have fathomed this you cannot be turned around by external causes or conditions. This empty, wide open mind is subtly and correctly illuminating.... Here you can rest and become clean, pure, and lucid. Bright and penetrating, you can immediately return, accord, and respond to deal with events.[49]

In a later section of this volume of his *Extensive Record*, Hongzhi says, "Sit empty of worldly anxiety, silent and bright, clear and illuminating, blank and accepting, far-reaching and responsive."[50] As Dōgen would do in his own way a century later, Hongzhi elaborates the workings of a meditation of open, responsive presence in which subtle awakened awareness is enacted.

ZAZEN AS RITUAL ENACTMENT IN SŌTŌ AFTER DŌGEN

Teachings on meditation as enactment ritual continued among Dōgen's successors in Japan. Keizan Jōkin (1264–1325), a third-generation successor of Dōgen, is considered the second founder of Sōtō Zen after Dōgen. Keizan's manual on Zen meditation, "Zazen Yōjinki" (Writing on the Function of Mind in Zazen), begins, "Zazen just lets people illumine the mind and rest easy in their fundamental endowment. This is called showing the original face and revealing the scenery of the basic ground."[51] This resting in and revealing of the fundamental ground continues Dōgen's enactment practice. As this text proceeds, Keizan gives extensive ritual instructions in when, where, and how to perform zazen, incorporating much of the procedural recommendations of Dōgen's "Fukanzazengi," while adding much more detail.

In the midst of these ritual instructions, Keizan also provides detail on how he sees zazen's relationship to and enactment of teaching, practice, and realization.

> Zazen is not concerned with teaching, practice, or realization, yet it contains these three aspects.... Although teaching is established within zen, it is not ordinary teaching; it is direct pointing, simply communicating the way, speaking with the whole body.... Although we speak of practice, it is practice without any doing. That is to say, the body doesn't do anything, the mouth does not recite anything, the mind does not think anything over.... Though we may speak of realization, this is realization without realization,... the gate of illumination through which the wisdom of the realized ones opens up, produced by the method of practice of great ease.

Here clearly Keizan is not espousing zazen as some technique to gain enlightenment, or some perfected practice or expounding, but simply is affirming the full endowment of realization already expressed in zazen.

This approach continues in much of later Sōtō Zen. The Sōtō scholar-monk Menzan Zuihō (1682–1769) significantly influenced the development of modern Sōtō Zen. Among his many writings is a long essay called "Jijuyū-zanmai" (The Samādhi of Self-fulfillment), in which he includes excerpts from many of Dōgen's writings about meditation, including "Bendōwa" and "Zazenshin," discussed above.[52] Before the Dōgen selections Menzan comments briefly on many other Buddhist meditation teachings. Menzan critiques the dualistic meditation of those who "aspire to rid themselves of delusion and to gain enlightenment;...This is nothing but creating the karma of acceptance and rejection."[53] For Menzan, on the other hand, "zazen is not a practice for getting rid of delusions and gaining enlightenment." Commenting on a teaching attributed to the Third Ancestor, Menzan adds, "If you do not make mental struggle, the darkness itself becomes the Self Illumination of the light." Later he says, "This is the culmination of the Buddha-Way and the unsurpassable samadhi which is continuously going beyond. For this reason all buddhas in the world of the ten directions...always dwell in zazen."

The approach to zazen as an enactment ritual is not the only mode of zazen in the Zen tradition or in modern Zen. The Rinzai Zen incorporation of koan introspection into zazen has its own set of associated rituals, many related to private interviews with the teacher. This praxis dates back to the great Japanese Rinzai master Hakuin (1686–1769), contemporary with Menzan, and has roots back to Dahui Zonggao (1089–1163; Jpn: Daie Sōkō) in Song China. This koan introspection approach includes a curriculum that at least has the appearance of fostering attainment of stages of mastery of koans, and seeking to obtain dramatic experiences of kenshō, or "seeing into [buddha] nature." But for Japanese Rinzai adepts, kenshō is not an object to acquire but a verb, the act of seeing into a situation or case, and the koan praxis includes significant ritual performative aspects.[54]

In the West, Zen meditation traditions continue to be influential among a range of spiritual practitioners and contemplatives. And recently, along with Buddhism's philosophical insights, Buddhist ritual practices are being studied more closely by religious and historical scholars. The enactment ritual approach to zazen may serve as a helpful antidote and be particularly illuminating in Western cultures dominated by materialist and consumerist orientations, where a bias toward acquisitiveness often colors even spiritual activities.

The Gateway to Repose and Joy

THE RHYTHM OF REGULAR ZAZEN

S ESSHIN MEANS "gathering the mind," or "gathering the heart," and refers to sitting for three, five, or seven days, or sometimes one day, in meditation retreat. It can be powerful and quite helpful. But while many find sesshin valuable, its importance may be questionable. Not everyone needs to do sesshin to fully benefit from this meditation practice. Having sat for many years, including many sesshins, I believe that sustaining a regular rhythm of ongoing Zen meditation through the week, just being present on your cushion in this body and mind, is more important long-term in developing and unfolding our awareness.

Dongshan Liangjie (807–869; Jpn.: Tōzan Ryōkai), the founder of the Sōtō lineage in China and the author of "Song of the Precious Mirror Samādhi," encourages achieving continuity.[55] Finding a way to sustain a regular attention to the quality of your life and your experience really reaches the heart. In his instructions for zazen, Dōgen spoke of zazen as the gateway of repose and bliss, or "the Dharma gate of joy and ease."[56] This may be especially difficult in the beginning, sitting for a day or two, or for forty minutes. What about the pain in my leg, or my shoulder? What about the confusion in my heart? How could it be that this practice of sitting upright, settling into relaxed attention to enjoying inhalation and exhalation, is the entryway to joyful ease?

DON'T HOLD BACK

Just sitting focuses on not trying to get anything from our investment of time from showing up, but not trying to get rid of anything either. Can we actually be present with *this* body and mind as it is, not our ideas of who we are, but actually be present with the physical sensation and the swirling thoughts that are happening on our cushion, right now? Without trying to get anything from it, and also not trying to get rid of it, do not hold back at all. Do not hold back from just being yourself, from just fully enjoying or engaging this present experience, whether you feel good, bad, or indifferent about it. This is the heart of zazen practice, at least in Dōgen's tradition.

This suggestion to not hold back is expressed in *Living and Dying in Zazen*, a book about teachers in the lineage of Sawaki Kōdō Roshi, the teacher of Uchiyama Roshi, who was the teacher of my friend and translation collaborator Shohaku Okumura. Sodō Yokoyama, a student of Sawaki Kōdō, says:

> Don't spare any effort. People always hold back something when they make any kind of effort. When you hold something back, no matter what you are doing, your effort never amounts to anything. You are holding back when you say "It's no good" or "I can't do it."[57]

You also are holding back if you are trying to get something. If you think about what you are going to get out of this experience, that is just consumerism, or turning your experience into some kind of commodity. If you try to get rid of anything, that is also a kind of holding back from actually just being yourself. This is a practice about learning to be radically yourself, to be completely ordinary, to be a human being, in fact, to be the human being on your cushion right now. People are hindered by many unhelpful delusions about Buddha and Zen masters and by hoping to achieve some perfect, great experience. Sodō Yokoyama adds:

> Śakyamuni was enlightened beyond all doubt to the fact that he was an ordinary person and became a buddha. Then he began to live the life of a buddha. When you realize your ordinariness, you

are a buddha, and when you are a buddha, no matter how many distracting ideas or irrelevant thoughts appear they are no match for a buddha and hence no longer remain obstacles.

In our body, in this skin bag here and now, are various sensations, aches and pains, tensions in our muscles, and also in this body are the swirling of thoughts and feelings. Your whole world is on your cushion right now. Can you be this ordinary person, not holding back, even a tiny bit, from being yourself?

The usual way we hold back is to try and get something, to think of some benefit that we will get in the future. Or we may think of something that we want to remove. If you sit for fifteen or twenty or forty minutes, every day or so, if you just sit and are relaxed and present and enjoy your breathing, among your experiences thoughts and feelings will arise. These will include our human entitlement of greed, hate, and delusion, of craving, anger, frustration, and confusion; that is, unless you are forcing yourself really hard not to be the body or mind on your cushion (and there do exist exotic practices that you can perform to run away from yourself, for a while). But do not try to force away any of those thoughts and feelings. Just sit and be with this as this. Be with that just as that. Do not hold back from yourself.

THE DISTRACTION OF SEEKING KENSHŌ

People come to sesshin with many ideas about intensive retreats involving some flashy experience. Some people may think, in subtle ways, that they are supposed to get rid of something or to reach some special experience. Some branches of Zen do emphasize what is called *kenshō* (seeing into buddha nature) and stress the urgency to experience that as the point of intensive practice. That might be a helpful approach for some people. But I respectfully suggest that trying to get some particular experience in sesshin is wasting your time.

Such dramatic experiences do occur, and can be very inspiring, but the point is to settle into a practice of actually facing ourselves in a sustainable manner. Our consumerist culture particularly, but also our human faculties of discriminating consciousness, lead us into thinking we have to get some benefit from our activities. People come to spiritual practice as well with consumerist attitudes. They want the coolest teacher, or the flashiest experience, or the neatest zazen. This happens on subtle levels. But our idea of what we think we want to get, and of what we want to get rid of, is not how we deepen our realization and not how we may loosen our attachments.

Zazen and buddha heart are much deeper than our ideas about them. Simply do not run away from yourself. Our society and culture offer us many distractions, many entertaining toys to help us run away from ourselves, to not be present with this body-mind right now. So our practice is fairly radical, an entryway to true joyful ease. Just sit and be present with this body-mind as it is, enjoy your breathing, not trying to avoid thoughts and feelings, just breathe into them. Do not try to do anything with them either. This buddha nature is present whether or not we have some particular flashy experience of seeing into it. Suzuki Roshi, my teacher's teacher, said once that you might get enlightened and not like it. Believing that having some flashy experience will settle things is a way of running away from our real responsibility. Kenshō is not the end of practice, but just an occasional pleasant jolt on the path.

THE RANGE OF ZAZEN EXPERIENCE

In this practice of upright sitting, it may happen that we experience some realization. We can have some insight or see things in a fresh way. We are open to not holding on to our idea of this body and mind. It is not that there is no realization in the midst of sitting and just being yourself. Also there is the possibility of letting go. If we sit, breathing into this being, into these thoughts and sensations, exhaling from them, being willing to face all of the repulsive feelings and the thoughts about ourselves that we do not like, just being present with them, at some point there may be transformation. Some attachments let go. But it does not happen based on our ideas about them. As we sit, naturally our brain notes thoughts, just as our ears notice sounds, and our nose scents. We do not need to eliminate the brain's secretions, any more than we need to obliterate all ambient sound in our environment. But how can we be present without being pushed around by thoughts? How can Dōgen call this challenging practice of just being this body and mind on our cushion right now the gateway to peace and joy?

SETTLING INTO REPOSE

Just being present on your cushion you are open to being who you really are, beyond your idea of body and mind. This present attention is a way of giving yourself to yourself, presenting this body and mind to yourself. Dōgen says that zazen is the Dharma gate of *anraku*. Norman Waddell uses the word "repose," translating *anraku* as "repose and bliss."[58] I render it, "Joyful ease." But this English word "repose" is interesting, to re-pose or reposition yourself. This is to settle, to pacify yourself, to find your true place now. The original Chinese character *an* of *anraku* also just means "peace." I actually believe that if everyone in the world just sat upright, breathing calmly and attentive for half an hour several times a week, maybe we would not need wars. That is a radical thought.

Can we be at peace with ourselves without thinking we need to get something else? Of course the phenomenal world is constantly changing, and we are all constantly changing. We develop attachments, we drop attachments, we take on new practices, and so forth. We find new ways to give this self to ourselves.

TRUE REST IS NOT PASSIVE

What I am suggesting as a practice is not about being passive. This is attentive, calm, settled, attention to body and mind, without trying to manipulate or turn ourselves into yet another commodity that we are trying to get something from. It is not easy to let go of that manipulative habit. Thinking if I could just improve this or that, we get caught and become commodities.

Such practice is not passively letting it all be, because *you* are there. Do not run away from yourself. Perceiving whatever comes to mind or body and letting it arise and pass without intervening or forming a response might seem to approach passivity. And yet, someone is paying attention, and that attention is important. It is not enough that the body and mind is giving rise to sensations and notes them falling away. You are present. Pay attention without judgments, or when making judgments, not making judgments about that, simply acknowledging a judgment about judgments without making a judgment about those judgments. Really pay attention, without trying to manipulate reality, without trying to get something or get rid of something. Just to become intimate with this experience takes some attention.

How can we sustain a practice of taking responsibility for this person, becoming friendly with ourselves? We must forgive ourselves for the fact that as human beings we arrived here because we have cravings and anger and frustrations and confusion. How can we breathe into that and pay attention, not trying to push it around as our human consciousness and culture may encourage us? How can we pay attention without being fooled? When truly settled and poised, we are not passive but are willing and ready to respond helpfully to the situation before us and even to respond more effectively to the suffering in our society and the world.

RESTFUL RESPONSIBILITY

We have the ability to respond, and we must engage this responsibility. The bodhisattva precepts provide guidelines to how we may respond and how to return home to Buddha. We return home to reality, to community, to fellowship, to friendship. How do we settle into a way of taking responsibility for how we see the world, acting on that, coming from a settling place, and forgiving ourselves for being human beings? We allow ourselves to be the human being on our cushion right now. This is true joyful ease. From that position, we repose in that pose of zazen, and we find our deep rest from settling, not into our ideas and attachments, but into what we actually experience as we are willing to face our own body and mind. From that place, we can support nonharming, the first precept against hurting life, and we can actually bring our life to life. We can take responsibility and speak our truth, and we express generosity rather than taking what is not given.

The twelfth-century Chinese Sōtō Zen teacher Hongzhi speaks from this place of great rest, when he says:

> Just resting is like the great ocean accepting hundreds of streams all absorbed into one flavor. Freely going ahead is like the great surging tides riding on the wind, all coming onto this shore together. How could they not reach into the genuine source? How could they not realize the great function that appears before us? A [Zen practitioner] follows movement and responds to changes in total harmony. Moreover, haven't you yourself established the mind that thinks up all the illusory conditions?[59]

When we settle into being present with this body and mind, we see how we are constantly giving birth to thoughts, feelings, and sensations, and we can start taking responsibility for ourselves. We can become friendly with ourselves. This can be very challenging. Yet simply to settle in and find this deep peace can transform the world. This is available, not just in longer sittings or retreats, but is incorporated fully when we practice several times a week at least, supporting some regular rhythm of settling. Sometimes we do need some particular focus, a meditation object to help us settle into this possibility of joyful ease or repose and peace, or perhaps an intensive period of focused zazen.

A PRACTICE FOR HUMAN BEINGS

When we really pay attention to this body and mind, we see how deeply we are connected with everyone and everything, right as we sit here now. All the people you remember are present on your cushion with you. Many beings and the whole world are on your cushion. If we really take care of ourselves, and see that we are not separate from our communities of people we see during the week, our family and coworkers, then our responsibility is not just to ourselves because "ourself" is not just ourself. We can see this as a moral precept, but how we take responsibility for the precepts and for alleviating the suffering of all beings, including ourselves, is to see that we each are deeply, deeply interconnected. What happens across the world, in Iraq, or Africa, or South America, affects us. We can see that interconnection now maybe more than people did centuries ago, and we can respond helpfully to the whole world. If the person next to you is unhappy, you cannot really be totally happy yourself. Hearing someone weeping is helpful to remind us of the reality of suffering. We all have felt damaged in some way. Not turning away from who we are means being willing to face the sadness that is part of reality.

The more you settle into this practice, the more subtly you can perceive the reality of suffering. We develop the craft of attending to it. With some sustainable way of regularly practicing, without trying to arrange or fix or manipulate it, we start to become more deeply familiar with our own physical and mental habits. Reality never happens according to our expectations. Reality is not our little meager idea. And yet we can take responsibility for our efforts. When we show up and befriend ourselves, we start to see more subtly the ways we try to grab on to or get rid of things. But we have to forgive ourselves for being human beings. Zazen is a practice for human beings, not for some super-beings.

Most of the trouble of the world comes from people trying to get something they do not have but think will make them happy, or trying to get rid of something they think prevents them from being happy. Can we just be content with this situation? Can we appreciate and respect ourselves and the world enough to be as we are? Then how do we take care of that, take care of all the suffering beings of the world and in our own hearts and minds?

Suzuki Roshi said that our practice is constantly losing our balance against a background of perfect balance. That is what re-pose is about, to lose our balance constantly—and to return to some upright, dignified posture.

PART 2

Reflections on Eihei Dōgen

Reflections on Translating Dōgen

THE JEWEL OF DŌGEN STUDY

TRANSLATING DŌGEN, like reading Dōgen (in the original or in reasonable translations), is a richly rewarding art. I am grateful to have
been able to make a contribution to the burgeoning body of translations
of Dōgen into English. My own study of Dōgen has been inextricably connected with my practice of zazen. My first zazen instruction in New York
City from my first teacher, Rev. Kandō Nakajima, was also my first time
hearing a Dharma talk about Dōgen's teaching. Something struck home.
Since that time, more than thirty-five years ago, I have continued everyday
zazen practice, as well as regular study of Dōgen. I feel that the two belong
together, and the wealth of new Dōgen material in English since then has
been very helpful.

A year or so after starting formal Sōtō Zen practice and listening to talks
on Dōgen, I returned to school to study Japanese language and Chinese
and Japanese history, literature, and philosophy. I did this simply to receive
some background for more fully understanding this Dōgen person. Since
then I have continued studying Dōgen, both academically and in practice contexts with my teacher Reb Anderson and other San Francisco Zen
Center teachers, and later for one practice period in a Sōtō monastery in
Japan.

DŌGEN'S IMPACT TODAY

The current interest in Dōgen comes in large part simply from the power
of his writings as poetic, evocative texts that yield subtle philosophic truths.

Dōgen has become a world figure in the history of spiritual literature. His name now shares a place for many with such luminaries as Rumi, William Blake, Rilke, Tsongkhapa, Saint John of the Cross, Hildegard of Bingen, Śāntideva, Meister Eckhart, Nietszche, Thoreau, or whichever particular dozen or so names we each might choose to suggest. But Dōgen is notable in that he is not primarily interested in religious doctrine or literary virtue but rather is a dedicated meditation teacher. His focus is to encourage the sustaining of a specific practice tradition, that of ongoing awakening, or going beyond buddha.

It is ironic that Dōgen's writing has been so meaningful to the introduction to the West of Zen (and even Buddhism generally) in the last half of the twentieth century. In terms of Dōgen's importance to the historical development of Japanese Sōtō Zen, study of his writings was nearly insignificant. Since a generation or two after Dōgen, his writings were basically unknown for many centuries except to a small number of Sōtō scholars and priests, until the popular revival and interest in Dōgen in Japan beginning in the 1920s. In terms of the historical development of Japanese Sōtō Zen, Dōgen was much more important, firstly, for his training of a fine core group of dedicated and skilled Sōtō disciples and, secondly, for his emphasis on precepts and his introduction of the lay bodhisattva precept ceremony, which helped develop wide Sōtō Zen support throughout the Japanese countryside and is still important in modern Sōtō Zen.

And yet, the rediscovery of Dōgen's writings and their popularity in translation in the West seems highly appropriate to our current situation. Dōgen's writings are profound and illuminating. While often poetic and provocative, Dōgen's writings also present a perspective appropriate to modern spiritual concerns. His writings are both challenging and sometimes deeply comforting. His radical nondualism offers a stimulating alternative to our sense of alienation from the surrounding "other" and to a consumerist culture that skillfully aims to turn our world and our lives into objectified commodities. His nonanthropocentric, inclusive worldview provides a fresh spiritual context for seeing our intimate connection and responsibility to our environment.

JOYS AND CHALLENGES OF TRANSLATING DŌGEN

The best way I have found for myself to study Dōgen has been attempting to translate him. I have had the great privilege to work extensively on translations of Dōgen in collaboration both with Kazuaki Tanahashi and with Shohaku Okumura. With Kaz I have worked on several *Shōbōgenzō* fascicles and some of Dōgen's poetry, and I have appreciated and learned from Kaz's incisive and poetically elegant approach to expressing Dōgen's essential meaning. With Shohaku I have translated "Bendōwa" (in *The Wholehearted Way*), *Eihei Shingi* (as *Dōgen's Pure Standards for the Zen Community*), and *Eihei Kōroku* (as *Dōgen's Extensive Record*). I have enjoyed and benefited from Shohaku's careful faithfulness to Dōgen and patient investigation of his teachings. I have also had the pleasure of working with, in various capacities, a half dozen or so other fine Dōgen translators or scholars, including Norman Waddell, Steven Heine, Carl Bielefeldt, Thomas Cleary, Tom Wright, Will Bodiford, and Griffith Foulk. I have learned much about Dōgen, and about translation, from each of them.

There are many challenges to translating Dōgen's writings. Some of these are inherent in the Japanese language he uses, as well as in the Chinese in which some of his works are written. Often subjects are not stated, pronouns are indefinite, and singular or plural is unspecified. Sometimes these are clear in the context of what is being said. But often the translator must make a decision about what and how much to add, just to make the English reasonably coherent. Not infrequently, even where a sentence should break is unclear in Dōgen's original, as phrases might be read either in connection with the phrase before or after.

Another main issue is how to include in English the ambiguities that are abundantly present in Chinese and Japanese. These can arise in the multiple meanings of some Chinese characters and compounds, as well as in Dōgen's abundant references to Buddhist teachings and Zen lore, along with Chinese literary classics. Usually, in the more precise English language, it is difficult to suggest all the overtones or nuances that exist in some of Dōgen's sentences (although footnotes can help). Often the translator can clearly sense from the context Dōgen's primary intended meaning, but there are instances where a multiplicity of meanings is clearly relevant. In such cases, occasionally, I have discovered a way in English to suggest the same range of ambiguities as the original— such are the small "victories" in translating Dōgen.

DŌGEN'S PLAY WITH LANGUAGE

Dōgen is famous for his intricate play with language, turning inside-out conventional phrases from the sutras and koan collections to yield their deeper meaning. Further, many of his sentences at first may seem unnecessarily lengthy and complex. Indeed, at times a literal English reading of his Japanese style might produce something that seems childish or repetitious in a way that is not at all the case in the original Japanese or Chinese, where it is simply natural. And simplified paraphrase is often an injustice to Dōgen's original. Norman Waddell told me that when he was studying Dōgen's writing with Kyoto School philosopher Nishitani Keiji, Nishitani once took apart one of Dōgen's long, complicated sentences to show that there was no other way Dōgen could have said what he wanted to say. Nishitani believed that all of Dōgen's seemingly convoluted sentences were completely necessary to the teaching Dōgen intended.

The following two complex sentences from the "Self-fulfillment Samādhi" section of "Bendōwa," an essential early work, are examples of Dōgen's intricate, precise utterances that cannot casually be condensed or simplified into short sentences:

> Therefore, this zazen person without fail drops off body and mind, cuts away previous tainted views and thoughts, awakens genuine Buddha Dharma, universally helps the buddha work in each place, as numerous as atoms, where buddha-tathāgatas teach and practice, and widely influences practitioners who are going beyond buddha, thereby vigorously exalting the Dharma that goes beyond buddha. At this time, because earth, grasses

and trees, fences and walls, tiles and pebbles, all things in the Dharma realm in ten directions, carry out buddha work, therefore everyone receives the benefit of wind and water movement caused by this functioning, and all are imperceptibly helped by the wondrous and incomprehensible influence of buddha to actualize the enlightenment at hand.[60]

This passage follows shortly after, and helps to amplify, one of Dōgen's most radical statements. "When one displays the buddha mudra with one's whole body and mind, sitting uprightly in this samādhi even for a short time, everything in the entire Dharma world becomes buddha mudra, and all space in the entire universe becomes enlightenment." The astonishing notion of space itself awakening, or becoming enlightenment, is elaborated in Dōgen's careful description of the mutual, incomprehensible influence between the practitioner and the grasses and trees, fences and walls, tiles and pebbles.

PROCLAIMING THE MEANING

The primary questions while translating such passages from Dōgen are, "What is the Dharma here? What does Dōgen mean? Why is he saying this?" It is not enough to just translate the words without considering their spiritual meaning. But on numbers of occasions after a few hours of wrestling over the teaching of a particularly difficult passage, considering various possible meanings, I have found that upon returning to reconsider Dōgen's original sentence structure, suddenly the meaning becomes clear. Then, of course, how to put his meaning into readable English that as accurately as possible conveys the teaching Dōgen is offering, with something of the same feeling and tone as Dōgen, is the next part of the challenge.

I came to refer to my regular collaborative translation sessions as "Dokusan with Dōgen" (Dokusan is the Zen practice of face-to-face teaching with a Dharma teacher). In encounter after encounter, Dōgen presents profound nuggets, sometimes playfully twisted inside-out, that challenge both understanding and response. The only appropriate response is somehow to clearly express Dōgen's Dharma in English. One can only hope that the attempts offered will be helpful to others' partaking of Dōgen's insight.

I especially have come to enjoy Dōgen's forthright style of proclaiming the Dharma. He does not follow what we might consider conventional logic, but his mind works and plays creatively in the connections he makes in order to express and declare the reality of awakening. In his essays in *Shōbōgenzō*, but also in the short Dharma hall discourses to his monk disciples in *Eihei Kōroku*, Dōgen interweaves connections between major themes, imagistic motifs, and the celebrated Chan figures upon whose dialogues he comments. He plays freely with this material to proclaim his own deeply experiential sense of the teachings and their expressions of wisdom and compassion.

Increasingly I appreciate Dōgen's playfulness and joy in simply expounding and expressing the Dharma, radically going beyond any dualism his students might be caught in. Dōgen's teaching is also very practical. The point of his wisdom is to encourage expression of this awareness throughout all our activity. In one of his short talks to his monks in *Eihei Kōroku*, Dharma hall discourse 239 from 1247, Dōgen expresses how this wisdom must be applied to expression in everyday activity:

> Entering the water without avoiding deep-sea dragons is the courage of a fisherman. Traveling the earth without avoiding tigers is the courage of a hunter. Facing the drawn sword before you, and seeing death as just like life, is the courage of a general. What is the courage of patch-robed monks?

> After a pause Dōgen said: Spread out your bedding and sleep; set out your bowls and eat rice; exhale through your nostrils; radiate light from your eyes. Do you know there is something that goes beyond? With vitality, eat lots of rice and then use the toilet. Transcend your personal prediction of future buddhahood from Gautama.[61]

The Practice of Genjōkōan

THE MEANING OF GENJŌKŌAN

PERHAPS THE MOST fundamental writing of Eihei Dōgen is "Genjō-kōan," an essay written in 1233. As it was addressed to a lay practitioner, it is particularly relevant to our practice in the West, practicing within the world.

The name of this essay, and of this practice, genjōkōan, comes from a phrase that was used in China to indicate resolving a koan, which is traditionally a teaching story from encounters between Chan teachers and students. However, this is not how Dōgen is using this word, and it is not the meaning of this term in our practice. The word genjō means "to fully or completely manifest," or more loosely "to express or share." And in this context kōan does not refer to these teaching stories but to the heart of the matter. So our practice in our sitting or when we get up from our formal sitting is to fully manifest, express, or share what is essential in the situation in front of us, and to do this within ourselves, together in sangha, and for our world as a whole. Expressing what is most essential is a very rich teaching.

DELUSION AND ENLIGHTENMENT DEFINED

In a passage from early in the essay, Dōgen says:

> To carry your self forward and illuminate the myriad things, the myriad dharmas, is delusion. That the myriad things come forth and illuminate themselves is awakening or enlightenment.

Those who are greatly enlightened about delusion are buddhas. Those who have great delusions about enlightenment are sentient beings or deluded beings. Moreover there are those who continue awakening beyond awakening, and those who are in delusion throughout delusion.[62]

Dōgen is defining things for us here very clearly. First, to carry your self forward and illuminate the myriad things is called delusion, and this is our normal human life. What we do in our world is to bring our selves forward. We experience the things of our life. We experience the teachings too from the context of projecting our selves forward onto them. We see ourselves as a subject, observing, manipulating, working with things of the world. We imagine the world is outside us, with a separation between ourselves and the world. We all have some story or idea about this self that we carry forward to illuminate the myriad things. Everyone could probably recite their address and social security number and many other things about this self that they are carrying forward. This is our ordinary human world of delusion.

On the other hand, Dōgen says enlightenment occurs when the myriad things come forth and illuminate themselves. As we do this practice of sitting and being present and aware of this process, we start to glimpse how the world arises with each inhalation and exhalation. The world experiences itself. This is not the subject-object world. It is not that the objects are coming forth and experiencing me; it is not that all of the readers are creating this book. Actually we are all creating it together. All the myriad things and all the myriad teachings come forth and illuminate themselves. This is enlightenment in Buddhism. The world is not some object that we can control. The world does not belong to people; we belong to the world, and we are part of the world, one of the myriad things. This description of enlightenment is not a description of passivity. It is not that everything comes forth and experiences itself and that this happens out there on some external TV screen. We are each integral pieces of that all-togetherness. Everything arises right now. This is the site of enlightenment.

However, the important point is not to think that you have to get rid of one and find the other. Dōgen says those who are greatly enlightened about delusion are buddhas, and those who have grand delusions about enlightenment are deluded beings. It is not that we should have some preference. These are both aspects of our life. We carry ourselves forward and we illuminate the myriad things based on this self that we have constructed. This is our world of delusion. Myriad things come forth and experience themselves, experience all things, experience our togetherness. This is awakening. Both sides are genjōkōan.

THE ACTIVE GENJŌKŌAN OF BOTH DELUSION AND ENLIGHTENMENT

"To genjōkōan," as a verb, is to fully express our hearts, to be present in all aspects of our life, to bring our life to life, to allow ourselves to express the world, to allow the world to express ourselves. We need to "genjōkōan" both delusion and enlightenment.

Each of us individually and all of us together, beings seen and unseen, beings human and otherwise, are all completely a subset of the myriad things, of reality arising right now. Our practice is actually to wake up to our delusions. We sit upright and present, settling down into our inner dignity, and when we do that we see delusions everywhere. We see our habits of attachment and of grasping. We see our conditioned patterns of reaction. We see our fears and sadness and all of the aspects of our life in which we feel damaged or hurt. We see our own patterns of creating more difficulty for ourselves and for others. This all takes a while. To see delusion and enlightenment is easy. That can happen any time. But then to actually bring this fully into our life is the endless practice of studying ourselves, just being there as ourselves. Buddhas are greatly enlightened and awakened to their delusions. This is our practice.

I remember receiving my first zazen instruction, and I felt like I had come home. The first time I sat was wonderful, and I knew it, and I have done zazen every day since. Yet when we start getting into the practice of sitting upright, and observe how we carry ourselves forward and impose and project ourselves on to things, and also as we start to see that things are arising together, we feel this tension and our habits of grasping, of aversion, and of confusion. You might feel happy when you start sitting and you might also feel terrible, as you were not aware that your mind was so actively chattering. You may have had the delusion that you are what you think, and that you can control your thoughts. But when you actually sit down and just breathe and are upright, the tapes can start rolling. Our practice is just to hang out there. It is not that you are supposed to fix that, not that you are supposed to get rid of delusion. Instead illuminate delusion; study it. Become familiar and intimate with yourself. See what it is really like to be in this body and mind, today, with each inhalation and exhalation.

On the other hand, if you have a lot of delusions about enlightenment, that is what Dōgen calls delusion. Nevertheless these two sides are present, and Dōgen says there are those who continue awakening beyond awakening. In fact, buddha is always ongoingly awakening. You may have some glimpse of enlightenment, or you may have some deep, dramatic, flashy, transformative experience of awakening. But that is just the beginning, because we can continue awakening beyond awakening and we can be in delusion throughout delusion.

When you are deluded, be deluded. See delusion. Delusion is the genjōkōan of delusion. Seeing this, genjōkōan your delusions. See how you are confused. See how you are caught up in grasping and attachment, in aversion and trying to get rid of things. From the point of view of awakening there is no difference at all between awakening and delusion. From the point of view of enlightenment, here we all are on the path together. How strange; how wonderful. Of course from the point of view of delusion, there is a huge difference. In delusion we actually do cause difficulty; we see ourselves as separate from others. We think we can manipulate the world to get what we want. We think it is okay to invade other countries to take back our oil from under their soil. We actually believe that we can manipulate the world to get what we want. This is delusion. Awakening is just sharing this realization of togetherness, this love, this possibility of being together. From the point of view of delusion, there is a huge difference.

Our practice is not to get rid of one and grab hold of the other. Trying to grab hold of enlightenment and get rid of delusion is more delusion, a big delusion. We have to genjōkōan delusion and genjōkōan awakening. Our practice, this practice that Dōgen is recommending, is about how we live in the world, how we bring our life into the world, and how we share what is significant in our life.

FULLY ENGAGING BOTH SIDES

It is important to see both sides as genjōkōan. Even after much experience of ongoing awakening, delusion can arise. We imagine there is something over there that we want to grab. We can imagine there is somebody over here we want to push aside. Or we can do that within ourselves in our own hearts, with our own body and mind. We can think that this part of me is wonderful but that part of me is ghastly, and thus we try to get rid of it. That kind of thinking is just delusion, yet that is how we think. This is a practice not for some fancy ideal buddha image on an altar, but for human beings. We are deeply deluded, living in difficult times in a troubled world. We are all confused and greedy, and we are all picking and choosing. This is the world of delusion that we live in. And yet, when all of the delusions arise and experience themselves, here we are, awake.

The practice of genjōkōan is about actually fully engaging both sides, first to see how we do have this deeply ingrained pattern of seeing ourselves as separate from the world. Our language and way of thinking is determined by syntax of subject and object. We think that we are subjects "verbing" objects to get what we want or get rid of what we do not want. Or we might feel that we are objects trying not to be "verbed" by subjects out there. Either way, this is our world of delusion; this is how we think.

And yet, also, this other side starts to arise in us. As we are willing to just settle down and be present and upright, we can see that we are all breathing together. The myriad things arise. This is our world too. Do not try and get rid of one and grab a hold of the other. Just to dance in this dynamic tension of delusion and awakening is our life; this is how we express ourselves. We can share our deepest wholesomeness with the world, not turning away from either side. Of course it is important to see the difference, to become intimate with this whole process and try not to cause harm, not to make problems for one's self or for others.

STUDYING THE SELF

In "Genjōkōan," Dōgen also talks about studying the Buddha Way and studying the self. He says:

> To study the Buddha Way is to study the self. To study the self is to forget the self. To forget the self is to be actualized by myriad things. When actualized by myriad things, body and mind as well as the body and mind of others drop away.

Often Zen students, when they hear, "To study the Buddha Way is to study the self. To study the self is to forget the self," think they are supposed to forget the self. But actually our practice is just to study the self. Studying the self is already exactly forgetting the self. Our practice is just to be the person on our cushion right now in this body and mind. Really, fully just genjōkōan this person here. Look at the delusion and the awakening happening as you sit. Doing that is exactly forgetting the self.

This study of the self is not about psychologically analyzing our self. That might be part of it, and psychology and psychotherapy can be complimentary and helpful to Zen students, but the practice that we do, sitting upright, observing this body and mind from within our body and mind, not from some idea of it, goes much deeper than just our psychological analyses. It may include those, but it is about how to actually be present in this body and mind, a yogic practice to really feel our presence physically. This is our work. This is the ongoing awakening beyond awakening.

SOMETHING IS MISSING

Another couple sentences later on in "Genjōkōan" fully express something very important. These two sentences have always struck me as strange and somewhat paradoxical. I have been chewing on them for thirty years, and they are worthy of remembering, considering, and sitting with. Dōgen says:

> When Dharma does not fill your whole body and mind, you think it is already sufficient. When Dharma fills your whole body and mind, you understand that something is missing.

The line "When Dharma fills your whole body and mind, you realize that something is missing" goes very deep. The first Noble Truth of suffering or unsatisfactoriness says that things are a little out of alignment, at least. It is all right when you think that your practice is okay just as it is. It means the Dharma is not yet filling your body and mind, but still, if that is what is happening, if you think it is fine as it is, please enjoy that. But please hear Dōgen saying that when Dharma fills your whole body and mind, when the teaching and reality occupies you, expresses you, and arises in you completely, then you realize something is missing. The reality of our life and of the world is that there is this lack. You may feel it in yourself but it is not just you. You might feel that you are the only one who feels some lack, but actually this is our situation as human beings and as buddhas. Something is missing.

The phenomenal world manifests in many particular ways. Each breath is unique. You may all be very experienced in inhaling, and in exhaling, as we share this air together. And yet every single inhalation and every single exhalation is completely unique. Even while we create this teaching together in each moment, the situation is changing. Everything is flowing. Who you are is shifting even though you might still remember your social security number. Reality is alive, dynamic, and flowing in all directions. When we really settle into being willing to be this person, we can realize that many things are possible and also that there are many limitations. We should not get rid of our limitations, but right in our limitations, right in this particular situation of the body and mind sitting on your chair right now, many things are possible. Many things also may *not* be possible, but something is missing and actually it is very fortunate that something is missing. If you truly were complete right now, there would be nothing else to do. You would not have to take another breath. But the reality is that each breath you take, whether you are aware and enjoying your inhalations and exhalations or not, is completely necessary. If you do not take another inhalation you never will take other inhalations in the future. And every inhalation you ever took in the past is absolutely necessary to this next one. This is how our ongoing awakening works. In each situation we still, afresh, must genjōkōan, must find our way of expressing and sharing what is important. There is an old saying that Śākyamuni Buddha only got fifty percent. Something is missing.

Another way to see this is in terms of the precepts. Because something is missing, because we are indeed alive, we need guidance in how to take care of our lives together, how to be kind to each other, how to see our limitations, and how to realize our mistakes and hopefully not make the same mistake too many times. We can see that there is something missing. Something more can be present. There is a limitation, but also other possibilities. Our practice of genjōkōan is just to find how to more and more fully express and share our caring and our love in the world. Meeting each situation, new possibilities and fresh challenges arise. In the middle of delusion and in the middle of enlightenment, we more fully express, share, and manifest our genjōkōaning, our caring, our expression of loving and receiving love in this troubled world, in the troubled world of our own hearts that are still grasping in delusion. We also manifest our genjōkōan in the troubled world of whatever sangha or community we are in, with the inevitable limitations that happen when particular examples of delusion and awakening rub up against each other. In our world at large, how do we share our caring with the world?

Practicing the Awesome Presence
of Active Buddhas

WHAT ARE ACTIVE BUDDHAS?

K AZ TANAHASHI and I translated an essay from Dōgen's *Shōbōgenzō* called "Gyōbutsu Īgi," translating the title as "The Awesome Presence of Active Buddhas."[63] *Gyōbutsu* are active or practicing buddhas, and *īgi* could be translated as "dignified manner." This *gyō* has many meanings. Literally it means "active" or "practicing"; it is one of the characters in the usual word for practice, *shugyō*. It also means "to walk" and implies performing. So this essay is about buddhas who are performing buddhas' work in the world, actual buddhas who are active. Gyō also means "conduct."

In the essay, Dōgen begins by talking about all the things that active buddhas are not. He mentions other categories of buddhas, bliss-body buddhas, incarnate buddhas, buddhas who acquire enlightenment, or buddhas who are fundamentally enlightened, and he says that active buddhas are not any of those. They are just lively buddhas.

In a story in the Lotus Sutra, ancient bodhisattvas in the open space beneath the earth spring forth from under the ground as needed to make offerings to Buddha and to help beings.[64] These ancient bodhisattvas are under our seats and ready to spring forth to help. The four leaders of these bodhisattvas all have this character *gyō* as part of their names. This *gyō* implies the activity of these bodhisattvas as buddhas in the world. We could also say gyōbutsu is "expressive buddha," the buddha who expresses himself or herself in the world in our lives. Gyōbutsu do performance art. How do we perform buddha in the world? Gyōbutsu are not static or dull, but lively, vital buddhas. This is buddha as responsive, and sustainable, buddha going beyond buddha. Active buddhas are buddhas who express buddha in a sustainable way in the world, as a renewable resource. How do we renew this awakened awareness every day, every breath?

DIGNIFIED PRESENCE

The second half of the title, "Īgi," is in some ways more mysterious, more complicated. We can misunderstand it easily. Kaz and I translated it as "awesome presence." But it also means "dignified presence," "decorum," even "etiquette." What is the form, the īgi, with which active buddhas express themselves? Īgi implies inner dignity, inspiring presence, the attitude or manners that inspire us to find our own īgi. We have external forms in Zen, including bowing, chanting, or simply how we stand in the meditation hall, all helpful in finding our presence. But īgi is really about our inner posture, which we form and learn in zazen, returning again and again to this possibility of sitting upright and finding our inner dignity. This īgi is not about becoming stern and formal. It is not about being aloof and beyond the world, but it is right in the middle of our world. Īgi is not about being correct, right as opposed to wrong. How do we bring īgi to life? How do we find our own inner dignity and vitality?

Dōgen tells us many things gyōbutsu is not, but he does not, I believe, do enough of the same for īgi. This īgi is a problem for us. Perhaps Emily Post was a Zen master, but etiquette is part of Western culture that many people might see as stiff or uptight. In Zen we have many forms. By doing prostrations, bowing, and sitting upright in a sustainable manner, we start to connect with this inner dignity and respectfulness, this inspiring awesome presence.

One of the unhelpful approaches to Zen that is available in America takes these Zen forms and tries to perform them perfectly. Among the different branches of Sōtō Zen in twentieth-century Japan, one style or branch emphasizes beauty, doing the forms beautifully to find one's inner presence. But at heart this is not the approach of Zen zombies, working to follow the forms perfectly as if that were the main purpose of practice. This īgi is not about repressing or getting rid of all feelings; it is about discovering, as we will see Dōgen says, "the home village of the self." One must deeply enter this practice and find oneself, explore how this body and mind right now takes on this expressive presence. This is not accomplished simply by copying external forms. One uses the outer forms to find one's inner dignity. They are like a trellis made of straight lines upon which the twisting vines of our true life can flourish.

Another nonhelpful approach is "lobotomy Zen"—thinking that in Zen practice just getting rid of all your thoughts is enlightenment. Do not fall for that one either. What is this mysterious inner dignity and awesome inspiring presence that is already on your cushion right now? It cannot be found by going out and buying a six-pack of īgi. It involves finding what is already somehow present, this inner inspired awakened, responsive, caring īgi. Bob Dylan has a song about īgi, called "Dignity," in which he sings, "Someone showed me a picture and I just laughed, Dignity never been photographed."[65] Dignity is not about the outer forms, and yet we use the outer forms. These active buddhas are performing in the world in many contexts and expressing this, each in his or her own way. Each of us has our own particular way of expressing the awakening heart/mind and inner dignity and presence on our seat right now. It takes a while, and actually it is endless, to find that dignity and allow it to open up and blossom in our lives.

NO WAITING FOR BUDDHA

One of the first things that Dōgen says in "Gyōbutsu Īgi" is "Know that buddhas in the Buddha Way do not wait for awakening." This practice is not some method by which, if you log enough cushion hours, or read enough Zen texts or sutras, or make enough prostrations, then eventually in the future something called awakening will appear. Buddhas do not think like that. They do not wait for awakening. The actual active, lively, performing buddhas know that awakening does not happen later as a result of spiritual practice. Practice is not about getting something later. This is a very central teaching of Dōgen, the oneness of practice and enlightenment. There is no enlightenment that is not practiced. When Śakyamuni Buddha had his big enlightenment he did not stop practicing. That was just the beginning of his practice, and he continued to sit in meditation every day. Enlightenment, if it truly is enlightenment, needs to be expressed, needs to be performed in the world. One way we do that is through zazen. Furthermore, practice is not really practice unless it is the expression of awakening. Even if you attend a Zen temple for the first time, just showing up to hear about practice proves that already, whether you know it or not, there is already awakening happening somehow around your body and mind. Of course, this develops and unfolds. But this practice, the engagement with the outer and inner forms of dignity and awesome presence, is an expression of awakening. Practice and awakening are not separate at all.

This is why Dōgen says that buddhas in the Buddha Way, which means active buddhas, do not wait for awakening. Awakening is not just some flashy experience. It happens sometimes that things drop away. These dramatic opening experiences are fine, but that is not what is emphasized by Dōgen. Just to sustain and renew the actual practice and engagement of awesome dignified manner is the point. In another writing, Dōgen describes how not just practice and enlightenment are one, but practice, enlightenment, and expounding the Dharma are one.[66] There is no true practice that is not an expression of enlightenment, and there is no enlightenment that is not an expression of practice, and there is no expounding of the Dharma that's not the practice of enlightenment. They all happen together. Dōgen states later in "The Awesome Presence of Active Buddhas" that buddhas also just sit and listen to the Dharma. Expounding the Dharma from a seat up in the front of the hall is not superior to listening to the Dharma in the moment it arrives on your seat.

THE VITAL PROCESS ON THE PATH OF GOING BEYOND

After saying that all buddhas in the Buddha Way do not wait for awakening, Dōgen offers one of my favorite lines in all of his writing, which I have recommended people memorize. "Active buddhas alone fully experience the vital process on the path of going beyond buddha." Our practice is just to fully experience this, not to understand it. He talks later about the impossibility of understanding this in a linear manner. This practice, awakening, and expounding of reality is a vital, dynamic, organic process, an alchemical process. It cannot be fabricated or manufactured. We cannot usually track it. Sometimes we may have a period of zazen where we feel very groggy and sleepy and think that was bad zazen, or we have a period of zazen where we feel very clear and think that was good zazen, but those are just our limited human calculations and judgment. We cannot know and grasp how this organic, alchemical, vital process is happening. We sit in the cauldron of the forms and structures and guideposts of the buddhas and ancestors, going back twenty-five hundred years and actually much more. So just surrendering to this organic path, allowing this dynamic active buddha to take form, *is* this vital process.

There is a path, an endless path. And congratulations for finding it! This path has its own organic dynamic process, which is the path of going beyond buddha. This is the path of living, vital, lively buddhas. Buddha cannot be a dead buddha. How do we bring buddha to life in our world with all its problems? "Going beyond buddha" is a common phrase in Dōgen's writings, indicating the ongoing nature of awakening and of the active or practicing buddhas' conduct. For Dōgen, buddhahood is not some one-time attainment to be cherished thereafter, but an ongoing vital process, requiring continued reawakening. The historical Śakyamuni Buddha and all the other many buddhas do not stop practicing and they do not stop awakening. The only real buddha is a buddha going beyond buddha, this ongoing sustainable, renewable resource of buddha.

Just fully experience the vital process. This dynamic, vital, alchemical process involves opening up to our feelings, to the first Noble Truth of the pain of the world, the sorrow of the world, the cruelty, loss, wars, and injustice, the truth of old age, sickness, and death. On the path of going beyond buddha sometimes this dynamic vital process does not feel so good. But we have to fully experience it and learn to trust that we are on this path, and feel what we are feeling, including feeling the sadness. Again, this īgi is not about being a Zen zombie. I often recommend as a mantra, even to use during zazen, Bob Dylan's mantra: "How does it feel?"[67] Just feel what you are feeling as you meditate. This is the vital process of finding your own way of expressing buddha, this inner dignity, this awesome presence, and that is not too small a word nor too big a word. Feel sadness when you feel sad; feel anger when you feel angry, not holding on to it and not turning it into grudge and revenge. Feel fear when you feel fear. It is very important these days not to be afraid of feeling fear and of being afraid. This is all part of this active process of expressing the active buddha on your seat. This dignified presence is how we express bodhisattva precepts.

WORKING BUDDHAS AND MEANINGFUL PRACTICE

Dōgen says, "Because active buddhas manifest awesome presence in every situation, they bring forth awesome presence with their body." This is not some theoretical abstraction, but something we actually do. Of course it is not separate from our mind. But this is a physical practice engaging the world. Dōgen then says, "Thus, their transformative function flows out in their speech, reaching throughout time, space, buddhas, and activities." We are sitting in the middle of the transformative function of the workings of buddhas. Everything is being transformed, digested, and spit out in each moment. Each moment there is this transformation. Everything is alive and changing, far beyond what we can see, hear, smell, taste, touch, or think with our limited human apparatus. And yet it depends on us. This transformative function happens because of your dignified presence, with all beings together, right now, today.

It is very important that there is a transformative function and that it flows out in speech, I would say also in body and mind, and reaches throughout time, throughout all the times. We can transform the past, and its meaning, just by how we see it now. This work also reaches throughout space. Your zazen is not just what happens where you are. This vital process of your own inner dignity reaches throughout time, space, buddhas, and activities. This transformative process functions when we set ourselves down on the path, taking care of our everyday activities and our relationships in our work life and with our families. This transformative function flows forth from this lively buddha and her dignified, inspiring presence.

Suzuki Roshi talks about nongaining mind. Hearing that, we may misunderstand and think we should not get anything out of the practice. We do not try to get something specific from this practice, because if we have some outcome we want to get, that is just consumer Zen, just trying to acquire more goodies. But our practice is not meaningless or purposeless. We have bodhisattva precepts to guide us in how this transformative function works. It does work. I know this, having seen it in myself and in many other people. But it takes time. This mysterious, organic, alchemical process happens with its own lawfulness, not according to our limited human conceptions.

EVERYDAY ACTIVITIES PRACTICE

In another passage Dōgen says, "Although the everyday activities of active buddhas invariably allow buddhas to practice, active buddhas allow everyday activities to practice." What does Dōgen mean that buddhas allow everyday activities to practice? The traditional Zen forms in the zendo and the sangha provide a structure in which to find our practice heart. But even when you are doing laundry, taking out the trash, or at the grocery store, these activities give you an opportunity to perform expressive, sustainable buddha work. Maybe you can get a taste of that driving down the street, for example. You have a chance to see yourself, to express kindness, maybe not to get upset at someone driving foolishly, but give him enough space. How can you allow washing the dishes or walking down the street to be this awesome, inspiring presence? How can you allow the exchange with the cashier at the grocery store, not just you or her, but the whole activity, to be active presence? That is the challenge Dōgen offers us.

There is a kind of craft involved. If you take on this practice in an everyday kind of way, offer the everyday activities of your life to practice, and take advantage of the opportunities of the situation of this world with all of its difficulties, sadness, and all its frustrations and confusion, then you can bring alive your life and its everyday activities. This transformative function will not fix the world according to our ideas of what it should be, but our ideas of what it should be are also part of the transformative function. Birds sing; people drink tea. The world is in the midst of transformation right now, as is your body and mind and heart.

LETTING GO AMID MUD AND WATER

Dōgen says:

> This is to abandon your body for Dharma, to abandon Dharma for your body. This is to give up holding back your life, to hold on fully to your life. The awesome presence not only lets go of Dharma for the sake of the Dharma, but also lets go of Dharma for the sake of mind. Do not forget that this letting go is immeasurable.

This dynamic, active process requires letting go. Zazen teaches us about letting go, letting go of the pain in the knees or wherever, and letting go of some encrusted holding on you do with some pain in your heart, allowing it to open up. This is letting go of holding back from your life. We have so many reasons and encouragements to hold back, to get distracted by all the sophisticated entertainments that our culture provides us, and to retreat from living our life. Dōgen says give up holding back your life so as to hold on fully to your life. Actually hold on fully to the experience of lively buddha, awakened vitality, inspiring presence, responding to the situation of your friends and family, responding to the pain in your own heart or the fear in your own body. How can we give up holding back our life? How do we give up holding back our engagement in this vital process so as to hold on fully to our life? "Do not forget that this letting go is immeasurable."

Continuing a little further, Dōgen says, "Who would regard this apparition of blossoms in the sky as taking up a mistake and settling in with a mistake?" Can you do that in the midst of the flowers falling from the sky, falling from the roof, and falling from the floor right now? "Stepping forward misses, stepping backward misses, taking one step misses, taking two steps misses, and so there are mistakes upon mistakes." Performing this transformative function, enacting this awesome dignified presence, is simply mistake upon mistake. We are actually alive in this vital process.

"You should thoroughly understand that in the awesome presence, and in the presence of awe, the great way is wide open." We can actually enact this presence and openness in this world, and sometimes it hurts. Just because we are living in the world of the majestic presence and dignity of practicing buddhas does not mean that there are no tragedies, sadness, loss, confusion, frustration, craving, anger, wars, and corruption. That is exactly where we practice. And because of such practice, the awesome presence of active buddhas right now is beyond obstruction. "Totally encompassed by buddhas," Dōgen says, "active buddhas are free from obstruction as they penetrate the vital path of being splattered by mud and soaked in water."

We do not engage this practice in some beautiful, ethereal, heavenly, mountaintop realm. Right in the middle of the mud and water we practice dignified presence and engage the transformative function, and so we can make a big difference. *Your* practice is very important and does make a difference in the world, just by your kindness, thoughtfulness, awareness, and consideration. Right now, this year, is very important to the whole history of the future of the human species. We are living in one of those very pivotal times. Pay attention and do not be afraid to be afraid; do not be afraid to speak your truth. We are completely in the mud and water. Take on this wonderful opportunity. Please enjoy the mud and water, but do not imagine that it is not mud and water. Out of this mud and water the lotus grows.

In this essay Dōgen further says, "The teaching of birth and death, body and mind, is the circle of the way, and is actualized at once. Thoroughly practicing, thoroughly clarifying, it is not forced." There is some effort involved in sitting upright for forty minutes, and there is some effort involved in showing up. Some effort is involved in being yourself, but it is not forced when we practice this dignified presence. You do not have to be somebody other than who you are, reach some higher state of consciousness, or higher state of being. You do not have to crawl through the desert on your knees. You just have to be who you are and express the dignified presence of the awareness and awakening that brought you here.

Dōgen adds, "It is just like recognizing the shadow of deluded thought and turning the light to shine within." Study your delusions without turning away from the shadows. This is what buddhas do. Deluded people have delusions about enlightenment and buddhas. Practicing buddhas, active buddhas, actually are awakened about their delusions. Do not be afraid of your fear or your craziness. Perhaps it is not possible to be truly sane in this corrupt, crazed society. Studying their own difficulties is the dignified presence of active buddhas that buddhas perform. "Recognizing the shadow of deluded thought and then turning the light to shine within" is the basic zazen instruction. As Dōgen says in his "Fukanzazengi," "Take the backward step that turns the light and shines it inward."[68] Do not try to run away from yourself, or become somebody other than the person on your seat right now. Everything you need is right here, now, in this skin bag. Willing to be the person you are, face the wall of your self. This is the practice of active buddhas.

CLARITY BEYOND CLARITY

Dōgen says, "Thoroughly practicing, thoroughly clarifying, it is not forced, it is just like recognizing the shadow of deluded thought and turning the light to shine within. The clarity of clarity beyond clarity prevails in the activity of buddhas. This is totally surrendering to practice." What is this clarity of clarity beyond clarity, which prevails in the activity of buddhas?

Each of you has your own special gifts, talents, and interests, and you may have sophisticated understandings about these. But this practice, this awesome dignified presence, is about finding the clarity of clarity beyond clarity, the understanding beyond understanding. Anything I say about this will be a mistake. I trust that as active buddhas reading about the Dharma, you will find your way to use this, even though each of my words is a mistake upon a mistake. There is a clarity that is beyond your idea of clarity. "Clarity" in Dōgen's passage above could be translated as "understanding." The same character also means "brightness," so it is the brilliance of your brilliance beyond brilliance, the understanding that goes beyond anything we can understand. Many things are happening right here where you are reading that you will never see or hear or understand.

Do not imagine that reality is simply what you think it is. This is not just some ancient Eastern inscrutable mystical philosophy. According to modern physics and string theory there are dimensions of reality happening all around us of which we are not aware. And yet there is a clarity beyond clarity, the true clarity for active buddhas. There is a clarity that might perhaps be called faith. But it is not faith in something outside. It is not faith in self-power or something inside, either. It is not about any belief system but about actually being the dignified presence you are right now, right here.

Even though we cannot understand, see, or hear it, we have some relationship to this clarity. In some way we can fully experience it, even though it is far beyond our experience. This clarity of clarity beyond clarity prevails. Dōgen adds some other sayings that point to it, other fingers pointing to the moon. He continues, "To understand the principle of total surrendering, you should thoroughly investigate mind. In the steadfastness of thorough investigation, all phenomena are the unadorned clarity of mind." Every single thing that happens is intimately related to your mind/heart.

THE HOME VILLAGE OF THE SELF AND THE MOUNTAIN SPIRIT REALM

Dōgen also says, "You know and understand that the three realms of desire, form, and formlessness are merely elaborate divisions of mind. Although your knowing and understanding are part of all phenomena, you actualize the home village of the self." It is not that you should get rid of your understanding and your intellectual knowledge. It is fine to work on trying to understand more, but that is not the clarity beyond clarity. However, it is still a part of all phenomena, a little piece of the clarity beyond clarity. You do not need to get rid of your thinking in zazen, or any other time. Your thinking is just your thinking, just like the bird singing is just the bird singing. Just allow your thinking to be your thinking, allow your bowing to be your bowing, allow your posture to be the dignified presence of your posture, as you realize that although your knowing and understanding are part of all phenomena, really you are "actualizing the home village of the self. This is no other than your everyday activity. This being so, the continuous effort to grasp the point in phrases and to seek eloquence beyond words is to take hold beyond taking hold, and to let go beyond letting go."

Where is your home village, this home village of the self? The home village of the self is not about your small ego self. But it is not separate from that either; that is included. All phenomena are the unadorned clarity of mind. To let go beyond letting go and actualize the home village of the self is simply another way of saying to take refuge in Buddha. Return to the home village of the self, the ordinary simple activities of taking out the trash, doing the laundry, washing the dishes. Take good care of the home village of the self.

This reminds me of a saying in one of my favorite koans in the *Blue Cliff Record* collection, case 61. In the main case, a teacher asks, "Are there any patch-robed monks who can live together and die together?" In his commentary Yuanwu says, "He has his own mountain spirit realm."[69] Realizing that you have your own mountain spirit realm, you actualize the home village of the self. This is exactly the clarity of clarity beyond clarity. Settle in there. Find your own way to be at home in this home village of the self. Express the dignified presence of completely inhabiting the home village of the self, in your own mountain spirit realm. Take on working in the mud and water of the home village of the self.

Another old Zen saying goes, "The ride home always seems shorter." This home village of the self is very close to the mountain spirit realm. The ride home always seems shorter, very close. Turn the light to shine within. All these fancy Zen words are about something that is very close, so close that you cannot see it. It is like trying to see your own eyeballs. Find your own home in the home village of yourself. Sit upright. Just take the next breath. Thoroughly practicing, thoroughly clarifying, it is not forced. And yet it depends completely on you.

Expressing the Dream within the Dream

OVERTURNING CONVENTIONS

ONE OF DŌGEN'S colorful essays from *Shōbōgenzō*, which I translated with Kaz Tanahashi, is called "Muchū Setsumu," or in English, "Within a Dream Expressing the Dream."[70] This essay provides a characteristic example of how Dōgen plays with and turns inside out conventional understandings, certainly from worldly society, but also conventional understandings within Buddhism. Usually in Buddhism dreams are understood as the opposite of awakening. Buddhism is the study of awakening; how we wake up to this nature of wisdom and kindness and awareness that is always present, but because of our dream-like conditioned mind and our habits of grasping and attachment we do not recognize it. Awakening is to actually be present and see this reality. Usually in Buddhist language and discourse there is this opposition of awakening to dreams. In this writing Dōgen completely turns that inside out.

JAPANESE DREAM AWARENESS

Another context is that in medieval Japan generally and medieval Japanese Buddhism especially, dreams were considered important. In both medieval China and Japan often bodhisattva figures, the great enlightening beings, appeared to people in dreams. One of Dōgen's important successors three generations later, Keizan Jōkin (1264–1325), is considered the second founder of Sōtō Zen in Japan, and Keizan's grandmother was a close student of Dōgen. Keizan respected dreams quite a bit, using them to help decide where to build his temples and how to conduct his practice.[71]

Medieval Japanese had the idea of a continuum of awakening. Now we also say that the practice of awakening is not just about what happens in our formal upright sitting meditation. Zazen also happens in how we bring the awareness that we taste in zazen into our everyday activity and interactions, and our work in the world. We recognize a continuum of practice, and there actually is traditional guidance for how to practice even while sleeping. In the monastic monks' hall one sleeps on one's right side, head facing toward the Buddha. This goes back to the Buddha's death or *parinirvāṇa*, which is depicted with the image of him lying on his right side. There are also biological and anatomical reasons why this sleeping posture is considered healthy, in terms of pressure on organs. When we get deeper into this engagement with awakening, we find a sense of a continuum of awareness within our mind. Awakening is not just one experience or state. This continuum of awareness is one context for this *Shōbōgenzō* essay, "Within a Dream Expressing the Dream."

BUDDHAS PRECEDE CREATION

Dōgen begins indirectly, as he does in many of his *Shōbōgenzō* essays, by proclaiming some fundamental background first, and then he returns to a main theme. He begins, "The path of all buddhas and ancestors arises before the first forms emerge." This path and its process of awakening followed by the Buddha and ancestors arise before the first forms emerge, so they are not a function of the creations of this world. "It cannot be spoken of in terms of conventional views. This being so," Dōgen says, "in the realm of buddha ancestors there is the active power of buddhas going beyond buddhas." This phrase, "going beyond buddha," is a definition of Buddha for Dōgen, and one of his basic teachings. Buddha is the one going beyond buddha ongoingly; awakening is not something that happens just once. The purpose is to gain not some dramatic or even nondramatic experience of awakening but this sustainable, ongoing "buddha going beyond buddha." Buddhas do not hold on to the buddha they may have realized or expressed yesterday or today or in the middle of zazen a little while ago. Dōgen speaks frequently about this going beyond.

This idea of going beyond is a basic context for Dōgen talking about dreams and their expression. Dōgen is not primarily interested in our reaching some experience or understanding, but he is interested in how we express this awakening. How do we make it real, how do we actualize it in our world? In "Within a Dream Expressing the Dream" Dōgen continues, "Thus the Dharma wheel has been set to turn since before the first sign of forms emerged." In the undergraduate introduction to Buddhism course I teach, students often ask: where is God in Buddhism? The idea of God as the Creator so central to Western religion is simply not relevant in Buddhism. Without making any judgments about any particular perspective, I simply note that Dōgen says the Buddha's Dharma wheel has been set to turn since before the first forms emerged, before any creation of this world. This teaching of awakening is more fundamental than the array of forms in this universe and world. But the point is, how do we express it in this world?

Dōgen continues, "The great merit needs no reward, and becomes the guidepost for all ages." The bodhisattva precepts are part of our basic practice and teaching and become this great merit. It needs no reward. We do not need to gain any personal benefit, which would actually diminish the merit and its practice, instead of it becoming a guidepost for all ages. What are appropriate standards, not from our conventional way of thinking, but from awakening? We can observe key criteria based on bodhisattva precepts such as supporting life rather than harming, speaking truth, and benefiting all beings. This standard is exceedingly radical in our age, and perhaps in all ages, but this is the dream that we have been given to express.

THE SITE FOR EXPRESSING DREAMS

Then Dōgen proceeds to get to the heart, saying, "Within a dream, this is the dream you express. Because awakening is seen within awakening, the dream is expressed within a dream." He adds, "The place where the dream is expressed within a dream is the land and the assembly of the buddha ancestors." From the usual Buddhist viewpoint this is highly radical and controversial, topsy-turvy. But Dōgen is going very deep here, as he does when he turns language and usual ways of thinking inside out. He claims that the buddha land and the assembly of the buddha ancestors is the place where the dream is expressed within a dream, not where delusory dreams are discarded or transcended.

He continues, "The buddhas' lands and their assemblies, the ancestors' way and their seats, are awakening throughout awakening, and express the dream within a dream." We have our particular dream and world with all of its problems. We have this dream of our own lives, each of us in our place. Is it derogatory to call this a dream? From the point of view of awakening it is just confessing our true situation, that we are human beings with attractions and aversion, with thoughts and feelings, with images or song lyrics or laundry lists, or whatever thoughts and feelings were floating through your heads along with reading the last paragraph. This is the dream we are in. What Dōgen emphasizes is *expression*. How do we express this dream within a dream? This Chinese character, *setsumu* in Japanese, which I translate as "express," could also be translated as "explain" or "expound" or "disclose."

How is it that each of us express, expound, or disclose this dream within a dream, here where we are? This is how Dōgen explores our practice, a provocative and helpful approach. The expressive quality of our practice pervades our everyday activity through various modes of expression, through music, art, athletic endeavors, helping others, listening to others, parenting, and through various organizational activities, we are expressing this dream within a dream. We are expressing, or rather awakening itself is expressing, the dream within a dream.

In "Genjōkōan," one of Dōgen's fundamental writings, he talks about being in awakening within awakening and being in delusions within delusion. It is not a matter of awakening as opposed to a dream. We awaken within a dream. This logic is fundamental to bodhisattva Buddhism. Early

Buddhists saw that we are in samsāra, we suffer. Through our grasping, through our desires, through our fundamental affliction of ignorance, we create a world of suffering. We grasp at things. We are not quite satisfied with all the wonders of the world. We want more. Or we want to get rid of some things that are unpleasant. We are beset with this dis-ease. This is the nature of this dream that we are all in, and the Buddha realized this. So he talked about samsāra and nirvāṇa. Samsāra is this cycle of birth and death, which happens lifetime after lifetime, and also occurs day after day, problem after problem, maybe job after job, relationship after relationship, city after city. We move around in this world of change, in this world where we are trying, sometimes in very wholesome ways, to make things better. There is nothing wrong with that. In early Buddhism the ideal of escape from this rat-race was seen through nirvāṇa as cessation, actually extinguishing all desires, all preferences, purifying ourselves of all discontent. And that is one way to be rid of suffering. But in the bodhisattva way one willingly returns again and again into this world of suffering, and all the problems we have in our lives and in our society, and tries to help. How do we express this dream within the dream, how do we make it real, as a dream? This is what buddhas do.

EXPRESSIVE GRASSES ARE NOT DREAMY

Dōgen adds, "Every dew drop manifested in every realm is a dream." Anything you can think of is a dream; any form you see is a dream.

"This dream is the glowing clarity of the hundred grasses.... At this time, there are dream grasses, grasses within, expressive grasses, and so on. When we study this, then roots, stems, branches, leaves, flowers, and fruits, as well as radiance and color, are all the great dream. Do not mistake them as merely dreamy."

He is not talking about dreams as something kind of fuzzy and groggy or sentimental, i.e. unreal and "dreamy." How do we express our true heart in the dream? He says, "When you say, 'Within confusion is just confusion,' still you should follow the path in the vast sky known as 'delusion throughout delusion.' Just this you should endeavor to investigate thoroughly." For Dōgen the point is not necessarily to obliterate all confusion and all of one's delusions. If it were, seeing how difficult that is, many of us would not even consider practicing the bodhisattva way. Rather, right within our confusion and delusions, how do we remain present and upright, and bring our awareness to that very experience? Continuing, he states quite strongly, "The expression of a dream within a dream is all buddhas." This strange and intriguing utterance might be read as "all buddhas just express a dream within a dream." How do we express our truth even amid confusion and delusion?

"To express the dream within a dream is the ancient buddhas; it is to ride in this treasure boat and directly arrive in the practice place....All things emerge and all things arrive right here." The place where buddhas practice is not in some exalted, lofty sacred site removed from our lives. As he says in "Genjōkōan," "Here is the place; here the way unfolds."[72]

Dōgen continues, "This being so, one plants twining vines, and gets entangled in twining vines. This is the characteristic of unsurpassable enlightenment." The enlightenment that Dōgen is concerned with, the unsurpassable enlightenment, is not some distraction or way of escaping from ourselves and from our world and from this dream. Buddhas are willing to be entangled in their life, and they notice sometimes when some of their dreams might untangle. Dōgen says, "Just as expression is limitless, sentient beings are limitless and unsurpassable. Just as cages and snares are limitless, emancipation from them is limitless." So the way to be free within the dream is by questioning, how do we express this dream? What is it we bring from our own particular mode of expression? How do you in your activity express this dream within the dream?

MEETING IN DREAMLAND

Typically Dōgen takes apart the language and warns of many ways we might misunderstand what he is saying.

There are inner dreams, dream expressions, expressions of dreams, and dreams inside. Without being within a dream, there is no expression of dreams. Without expressing dreams, there is no being within a dream. Without expressing dreams, there are no buddhas. Without being within a dream, buddhas do not emerge and turn the wondrous Dharma wheel.

This is reminiscent of the Lotus Sutra where it says the only reason for buddhas to appear in the world is because there are suffering beings to help lead onto the path of awakening.[73] Buddhas indeed show up to help others onto this path. Buddhas appear in dreams. They can only appear in dreams; this world of suffering created by innumerable causes and conditions is where buddhas show up. Buddhas do not hang out in some paradise up in the clouds, or if they take a rest there for a while, they return to meet beings in our dreams of suffering.

Dōgen continues:

Without being within a dream buddhas do not emerge and turn the wondrous Dharma wheel. This Dharma wheel is no other than a buddha together with a buddha, and a dream expressed within a dream. Simply expressing the dream within a dream is itself the buddhas and ancestors, the assembly of unsurpassable enlightenment. Furthermore, going beyond the Dharma body is itself expressing the dream within a dream.

This phrase, to express the dream within a dream, is challenging. In one other place he says, "The expression of a dream within a dream can be aroused by both ordinary people and sages. Moreover, the expression of a dream within a dream by both ordinary people and sages arose yesterday and develops today." This is ongoing buddha going beyond buddha, where we admit the dream we are in and say yes to it. And then, how is it? What is the most beautiful way to express this dream that we are in together within a dream? We each have our own particular, unique vantage point on the dream. And we each have our own special gifts and talents with which to express this dream within a dream. This is not a dream as opposed to awakening; it is the inner life of awakening.

This is advanced Zen teaching, but it is really how we bring our lives to life. How do we find what is important in our own life, and how do we express it? How do we face it, without escaping into dreamy dreams, but saying okay, here is this dream I am in, here is this Dharma position. Dōgen speaks elsewhere about abiding in one's Dharma position, which might be read as hanging out in your dream and really taking it on. What is it that I have to express in this dream, in this lifetime? This is challenging material and I have quoted only from the first half of Dōgen's essay. In the second half he cites a passage in the Lotus Sutra in which buddhas are described as awakening within a dream, and again Dōgen critiques the notion that this is not reality. He says, "This dream of buddhas is not an analogy."

CELEBRATING AND PLAYING WITH DREAMS

The dream delusion is not different from the delusion that we are in now. It is delusion throughout delusion and enlightenment throughout enlightenment. It is what is. There are many dreams, not merely one dream. But the buddhas and ancestors can hang out in all of them, all the different aspects of the suffering in this world. Include all the people you have ever known, all the people you care about in your world. This is the dream we are in right now. How do we embrace and celebrate that dream? It might be rendered as "Celebrating the dream within a dream." We see the dream for what it is and then say, what do we do to bring it alive?

It seems like the self that we impute on phenomena creates the dream, but it is not just that self. The dream is not only personal karma but our collective karma as well. This is an interactive process, not just about you. One implication is that in our idea of awakening, we think that as good Zen practitioners we should wake up and be like some buddha, but that does not happen separate from the nitty-gritty of cleaning the temple, making tea, brushing your teeth, going to the bathroom, meeting our friends, taking care of our situation. How do we care for our dream? Dōgen, being very playful, might have said, "Within a dream, play with the dream." How do we play with this dream, but in a way that is gentle, appreciating that this dream is a treasure?

Zen Rule-Bending and the Training for Pure Hearts

THIS CHAPTER is inspired in part by my observation some years ago that the "ancient ones" in my extended spiritual community of the San Francisco Zen Center, those with twenty or more years of steady practice experience, seemed distinctive in that they were most truly "themselves." Sometimes this takes the form of their being eccentric or even quite peculiar, but somehow also particularly true to themselves in some deep, and often inspiring, way. The fruits of long-term spiritual practice do not seem to be homogenized uniformity of character but rather the uniqueness of each person's sincere expression of that which goes beyond egoistic personality, but which might appear rather quirky and individual.

What are the qualities of the sincere, pure-hearted adept? Does the training in monastic, or semimonastic, practice communities help develop pure hearts and open minds? And if so, how? Below I will discuss how monastic forms in the Zen tradition might serve to grow this pure wholeheartedness, focusing on Dōgen's writings from *Dōgen's Pure Standards for the Zen Community* (Jpn.: *Eihei Shingi*).[74] As well as being a manual for procedures in the monastery, with instructions for everything from how to brush teeth to how to receive and eat food in the meditation hall, in this work Dōgen emphasizes attitudinal instructions and the psychology for taking appropriate responsibility for community well-being. His choice of illustrative stories and exemplary models is often unexpected and startling.

THE ROLE OF MONASTIC REGULATIONS

The Zen monastic regulations (Chi.: *Qinggui*; Jpn.: *Shingi*) are an out-growth of the early Buddhist Vinaya, the ethical injunctions dispensed by the Buddha. The first legendary Zen monastic rules are traditionally attributed to Baizhang Huaihai (749–814; Jpn.: Hyakujō Ekai).[75] Baizhang is widely regarded in the tradition as the founder of the Zen work ethic, for example with his famous statement, "A day without work is a day without eating."[76] Dōgen cites Baizhang as an inspiration for his own Shingi, which for procedural instructions liberally quotes both the old Vinaya attributed directly to Śākyamuni Buddha and also passages from the *Chanyuan Qing-gui* (Jpn.: Zen'en Shingi), the most comprehensive Chinese collection of Zen monastic regulations, compiled in 1103.[77]

The communal institution has been an important element of Buddhism since Śākyamuni Buddha began his monastic order twenty-five hundred years ago in northern India. The monastic enclosure developed during the Indian rainy season, when the monks halted their wandering mendicant practice to reside together for a few months of practice. This fellowship of practitioners, or sangha, has functioned ever since as a radical contrast to existing social conventions and conditioning. The Buddhist monastic com-munity has offered an alternative to the status quo of exploitative societies that disregard individual human potential.

The common designation of Buddhist monks as "home-leavers" implies the physical act of renouncing worldly ambition so as to join the monastic community and also the inner work of letting go of attachments from the bonds of social and personal psychological conditioning. In accord with this liberative purpose, monastic community life becomes an opportunity for its participants to develop their capacity for enacting the universal prin-ciples of awakening in the concrete affairs of their individual lives. The monastic procedural forms are designed to provide the monks a congenial space conducive to inner contemplation. Each ordinary, daily life function, from cleaning the temple to taking care of personal hygiene, is treated as a tool for enhancing mindfulness of one's moment to moment state of awareness and innermost intention. The monastic lifestyle, procedures, and forms act as supports for practitioners' immersion in the process of deepening personal experience of the nonalienated, integrated nature of reality described as the basis for Buddhist awakening. These monastic forms allow the psychic and physical space for self-reflection, a harmonious realm for supportive interaction with fellow contemplatives, and also function as practices with which to enact the fundamental teachings arising naturally out of meditation.

While Dōgen does offer in his Shingi detailed procedural instructions, often borrowed from the Vinaya or previous monastic regulations, his clear emphasis is attitudinal instruction and the psychology of spiritually beneficial community interaction. Zen monastic regulations function as a latticework for ethical conduct. The rules may be upheld and consequences enforced, but they are seen as guidelines rather than restrictive regulations or rigid proscriptions.

A major paradigm of Mahāyāna Buddhist monasticism has been oscillation between periods of training in the monastic container and reentry into the marketplace. Monks test their practice by returning to interact with conventional society, and they also help fulfill the developmental function of the Buddhist order by sharing with the ordinary world whatever they have learned of self-awareness, composure, and compassion during their monastic training. In Japan, from Dōgen's time to the present, monks finish a period of training and go out to function as temple priests, ministering to the laity. Some later return to the monastery for further development or to help train younger monks. Traditionally, monks would also leave their monastic community to wander around to other teachers and test their practice and understanding.

The essential insight of Buddhist awakening affirms the fundamental rightness and interconnectedness of the whole of creation, just as it is. But along with its effect on individual trainees, the sangha has also served at times as a historical instrument to perform the long-term work of civilizing and developing human awareness so as eventually to actualize and fulfill for all beings the vision of our world as a pure land, informed by wisdom and compassion. This effect has been accomplished both by the inspiration of exemplary individuals and on a wider societal level. Despite its sometimes compromised relationships and accommodations to the ruling powers throughout Asian history, in fact the Buddhist spiritual institution has had, from time to time, a civilizing effect on Asian societies, moderating the brutal tendencies of various rulers.

DŌGEN'S STARTLING MONASTIC EXEMPLARS

Until the twentieth-century popularization of his voluminous philosophical and poetic writings, Eihei Dōgen was more important historically for establishing a monastic order that became the basis for the Japanese Sōtō Zen school. In *Dōgen's Pure Standards*, written to instruct his monk disciples, he presents exemplary models of Chinese monks who had taken on the responsibility of administrative positions in Chan monastic communities. Dōgen emphasizes the importance of these positions, such as the administrative director and the chief cook of the monastery. People who hold these positions need to be devoted to the well-being of all the practitioners, and at the same time they must be exemplary in their own practice directed toward mastering the teaching and fully realizing and expressing spiritual awakening.

Given the emphasis Dōgen places on these administrative positions, it is remarkable how many of Dōgen's exemplars are involved in rule-breaking or at least rule-bending, precisely in the example or story that Dōgen cites. In the "Chiji Shingi" (The Pure Standards for the Temple Administrators), the final essay which takes up nearly half of the full text of *Eihei Shingi*, Dōgen talks about great historical Zen figures and their conduct in the monastic roles, specifically the roles of director, supervisor of monks (ino), chief cook (tenzo), and work leader, as well as some of the other supervisory positions.

Of the twenty exemplary anecdotes that Dōgen cites, ten of them involve actions by the exemplar in which he does something that would be seen from conventional morality as improper and a violation of monastic regulations. A number of them threaten to beat up their teachers or some other practitioner, and one actually does physically beat his teacher. One sets a fire in the monastery, another throws away the community's food. A few are shunned or even expelled from the community. After each of these stories the protagonist is praised by Dōgen for his sincere spirit of inquiry, dedication to practice, or commitment to the monastic community. The wildness and natural quality of true practice may involve the kind of deviation from the rule that Dōgen praises.

A TENACIOUS TENZO

Dōgen especially elaborates the importance of the position of the chief cook or tenzo, which he describes as equal in importance to the abbot's role. Dōgen dedicates a whole essay, the celebrated "Instructions for the Cook" (Tenzokyōkun) to the virtues of this position. In "The Pure Standards for the Temple Administrators," of all the tenzos he acclaims, Dōgen most lavishly praises Fushan Fayuan (991–1067), Jpn.: Fusan Hōen). After recounting stories about the virtue of a number of tenzos, Dōgen says, "Especially, we cannot fail to study the tenzo [Fushan] Fayuan's faithful heart, which can be met only once in a thousand years.... If tenzos do not experience dedication like Fayuan's, how can their study of the Way penetrate the innermost precincts of the buddhas and ancestors?"[78] And yet in the story told by Dōgen, Fayuan committed thievery while tenzo and was expelled from the monastery.

The story begins with a demonstration of the physical and spiritual toughness expected in the monastery in question. Fushan Fayuan and a monk comrade, Tianyi Yihuai, traveled to visit and train with [Shexian] Guisheng, a master with a reputation for being "cold and severe, tough and frugal. Patchrobed monks respected and feared him." Fayuan and his friend "arrived in the middle of a snowy winter" and joined the other traveling monks sitting in the monastery visitors' room while awaiting admittance. Guisheng abusively scolded the monks and poured cold water on them, so that the other monks left. When Guisheng further threatened

Fushan Fayuan and his friend, [Tianyi] Yihuai replied, "The two of us have come a thousand miles just to study Zen with you, how could we leave from just one scoop of water dumped on us? Even if you beat us to death, we will not go." Guisheng thereupon laughed and accepted them into the monastery.

After some time Fushan Fayuan was promoted to the position of tenzo. But the monastery was poor and the spartan diet coarse, and Fayuan was finally moved by his sympathy for the monks to commit a grave offense. Once Guisheng left for the village and:

> Fayuan stole the key [to the storehouse], and took some wheat flour to prepare a special flavorful gruel. Guisheng suddenly returned and went to the hall. After eating, he sat in the outer hall and sent for Fayuan. Guisheng said, "Is it true that you stole flour to cook the gruel?" [Fayuan] admitted it, and implored Guisheng to punish him. Guisheng had him calculate the price [of the flour], and sell his robes and bowls to repay it. Then Guisheng struck Fayuan thirty blows with his staff and expelled him from the temple.

Fayuan's offense was motivated only by concern for the monks' health and comfort. Shexian Guisheng instantly tasted the difference in the gruel, and Fushan was not spared prompt and severe consequences for his actions. However, the story continues that Fayuan remained in the nearby town, repeatedly making efforts to gain readmittance into Shexian Guisheng's monastery, but all were rebuffed by Guisheng. "Fayuan was not bothered, but carried his begging bowl through the city and sent the money he received [to the temple to repay his debt]."

Eventually, one day "Guisheng went to the town and saw Fayuan holding his bowl. Guisheng returned to the assembly and said, 'Fayuan truly has the determination to study Zen.'" So finally Fushan Fayuan was readmitted to the monastery, and he later became a Dharma successor of Shexian Guisheng.

Fushan Fayuan's sympathy for the monks' lack of food may have been misplaced, and his unswerving persistence after his expulsion may appear foolish or perhaps even obsessive. But it is precisely this kindness, and selfless dedication, even in the face of disgrace and loss of reputation, that seems especially to endear him to Dōgen. Fayuan violated the precepts and monastic rules but never abandoned his intention to express the way. His teacher Guisheng seems to have consciously used the rules, not for the sake of moral propriety, but to test and more fully mold Fayuan's commitment. The monastic regulations and precepts are at the service of the dual priorities of total dedication to one's own investigation of spiritual reality and commitment to caring for the practice community's well-being.

BENEFITING THE COMMUNITY

Another exemplary monk whom Dōgen esteems most highly, Wuzu Fayan (1024–1104; Jpn.: Goso Hōen), was shunned by his fellow monks for the monastic violations of drinking wine, eating meat, and entertaining women. The story goes that Wuzu Fayan had "settled his investigation of the great matter and deeply penetrated the bones and marrow" and was manager of the monastery's mill down the mountain. Wuzu Fayan devoted himself to the task of increasing the monastery's resources, but somehow he incurred the enmity of some of the monks. As even modern monks can testify, in the cauldron of monastic practice supposedly "worldly" human jealousy and pettiness can still arise. When Wuzu heard about the accusations, "He intentionally bought meat and alcohol and hung them out in front of the mill, and also bought cosmetics and makeup for his women friends. Whenever Zen monks came around the mill, [Wuzu] Fayan would touch the women and laughingly banter and tease them, completely without restraint." When his teacher finally questioned him, Wuzu Fayan made no explanation and accepted expulsion. But when he submitted the mill's accounts, including unusual profits for the monastery, his teacher was impressed, "and understood that petty people had just been jealous [of Wuzu Fayan]."

Dōgen praises Wuzu Fayan for his dedication to accomplishing his task of managing the monastery's business so as to best benefit the community and its assets. That he did this without any concern for his own personal reputation and standing in the eyes of his teacher is especially admirable for Dōgen. Wuzu was willing to accept the blame and punishment of his teacher, as had Fushan Fayuan, without becoming defensive or trying to protect or explain himself.

TRAINING, ICONOCLASM, AND LOVING-KINDNESS

I discuss these anecdotes of Zen rule-bending and Zen fools not to support an erroneous and misleading stereotype of Zen iconoclasm. In the initial importation of Zen to America, and its reception by what has been called "Beat Zen," the image of Zen "wild men" was provocative and attractive to many. But the history of Zen throughout East Asia has been very predominantly that of sincere practitioners quietly engaged in devotional rituals and contemplative practices. Dōgen's rule-bending exemplars of temple administrators were veteran monks steeped in conventional monastic practice and decorum.

Prominent in Zen culture far beyond their actual numbers are the colorful adept graduates from Zen monasteries who as outsiders or hermits exemplify foolishness and loving-kindness, figures such as Hotei, Hanshan, and Ryōkan. The historical tenth-century Chinese Zen monk Budai, whose Japanese name Hotei is probably better known in the West, is familiar as the fat, jolly "laughing buddha" whose statue is ubiquitous in Chinese restaurants and Chinese Buddhist temples. Hotei had completed his monastic training, but expressed his awareness as a homeless vagabond, a disheveled Buddhist Santa Claus displaying warmth and loving-kindness, carrying a sack full of candy and toys for the children. Known for his divine foolishness, in China Budai/Hotei came to be identified as an incarnation of Maitreya Bodhisattva, the next future buddha, to such an extent that Chinese images of Budai are now simply labeled Maitreya (Ch.: Milo-fe).[79]

The Chinese mountain recluse poet Hanshan, "Cold Mountain," apparently was a layman who lived near a monastery high up in the Tiantai mountains, probably in the ninth or tenth century. His poems, celebrated in American as well as East Asian Zen, set the mold for the carefree mountain hermit, joyfully immersed in nature apart from the world but not without occasional acknowledgments of loneliness. I have experienced in contemporary Zen monasteries, both in America and Japan, persons in proximity to the monastery but with similar ambiguous relationships to it. They may support the temple in various ways, but such characters also function, often through unconventional behavior, to remind the serious monks of the context of their liberative endeavors.

Ryōkan (1758–1831), the Japanese Zen monk and brilliant spiritual poet, was fully trained in a Sōtō Zen monastery, but instead of becoming a temple priest and teaching formally, he returned to a hermit's life of meditation in a hut near his home village and made a modest livelihood through begging rounds in nearby towns. Still a deeply beloved figure in modern Japan, Ryōkan chose the spiritual name Daigu, or "Great Fool," even though he was intelligent, a dedicated student of sutras and Dōgen's writings, a skilled meditator, and an elegant calligrapher, whose brushwork was already valuable and sought after during his own life. But Ryōkan is best known for many foolish anecdotes about him, many involving kindly play with children.

The innocence and kindness of these iconoclastic outsiders are often considered innate traits. Yet the effort to cultivate and train practitioners toward such openness and dedication seems to be part of the intention of Dōgen's pure standards and of the Buddhist monastic enterprise generally. Dōgen's chosen historical exemplars clarify that the training of pure hearts cannot proceed simply by following some prescribed routine or program. These monastic procedures rather serve as a cauldron for guiding the practitioner toward actualizing the inner spirit of the pure heart.

In considering Dōgen's description of Zen training, and its goal, it is notable that Dōgen does not hold to a literal interpretation of the regulations. This is so even though Dōgen is noted for his own emphasis on monastic forms. For example, he includes in his *Eihei Shingi* a short essay with sixty-two specific instructions for the manners and etiquette with which monks should defer to their seniors. Dōgen never advocates bending the monastic rules just for the sake of iconoclasm, and he strongly criticizes those who mistakenly believed that Buddhist liberation means freedom from ethical concern and proper demeanor.[80] Nevertheless, it is clear from his exemplars that Dōgen sees the purpose of monastic training not as the rigid alignment with some code of conduct, but as the development of kindly concern for the whole community and sincere, intent, persistent inquiry into the deep mysteries of awakening.

PART 3

Commentaries on
Dōgen's Extensive Record

Speak Softly, Speak Softly

I N ZEN we talk about the mind of the Way, sometimes called the mind that seeks the Way. In Sanskrit it is *bodhicitta*, literally, awakening mind. It refers to the arousing of our direction toward awakening and spiritual practice, our first thought of spiritual practice, and the arousing of caring and concern. In Suzuki Roshi's Sōtō Zen lineage we celebrate beginner's mind. We all aspire toward remembering that first impulse toward taking care of something as strange as sitting facing the wall, quietly, upright. This is bodhicitta, the mind of the Way.

This aspiration toward awakening, a deep concern and caring for all beings, is illuminated by a traditional Zen koan discussed by Eihei Dōgen in his *Extensive Record*. Koans are teaching stories, many of them dialogues between students and teachers, and the classical koans are attributed to persons from nearly twelve hundred years ago. We continue to study them because they have something to do with our life, today. If they were just about something that happened twelve hundred years ago, we would not bother.

Dōgen brought a great deal of the koan literature from China to Japan and has a unique approach to koan practice. Unlike Rinzai Zen practice where one passes through a curriculum of koan cases, in Sōtō practice generally the point is to engage the story and allow it to become part of one's practice body and awareness. In this way one never finishes with such a story, but digests and incorporates its teachings. Dōgen's approach to koan practice includes his expansive elaborations on koan cases and their themes in his essays in *Shōbōgenzō*. His koan praxis has been discussed by Dōgen scholar Steven Heine as the panoramic, scenic route, analyzed astutely in his book *Dōgen and the Kōan Tradition*.[81] The whole literature of Zen is composed to a great extent of these stories, most often attributed to Chan masters from the ninth century, and then many layers of commentaries on those stories.

The story "Speak Softly" was discussed in a short Dharma talk by Dōgen. Many of these stories refer to other stories, and that is very much the case with this koan, which involves a number of others. Dōgen himself provides a long introduction, and then he has his own comments. I will offer my own introduction to his introduction. The basic story itself is very short. It concerns a tenth-century Rinzai Zen teacher in China named Shoushan Xingnian (926–993; Jpn.: Shusan Shōnen). A monk came to him once and asked Shoushan, "All the buddhas come from this sutra. What is this sutra?"

Shoushan responded, "Speak softly, speak softly."

The monk understood. And he asked, "How should we receive and maintain it?"

And Shoushan said, "It can never be defiled."[82]

AN INDIAN BOY'S INTRODUCTION

Before returning to this primary story, I will offer an introduction. This is a modern story from a novel that reached the bestseller list, called *Life of Pi*, a very interesting book.[83] The novel is about a fifteen-year-old Indian boy who finds himself stranded on a lifeboat in the middle of the Pacific Ocean, together with a huge Bengal tiger, and about how the boy survives. But the part I want to talk about as an introduction to this old Zen story, and to Dōgen's introduction to it, happens before the boy ever gets to the ocean. This young fourteen- or fifteen-year-old Indian boy nicknamed Pi comes from a very secular background. His parents are not concerned with religion. His father is owner and manager of a zoo, which is how the tiger ends up in the story.

But when he is fourteen, a relative takes this young boy to a Hindu temple, where he is dazzled and amazed and very happy with all the colorful gods and goddesses and stories of the Indian tradition. And Pi becomes a devout Hindu, without his parents knowing about it. He is very involved in the practice and devotions in the local Indian temple. Then Pi happens to stumble upon a Catholic church and is startled, and he ends up talking with the priest. At first he is appalled that this religion has merely one god and that the image of the god is of suffering up on the cross. He cannot understand it. None of the Indian gods would be depicted in such a cruel setting. But finally Pi understands from the priest that this is about love. So, as well as a Hindu, he becomes a very devoted Christian and goes and studies the Bible and prays at the church.

And then Pi happens upon a humble baker who turns out to be a Sufi master. He sees this man praying to Allah, doing his daily prayers, and the boy becomes interested and ends up also becoming a devout Muslim. Since we have a problem with Islam in our country, here is a little bit about what Pi says about it. He recalls:

> I loved my prayer rug. Ordinary in quality though it was, it glowed with beauty in my eyes. I'm sorry I lost it. Wherever I laid it I felt special affection for the patch of ground beneath it, and the immediate surroundings, which to me is a clear indication that it was a good prayer rug, because it helped me remember that the earth is the creation of God, and sacred the same all over.

I feel like that myself about wherever I sit when I sit zazen. Anyway, this young boy from this secular background becomes very involved and committed with all three of these traditions.

One day Pi is out with his family, and lo and behold all three of his teachers see him at once, and they come over to meet him and meet his family. The family has no idea that Pi is involved with anything religious. And the three teachers come up to him and are appalled to see each other. Each of them says how wonderful Pi is, and they get into a big argument, each criticizing the others' traditions. Finally the Hindu teacher says that Pi cannot be a Hindu, a Christian, and a Muslim; it is impossible. He must choose. And the father, who is bewildered, says, I do not think it is a crime, but I suppose you are right. So they finally turn to the boy after criticizing each other's religion, and the boy tells them that Mahatma Gandhi says that all religions are true. And then Pi blurts out, "I just want to love God."

This is a story about bodhicitta, this thought of awakening. And I was reminded of when I was about that age, fourteen or fifteen. I could not have said, "I just want to love God," because I had decided that I was an atheist. And yet I was searching for something, avidly reading Dostoevsky, Kafka, and Sartre, listening to the questioning songs of the young Bob Dylan. I wanted to find some meaning. How do I live? What do I do with my life? Such a search for meaning, for spiritual integrity, has something to do with this bodhicitta, the arousing of the thought of awakening. In my generation existentialism was one way that people found this basic question. Back then there was no Buddhist practice available as far as I knew. Anyway, Pi provides my introduction to the introduction by Dōgen talking about this kōan, "Speak Softly."

THE MASTER DOES NOT TEND TO OTHERS

Dōgen's introduction is much longer than the kōan story itself. He was giving this talk in 1246 at his monastery Eiheiji, which he had founded not long before in the remote mountains, and which is still one of the headquarter temples of Sōtō Zen in Japan. Dōgen starts:

> In studying the Way the mind of the Way is primary. This temple in the remote mountains and deep valleys is not easy to reach, and people arrive only after sailing over oceans and climbing mountains. Without treading with the mind of the Way it is difficult to arrive at this field. To refine the rice, first the bran must

be removed. This is a good place in which to engage the Way. And yet, I'm sorry that the master [Dōgen] does not readily attend to others by disposition. However, by day or night, the voice of the valley stream happens to be conducive for carrying water. Also, in spring and fall, the colors of the mountain manage to be conducive for gathering firewood. I hope that cloud-and-water monks will keep the Way in mind.

He was giving this talk way up in the mountains, and monks and laypeople had come from a great distance to hear him and to practice with him. And yet I think it is still relevant to our situation, coming to Buddhist practice in America in the world today. He says, "In studying the Way, the mind of the Way is primary." The first point is just the mind of the Way, this direction toward awakening and caring for all beings. He says, "This temple in the remote mountains and deep valleys is not easy to reach, and people arrive only after sailing over oceans and climbing mountains. Without treading with the mind of the Way it's difficult to arrive at this field." That was certainly true for a place like Eiheiji, or for Tassajara monastery in the deep mountains in Monterey County, where I trained and where some of the students had come from distant countries. Although there are now Zen meditation centers in many parts of the United States and other Western countries, some close to many readers, deciding to visit may require varied life events and partaking of this mind of the Way at least to some extent.

"To refine the rice, first the bran must be removed." This is an image of the practice that we do once we recognize our mind of the Way: Sitting, watching ourselves, facing the wall, trying to be upright in the middle of all of our confusion and desires and frustrations and the difficulties of this world and our lives. Dōgen says, "This is a good place in which to engage the Way." And it is. Wherever you arrive, whenever you decide to sit and actually face your life, this is a good place. And then he says this very sweet thing, "I am sorry that the master (and here Dōgen is referring to himself) does not readily tend to others by disposition." Perhaps Dōgen was a shy kind of guy. Maybe he was not very good at "people skills"; at least he said he was not very good at engaging with his monks. But maybe, always, the teacher does not readily attend to others by disposition. Because nobody can do this for you. You have aroused the mind of the Way in some small measure at least, if you are reading this. Now how will you engage the Way? "I'm sorry. The master does not readily attend to others by disposition. However, by day or night, the voice of the valley stream happens to be conducive for carrying water. Also in spring and fall the colors of the mountain manage to be conducive for gathering firewood."

Even if you do not live in the deep valleys there is some voice in the world around you that happens to be conducive for your taking care of your life and living with concern for those around you. Even if you do not live amid the colors of the mountain, there are colors and shapes and forms in the world around you that can support you in your own practice of gathering firewood, of trying to take care of this life. So Dōgen says, "I hope that clouds-and-water monks will keep the Way in mind."

"Clouds and water"—*unsui* in Sino-Japanese——is the word for monks in China and Japan. It refers to roaming freely like clouds and waters. For modern Westerners I hope that householder practitioners also will keep the Way in mind. Even living in this world, what choice do we have when we recognize the suffering of the world around us, when we recognize our own confusion, when we recognize our own desire to live in some meaningful way, when we wonder how can I live this life, what is a proper livelihood in this place and time, in this society? How can I raise my children; how can I be friendly with my friends? Please, as you negotiate that way, keep the Way in mind. That is Dōgen's introduction before reciting the koan.

HOW DO BUDDHAS EMERGE FROM THE SUTRAS?

I remember a monk asked Shoushan, "All the buddhas come from this sutra. What is this sutra?"

Shoushan responded, "Speak softly, speak softly."

The monk asked, "How should we receive and maintain it?"

Shoushan said, "It can never be defiled.'"

Often in these stories it just says, "A monk asked the teacher." Sometimes it says the name of the monk, and that means the monk later became a famous teacher himself. This time it does not give the name of the monk, but I love this monk. He asks a wonderful question, "All the buddhas come from this sutra. What is this sutra?" There is a joke in this question. A sutra is a Buddhist scripture, the words of a buddha that can only be spoken by a buddha. And yet the monk asks, "All the buddhas come from this sutra. What is this sutra?" How can buddhas come from a sutra, if there are not buddhas there already to speak the sutra? And yet, there are the sutras that you can find in libraries, and there are also sutras found among the birds and trees and the sound of waves. But what is this sutra that all the buddhas come from? This is a fundamental question of the mind of the Way, an important question. What does our own awakening arise from? Where is it? What is it? How do we find it?

The Indian boy Pi had found three different collections of sutras. But still, where did they come from? Where did this impulse come from? What is it that inspires a buddha to appear; what is it that inspires our own awakening? All the buddhas come from this sutra; what is this sutra? The Lotus Sutra says that the single great cause for buddhas appearing in the world is simply to demonstrate the Way and help direct people toward finding it. So the single great cause is the recognition of the suffering of beings and the need to find our way. Still, this monk focuses in on this question. Shoushan's answer was, "Speak softly, speak softly." Maybe speak softly means to speak gently. Maybe this refers to kind speech. But speak softly also means speak up; speak the truth. Speak your truth, but speak softly, speak softly. This statement by Shoushan is worthy of deep reflection.

SUSTAINING SOFT SPEECH AND WHAT COMES THUS

Then the monk asked, "How should we receive and maintain it?" That question demonstrates that he got it. I do not know how softly the monk asked that question, but how should we receive and maintain it? In the teaching poem by the Chinese Sōtō founder Dongshan "Song of the Precious Mirror Samādhi" it says, "The teaching of suchness is intimately communicated by buddhas and ancestors. Now you have it, please keep it well."[84] Now that you have heard the first two lines of that poem, now you have it, please keep it well. Our whole practice of refining the rice, of refining our life, is about how we receive and maintain it. This was a very good monk. Shoushan said, "It can never be defiled." This answer is a reference to another, longer story. This is about Dajian Huineng (638–713; Jpn.: Daikan Enō), the Chinese Sixth Ancestor, one of the real founders of Zen in China. One time a monk came to see him at his temple, and we know this monk's name was Nanyue Huairang (677–744; Jpn.: Nangaku Ejō), because later he became a great teacher.[85]

Huineng asked Nanyue, "Where are you from?"

And Nanyue said, "I came from the place of the National Teacher."

Then the Sixth Ancestor looked at him and said, "What is this that thus comes?" This is a curious, probing manner of asking, "Who are you?" not assuming some fixed "self" or "you," antithetical to Buddhist teachings of nonself and emptiness. What is this that thus comes? Nanyue did not know what to say. And the story relates that he went and sat in the meditation hall for eight years considering this question.

Sometimes in these Zen stories it looks like these teachers and students are talking back and forth quickly. But sometimes there is a little space. Sometimes it happens that somebody goes and thinks about it for a little bit before replying. Usually the time lag is not mentioned. Sometimes there were also other people around listening, and they are not mentioned. But in this case it says explicitly that Nanyue went and meditated on this question for eight years.

After eight years Nanyue came back to the Sixth Ancestor and said, "I can now understand the question, 'What is this that thus comes?' that you received me with upon my first arriving to see you."

Huineng said, "How do you understand it?"

And Nanyue said, "To explain or demonstrate anything would completely miss the mark."

It took Nanyue eight years just to come up with that. But then he proved that he had not wasted his eight years. The Sixth Ancestor asked him, "Then do you suppose that there is practice-realization or not?"

Nanyue said, "It is not that there is no practice-realization, but only that it cannot be defiled."

And the Sixth Ancestor said, "This nondefilement is exactly what all the buddhas and ancestors protect and care for. I am thus, you are thus, and the ancestors in India also are thus."

As a wonderful example, Nanyue stayed with Huineng for another eight years thereafter, just to make sure it sank in.

THE MIND UNDEFILED WITH EYEBROWS REMAINING

This practice-realization, this practice of enlightenment, or enlightened practice, can never be defiled. That is what this student of the Sixth Ancestor said. It may be very easy to imagine all the ways in which we could defile our own mind of the Way, to imagine all of the terrible things we might do or say. One possibility of defilement warned against here is engaging meditation practice as a mere means, with enlightenment seen as a remote abstraction separate from our activity and awareness. But no matter how much we fail to take care of this mind of the Way, it is something that can never be defiled.

This "speak softly, speak softly," the sutra from which all the buddhas come, is beyond our ideas about it. As Nanyue said, no matter what he said it would miss the mark. All of our thinking, all of our talking, whether it is soft or loud, cannot get to the core of this mind of the Way. It is a great mystery. What makes an Indian boy suddenly want to love God? What makes someone suddenly decide, I am going to take on a spiritual practice? We cannot say where this comes from. But please, speak softly.

When the birds are singing outside, we might think that they are singing sweetly or harshly, softly or loudly, and yet can we hear how the birds sing softly, sing softly, just as they are? Can we listen to our own hearts as they speak softly, sometimes covered up by all of the enticements, entertainment, and all of the wonderful things to consume that our society presents to us?

After offering this story, Dōgen then comments, "Suppose someone asked me, 'What is this sutra?' I would say to him: if you call it this sutra, your eyebrows will fall out." In East Asia they had the notion that if you lie, or if you do not tell the truth, your eyebrows will fall out, like Pinocchio's nose growing for us. And Dōgen says, if you call it this sutra your eyebrows will fall out. Whatever you call it misses the mark. If you call it Buddhism, if you call it Hinduism, if you call it Christianity, if you call it Islam, whatever you call it misses the mark. And yet here we are, somehow concerned about this mind of the Way, wondering how can we find our way.

REACHING BACK FOR THE PILLOW

Dōgen adds, "As to how should we receive and maintain it, I would say, reaching back for your pillow in the middle of the night." This is a reference to yet another story, from the teacher of Dongshan, founder of Sōtō Zen in China, whose name is Yunyan Tansheng (781–841; Jpn.: Ungan Donjō). Yunyan and his brother Daowu Yuanzhi (769–835; Jpn.: Dōgo Enchi), who was also a monk, were talking one day about the bodhisattva, or awakening being, of compassion. One of the main forms of the bodhisattva of compassion in Buddhism has a thousand arms, with a thousand hands, and each hand has an eye in it. Many of the hands have tools: lotus flowers, sutras, whisks, daggers, hatchets, Dharma wheels, teaching sticks, perhaps watches, or sometimes a cup of tea. The name of this bodhisattva of compassion is Kanzeon in Japanese, Chenrezig in Tibetan, Guanyin in Chinese, and Avalokiteśvara in Sanskrit. The name of this bodhisattva of compassion means the one who hears the sounds of the world.[86] Thus compassion in Buddhism is about listening. When the truth is speaking softly, we have to listen closely. Just to listen, and just to be heard, is compassion. But also compassion responds with whatever is at hand. This story is about how this response works.

Yunyan asked Daowu, "Why does the bodhisattva of compassion have so many hands and eyes?" He was referring to this image with a thousand hands, each hand with an eye in it. Daowu replied, "It's like reaching back for your pillow in the middle of the night."[87] This is a wonderful image for this response of compassion in Buddhism. It is not something we plan, or calculate, but a hand reaching out. We respond to the problem in front of us, even if it is that we cannot sleep and we want our pillow. In the middle of the night—in the middle of darkness, uncertainty, and not being able to see anything—just reach back.

This is Dōgen's answer to how we may receive and maintain it; just reaching back for your pillow in the middle of the night. With whatever is at hand, we do our best to respond to what we see and hear in front of us. This compassion is essential to the mind of the Way. The mind of the Way has to do with our caring about the suffering of the world, which of course includes the suffering of ourselves, the suffering of our friends, the suffering of beings throughout the world. When we reach back for our pillow in the middle of the night, we do not know what to do. We do not know how to bring peace in the world. Sometimes we do not know how to take care of our own confusion, frustration, desires, or anger. Still, reaching back for the comfort of our pillow in the middle of the night, how can we respond from this place of "speak softly, speak softly" without calling it anything, or getting stuck on any particular definition?

TRUST YOURSELF

I like Shoushan's answers very much: "Speak softly, speak softly" and "It can never be defiled." I also like Dōgen's answers very much. One of the major traditional modes of koan commentary is for teachers to say what they would have said in the dialogues in place of the original participants' statements or questions. Offering my own commentary, if someone were to ask me, "All the buddhas come from this sutra. What is this sutra?" I would say: Do not look outside. Deeply trust yourself. Or maybe, deeply trust the ground you sit on.

There are many wonderful teaching traditions. These old Zen stories we play with can be very helpful, as is coming together and sitting zazen with other people. Meeting with a teacher with a little more experience in looking for the Way can also be very helpful. But again I say, do not look outside. Deeply trust the ground you are sitting on right now. This is not something we find someplace else. Whatever it was that brought you here, listen, it is speaking softly; trust yourself.

Suppose someone were then to ask me, "How should we receive and maintain it?" I would say: Keep returning to the question "How does it feel?" Right now, as you sit upright, in this life, with this body and mind, how does it feel? Dōgen and Shoushan borrowed from other stories, so I do not mind borrowing from my favorite American spiritual poet who likes to borrow from others too. "How does it feel, to be on your own, a complete unknown?"[88] How does it feel, right now, with this breath, with this bird song, with this inner voice, how does it feel? No direction home; or maybe, all directions home. In Asia people who found the mind of the Way left home and went off together into the deep mountains. Maybe in modern America we need to find our Way back home. We have been wandering for many generations in this country. We do not know our homes. Maybe all directions are home. But still, how does it feel? Listen closely, deeply trust yourself, but then: how does it feel? What is this that thus comes? Anything you say is going to miss the mark, so it is not a matter of getting an answer to this question, but simply of returning to awareness again and again. I have been recommending this as a mantra, or a kōan to use in zazen: How does it feel? How does it feel in your heart, in your body and your mind; in your elbows, shoulders, and knees?

In studying the Way, the mind of the Way is primary. We must take care of it and appreciate it. We must first of all recognize that we have heard it, speaking softly. These principles of hearing and speaking and receiving and maintaining the mind of the Way apply to your own search for the Way on your seat, in your heart, within your own life. They also apply to how we take care of our relationships and our world, how we try to speak softly and see, how does it feel? And what do we do when we make mistakes? Because we do, as human beings, make mistakes. How does it feel? Please do not be afraid to speak softly, but speak up, and enjoy your mind of the Way.

Dōgen's Five-Part Approach to Zazen

ZAZEN ALREADY was practiced in Japan before him, but Eihei Dōgen introduced a particular approach to Zen practice. In one of his Dharma hall discourses, number 266 in the *Eihei Kōroku*, given in 1248, Dōgen talks about five aspects of his teaching.[89] This extraordinary, concise talk is truly amazing in presenting Dōgen's sophisticated understanding of five fundamental aspects of practice and of his own particular way of teaching.

Dōgen had left Kyoto in 1245 and was up in the remote mountains in northern Japan where he built his monastery Eiheiji, still one of the two headquarter temples for Sōtō Zen and for which Eihei Dōgen is also named. This discourse was given a few months after he had returned from a visit to Kamakura, the capital then, where he had spent about six months teaching the samurai rulers. He came back and spent the rest of his life until his final sickness teaching his monks and other students at Eiheiji. This succinct but revealing discourse provides a road map or topography of zazen practice. Here is the entire talk:

> Sometimes I, Eihei, enter the ultimate state and offer profound discussion, simply wishing for you all to be steadily intimate in your mind field. Sometimes, within the gates and gardens of the monastery, I offer my own style of practical instruction,

simply wishing you all to disport and play freely with spiritual penetration. Sometimes I spring quickly leaving no trace, simply wishing you all to drop off body and mind. Sometimes I enter the samādhi of self-fulfillment, simply wishing you all to trust what your hands can hold.

I will discuss how this describes four aspects of zazen. Dōgen also adds:

Suppose someone suddenly came forth and asked this mountain monk, "What would go beyond these [kinds of teaching]?"
    I would simply say to him: Scrubbed clean by the dawn wind, the night mist clears. Dimly seen, the blue mountains form a single line.

That portrays a fifth aspect of zazen.
Dōgen was transporting and introducing the Zen tradition from China to Japan. We are involved in a much more extreme experience of translation and transporting, conveying Zen from East Asia to the United States in the early twenty-first century. I will interpret and demonstrate how this short talk presents a five-part pattern for zazen. These are not practices that we need to somehow figure out or attain, but they are already aspects of zazen.

THE ULTIMATE STATE SUPPORTING INTIMACY

Dōgen begins, "Sometimes I enter the ultimate state and offer profound discussion, simply wishing for you all to be steadily intimate in your mind field." A major aspect of zazen practice involves developing steadiness and intimacy with this present field of mind. This may be the most difficult part of Zen practice. Once we find our seat and figure out a way to sit relatively comfortably and settle into zazen, how can we be steadily intimate in our mind field? In his essay "Genjōkōan," Dōgen talks about how studying the way is studying the self. Part of our sitting is just settling, not getting rid of thoughts and feelings, but finding some space of steadiness in being ourselves. Intimacy develops with the whole field of awareness that includes everything, the siren out on the street, the taste of tea, thoughts, feelings, and sensations, including the ache in your shoulder or knee, as new thoughts arise.

The mind field includes everything, and Dōgen says he wishes "all beings," clearly including his audience of disciples, to be intimate in this mind field. Each of us is present now in our mind field, with our own realm of awareness. Becoming intimate includes becoming familiar and friendly with our own habits of thinking, our own modes of constructing this mind field that we think of as "mine." We construct an identity; we think "this is who I am." But beyond that identity lies this realm of awareness that we each are as we are sitting now. How do we get to know and become familiar with our patterns of thinking, of grasping, desire, and aversion? How do we become intimate with our patterns of reaction to our habits and also our own particular patterns of connecting with the wholeness that is here as we sit? Just becoming steadily intimate with our own mind field is a vital aspect of zazen.

Interestingly, Dōgen says that the teaching he does to encourage this intimacy for his students is *himself* entering the ultimate state and offering profound discussion. His own deep settling and connection with the ultimate universal awareness and openness encourages his students to settle. Developing this steadiness includes forgiving ourselves for being human beings. It also includes gratitude and appreciation for the mind field of awareness on your seat right now, which has its own pattern and shifting while sitting for a period of zazen.

PRACTICAL INSTRUCTION FOR PLAYING FREELY

Secondly Dōgen says, "Sometimes, within the gates and gardens of the monastery, I offer my own style of practical instruction, simply wishing you all to disport and play freely with spiritual penetration." This one is particularly interesting because he mentions "within the gates and gardens of the monastery." Shohaku Okumura and I translated Dōgen's writing about standards for the Zen community, and many American Zen students have practiced in a residential context or Zen monastery with lots of forms to support awareness and intention.[90] All the forms that may seem like restrictions and regulation are actually helpful guidelines to support attention. Dōgen offers such teaching "simply wishing you all to disport and play freely with spiritual penetration." This might not seem relevant to most Zen practitioners who live out in the world while practicing with smaller nonresidential groups, where we may not have the advantage of that traditional practice schedule and structure in our everyday lives. But I believe such instructions actually bear special relevance for lay practice in the world. The bodhisattva precepts and other guidelines aid in expressing zazen mind and heart. How do we express intimacy and steadiness in our life activities? How do we express Zen guidelines and heart in response to the great many difficulties of the world, and in the weekly activities with our work, relationships, neighbors, and family?

What Dōgen says he is encouraging with his practical instruction does not concern following rules but "wishing you all to disport and play freely with spiritual penetration." Spiritual penetration has to do with paying close attention. How do we pay attention as we engage each other in the world? This concerns sangha, the people we formally practice with, but also the people we work with and encounter throughout the week. These instructions also support zazen. We have forms for moving around the meditation hall, for sitting, and for ceremonies. But Dōgen says that the point is to play freely. Zen may look very austere, but the heart is about finding our own freedom and playfulness. For sitting facing the wall, assuming upright posture and mudra, Dōgen's practical instructions are aimed at support of your own playfulness. A teacher of mine once said, "Be wild on your cushion." This does not mean to move around or start howling, but in your settledness and your intimacy with your mind field, in this uprightness, as Suzuki Roshi suggested, "Give your cow a large, spacious meadow."[91] Allow your mind field to play freely, in zazen as well as in engagement with your life. How do we play and express ourselves freely, while supporting the spiritual penetration of sustained attention and caring? This practice is not about becoming a Zen zombie or mimicking wooden statues of Buddha. Becoming steadily intimate with your mind field requires "to disport and play freely with spiritual penetration."

STARTLING ACTIONS TO ENCOURAGE DROPPING BODY AND MIND

For the third aspect of his teaching, Dōgen says, "Sometimes I spring quickly leaving no trace, simply wishing you all to drop off body and mind." This phrase, dropping off body and mind, is another synonym Dōgen often uses for zazen, but also to express total enlightenment. Such dropping of mind and body is not the same as entering the heretical school of Lobotomy Zen, discarding your intelligence, or self-mutilation, or suicide. Dropping body and mind is just letting go. In his "Song of the Grass Hut," an eighth-century teacher honored by Dōgen named Shitou Ziqian (700–790; Jpn.: Sekitō Kisen) says, "Let go of hundreds of years and relax completely."[92] This is another way of saying drop off body and mind. It does not mean not to pay attention or take care of our bodies and mind. But this is fully accomplished by just totally letting go. There is not so much to say about this third aspect of zazen. Just let go. Dōgen's sometimes abrupt exclamations or enactments recorded in *Eihei Kōroku*, such as throwing down his whisk or just stepping down from his teaching seat, are demonstrations to spark this release.

SELF-FULFILLMENT PRACTICE AND CONFIDENCE

We can be playful in our awareness as we sit, or we can just let go. The fourth kind of teaching Dōgen offers is a little more intricate. He says, "Sometimes I enter the samādhi of self-fulfillment, simply wishing you all to trust what your hands can hold." This samādhi of self-fulfillment is a technical term, yet another name for zazen. This practice is discussed in one of his earliest writings, "Bendōwa," which Shohaku and I translated in *The Wholehearted Way.*[93] This samādhi of self-fulfillment, self-enjoyment, or self-realization is another way Dōgen elaborates the heart of zazen. Samādhi is a Sanskrit term that means concentration or meditation involving settling, attention, and focus. Many varied types of samādhi are named in Buddhist scriptures. But Dōgen designates this samādhi of self-fulfillment as the criterion for zazen. How do we enjoy, realize, and fulfill this constructed self, or this self connected beyond our self-identity to the totality of self, sometimes called nonself?

The three Chinese characters for self-fulfillment are pronounced in Sino-Japanese as *ji-jū-yū. Ji* means self; *jūyū* as a compound means enjoyment or fulfillment, but *jū* and *yū* read separately mean literally "to accept your function." These two characters might be interpreted as taking on your place or role in your life. When we accept our life, our potential and qualities, and enjoy these, we discover self-realization and fulfillment. This is not mere passive acceptance but actively taking on and finding our own way of responding. This experience is the samādhi of accepting our own karma, feeling and accepting this situation with its difficulties and its richness, while using our abilities and not turning away from our sadness or fear. Facing the challenging parts of ourselves we connect to our humanity. How do we accept our place in the world, in the totality of self?

Dōgen says he enters the samādhi of self-fulfillment so his followers can "trust what your hands can hold." Part of zazen is simply learning to actually take hold of who we are and the tools we have, and to trust that. Trust might be rendered as faith or simply as confidence. How do we learn to trust our own qualities and our ability to engage practice? How do we take hold? Discussing it in terms of hands feels appropriately tactile. How do we handle the tools in our everyday life? How do we meet each other, open hand to open hand? The image of what is held in the hands is reminiscent of the implements held in the many hands of the bodhisattva of compassion, sometimes depicted with a thousand arms, and evokes the practice of skillful means, using whatever is handy to help relieve suffering and awaken beings.[94] Dōgen's samādhi of self-fulfillment described here can thus be seen as intending to provoke faith and skillful means.

A TYPOLOGY OF PRACTICE TIME AND THE SINGLE DIM LINE

Dōgen has quite impressively provided four primary aspects of zazen and of his teaching strategy or pedagogy. They might serve as a typology of practice: to be steadily intimate in our mind field, to disport and play freely with spiritual awareness, to drop off body and mind, and then to trust what our hands can hold. These modes are aspects of our zazen already. Although I know of no other Zen writing that has described zazen in this manner, they are all aspects of what matures in the process of enjoying our breath and feeling our own uprightness.

It is noteworthy that each of these four is introduced with a term we translated appropriately in this context as "sometimes." However, the word Dōgen uses here for "sometimes" is ūji, also the title of a highly celebrated essay from Shōbōgenzō, which has been translated as "Being Time."[95] In this essay Dōgen presents a teaching about the multidimensional flowing of time as our very existence, which has been analyzed as a unique philosophy of temporality. For Dōgen our practice engages this present particular temporal situation of causes and conditions, not some abstracted eternal present. Time does not exist as some external, objective container, but actually time is exactly our current dynamic activity and awareness. The four aspects of zazen and teaching described in this 1248 Dharma hall discourse need not be seen in terms of Dōgen's teaching about being time, presented in the Shōbōgenzō essay from 1240. However, the overtones of his using this term cannot be ignored. Thus we might also see these four practices as four aspects of being time for Dōgen.

Concluding this Dharma hall discourse, Dōgen offers a fifth response, *not* introduced with the term "sometimes," which might be seen as going beyond any particular being time, while still invoking the specific occasion of dawn. Together these five approaches might be related to the Sōtō Zen teaching of the five ranks. The five ranks teaching first attributed to

Dongshan, founder of the Chinese Sōtō school, was initially expressed in his "Song of the Precious Mirror Samādhi." These are five interrelationships between the real and apparent aspects (also described as the universal and particular, or ultimate and phenomenal) of our life and practice. These five have been designated in various ways, one version being: the apparent within the real, the real within the apparent, coming from within the real, going within both apparent and real, and arriving within both together.[96] However, the five modes of practice described in this 1248 Dharma hall discourse should not be reduced to that five ranks system, as they are much richer than any limited formulation.

Dōgen adds after presenting the first four aspects, "Suppose someone suddenly came forth and asked this mountain monk, 'What would go beyond these kinds of teaching?'" Dōgen often talks about buddha going beyond buddha, or this practice of ongoing awareness or awakening. This dynamic process is not something to be figured out or grasped, but an organic engagement of going beyond. However well or poorly you may feel you are playing freely with spiritual awareness, there is possible an endless unfolding of all these approaches. Having presented a brilliant vision of the fourfold heart of zazen, Dōgen is everready to go beyond and further develop his awakening.

Dōgen imagines one of his students coming forward and asking, what would go beyond those teachings? Dōgen responds, "Scrubbed clean by the dawn wind, the night mist clears. Dimly seen, the blue mountains form a single line." This may be a better Dharma hall discourse to consider in the morning, closer to the dawn wind, rather than during dusk or some other time of day. Dōgen describes being "scrubbed clean by the dawn wind." He is concerned not simply with one time of day but with the sense of freshness available in any inhalation, or maybe even in an exhalation. "Scrubbed clean by the dawn wind, the night mist clears" speaks to the process of bringing oneself back to attention and awareness, waking up and realizing, "Here I am, this is where I live. Here is this body and mind." We actually experience this every morning, and we might realize that this occurs breath after breath as well. "The night mist clears." Sometimes it hangs around for a while; sometimes it suddenly clears. Either way we can feel "scrubbed clean by the dawn wind." Wind also serves as a customary Zen metaphor for the teaching, and for the flavor of our awareness.

Dōgen adds, "Dimly seen, the blue mountains form a single line." This concerns each mountain, each molehill, each situation, each problem, each aspect of our mind field, seen dimly, as they all form a single horizon. We can envision it as just this oneness, or we can see the single line as a circle. This describes our wholeness. As we awaken we can realize each diverse aspect of our practice, of our life, of the difficulties of the world, or of our perplexity at how to respond, and yet, all form a single circle or a single line. We might only see dimly, balanced between the sharpness of our life and the more amorphous wholeness. This might be envisioned as just this oneness, the single horizontal line for the Chinese character one, or the single line seen as a circle, thus describing wholeness or totality. Such a sense of wholeness is the fifth aspect of zazen, including all the others in some way.

MOUNTAIN BLUES

As to the blueness of mountains, when Shohaku Okumura and I were translating this we had a long discussion about mountains and color. The Chinese character often translated as blue also can mean green. But Shohaku was certain that in this instance Dōgen meant blue mountains. Maybe at dawn or at dusk they look more blue. Dōgen talks elsewhere, quoting Furong Daokai (1043–1118; Jpn.: Fuyo Dōkai), an important Chinese teacher in the Sōtō lineage, about the blue mountains walking. Here he talks about them forming a single line. This type of Zen talk is concrete, specific, and literal in one way, but metaphorical in another. Dōgen might well be referring to the lineage, the line of ancestral teachers, who are often called by their mountain names. I might also say, "Dimly seen, the Zen students form a single line," as in a row of meditators in the monks' hall or monks on begging rounds. The intervening space between mountains is also important, as in ink-brush landscape paintings, evoking the spaciousness of awareness accessible in zazen. Dōgen speaks here about dawn, the night mist clearing, and seeing dimly that spaciousness where we are aware and also open to the mist.

In Western Pennsylvania where I grew up are the Blue Mountains, and the Blue Ridge Mountains range from Georgia to Pennsylvania, covered with deep green evergreen trees. Mountains may seem blue at certain times of day, when arising from mist, or amid a little haze. When you approach individual trees they are not blue, but stepping back from the mountains, when we see the whole of them from a distance, they may appear blue. In some ways when sitting we have a particular kind of distance from our life and the aspects of this mind field we sit in. Turning our light within may allow the space where we can see our life from the viewpoint of dawn or dusk; we can see the wholeness or oneness of it.

Looking out over Lake Michigan the horizon also appears as one single line. But when close enough, you can see waves instead of a still mirror. Dimly seen, blue water also forms a single line. The single line acts as a metaphor for interconnectedness. But why does he say "dimly" of the insight into interconnectedness? With Zen discourse, do not worry about understanding clearly. We recognize something; it evokes something. Not that it is impossible to understand, but it is like listening to jazz and trying to discern the role of each note. Dōgen says very directly in "Bendōwa" that trying to compare different schools or teaching is irrelevant; the point is, how is the practice? The "dimly" here suggests this kind of oscillation between seeing each mountain and then seeing the single line. They are foreground and background, both in the picture. When we sit zazen formally, facing the wall, we keep our eyes open with this soft gaze, just as we keep our ears open, and we are open to both the wholeness and the details around and in front of us.

Almost Not Confused by Self

A STORY ABOUT RELEASING THE SELF

B EFORE DŌGEN DEPARTED the capital city of Kyoto in 1243 for the remote mountains of Echizen where he established Eiheiji, he gave many short talks referring to old teaching stories from China, recorded in the first volume of *Eihei Kōroku*. These include Dharma hall discourse 39, from 1241, which begins, "Jingqing Daofu (868–937; Jpn.: Kyōsei Dōfu) asked a monk, 'What is the sound outside the gate?'" In response the monk said, "The sound of raindrops."[97] Sitting zazen during rainfall is lovely. Sound pervades. Sometimes we may hear people moving or talking nearby, or sounds from above the ceiling, or sounds of traffic outside. Sometimes the sound of traffic flowing may seem like rain.

Responding to the monk's "The sound of raindrops," Jingqing said, "Living beings are upside down, deluded by self and chasing after things." This is our situation, upside down, topsy-turvy, "deluded by self and chasing after things." Our idea of a self is the primary opportunity for delusion and confusion, and our world is built on chasing after things. When not enough people are chasing after things, our economy collapses. Chasing after things is the ideal for our material, consumerist society, but it is also how our human consciousness functions most of the time. We try to move things around to get what we want or to get rid of what we do not want.

In response to Jingqing's "Living beings are upside down, deluded by self and chasing after things," the monk inquired, "Teacher, how about you?" Jingqing replied, "I'm almost not confused by self." What a wonderful, poignant statement. We might imagine as a goal not being confused *at all* by self. But pretty regularly we are all rather thoroughly confused by self. So why is this teacher saying, "I am almost not confused by self"? The monk asked, "What does it mean, almost not confused by self?" Jingqing responded, "It is most easy to be released by the self, but expressing this dropped-off body is very difficult."

That is their entire dialogue.

THE CHALLENGE OF EXPRESSING RELEASE

You may not feel that it is so easy to be released from the self. But when we sit, as we sometimes do all day, we have a chance to let go and be released from the self, from attachment to body and mind. Maybe just for a few minutes here and there throughout the day, or maybe, in some way, for the whole day, we might let go of our ideas of this body and mind.

Whether or not we agree with Jingqing about it being easy to be released from the self, we can all agree that expressing dropped off self is very difficult. When we have some feeling of letting go, of breathing into our body and mind and thoughts, and not trying to hold on or grab hold of self, how do we express dropped off body? How do we get up from our cushions and clean the temple, or get up from our cushions and go out into the world? How we express dropped off body is pretty challenging.

Such questioning is what Jingqing may mean by almost not being confused by self. In zazen self arises, as thoughts and feelings or perhaps an itch in our neck, but then we might almost not be confused by self. Releasing a bit from self as we sit is wonderful. Even during a period where some situation is churning around and you are not at all released from self, when something is troubling you, still, somewhere is this possibility of at least glimpsing, here I am; inhale, exhale. Yet expressing this dropped off body is very difficult. How do we express the self that has released the self, the self that is not confused by the self or almost not confused by the self?

When Jingqing asked, "What is the sound outside the gate?" this has to do with not only the sound outside our temple or sitting place. We think in terms of outside and inside, and part of the confusion of the self is we think of this self, this skin bag right here and now sitting on our cushion, as separate from all that other stuff out there. In response to Jingqing's question, the monk said, "The sound of raindrops." Does that mean there is in addition to self some "other," some sounds out there? We think the rain falls somewhere else; it is not falling on this cushion, even though our sensation of hearing rain is happening right on our own cushion. How do we see inside and outside? How do we recognize that there is a gate?

PRACTICING NEAR THE DRAGON GATE

An old Chinese story tells of an ancient dragon Zen gate for which the temple where I teach is named. When a fish swims through this gate at the bottom of one of the major rivers of China, suddenly it becomes a dragon. Are we inside or outside the gate? It might be best just to be a fish near the gate. Part of studying the self is simply to see that we see things as inside and outside; we think there are things that are other, outside, out there in the world.

Expressing this dropped off body is very difficult. Various forms of aware expression are available: expression through zendo forms, expression through art and music, expression through social activism, or expression through seeing each situation in our lives as an opportunity, as a Dharma gate. Maybe that dragon gate is not only in China and not only one place in the river. How do we find all things as Dharma gates? The monk replied, "The sound of the rain," which is a pretty good response.

When sitting quietly the sound of rainfall is wonderful. But Jingqing said living beings are upside down, deluded by self, chasing after things. Was the rain inside the monk or outside the monk somewhere, as he looked for relief from his squirming body and mind on his cushion, chasing after things? There is deep subtlety in chasing after things. When our thoughts chase after things, it does not mean we should destroy our thoughts, but how do we release this deluded self?

Practice involves learning about the self, learning to release the self, learning to stop grasping after body and mind, our confused self, and grasping after things out there. But there is another part of practice; not that one part follows the other. Practically speaking, they are intermingled when we study how to express this possibility of release from self and how to express this together.

THE TEXTURE OF DELUSION

In this Dharma hall discourse Dōgen comments on the story: "Since completely dropping the body, there is still the sound of the raindrops. Released from the self, what is the sound outside the gate?" Dōgen's style of working with these stories is to ask questions about each question and each section. He allows us the opportunity to consider for ourselves. Dōgen concludes, "As for deluding the self, which is difficult or which is easy I completely leave to you. As for chasing after things or chasing after self, are they upside down or not upside down?" Is deluding the self easy? It is how we have been positioned as human beings; we are constantly grasping on to things. Maybe it would be easier not to be deluded. Sometimes we feel not deluding the self is very difficult. Which is it? Maybe they are both easy; maybe they are both difficult. This is a practice question we can engage, if we choose. How is it when we delude ourselves? Can we see it, or do we see when we let go of delusions? We may feel a particular issue as difficult or easy. Sometimes we do not delude ourselves for a while, and then suddenly, we start deluding the self with thoughts and feelings or grasping after things, and then we realize it. Dōgen encourages us to look deeply at the texture of our experience.

Dōgen presents another interesting question: "As for chasing after things or chasing after self, are they upside down or not upside down?" Everyone has experienced chasing after things. This is the main mode of consumerist cultures, maybe all human cultures. How about chasing after self? Dōgen says to study the self. Part of practice is to sit and experience this confused self, and maybe at some point we hear the sound of raindrops outside the gate. Which one is upside down and which one is not upside down? It may be easy to say chasing after things is upside down. Is there a way of chasing after things that is not based on grasping? Is there a way of taking care of things that might not be upside down? Perhaps that is not chasing after things, but still, when we arise from sitting and act, is that upside down or not upside down?

When we sit with some idea to calm down and cool out, or to get some new perspective on a situation, that might be chasing after self. Or perhaps that is simply just our practice. This teacher, Jingqing, said that he was almost not confused by self. Something about that is very appealing. Saying "I'm not at all confused by self" might be a little too much. If you say that, some confusion appears. We may easily get seduced by the grand idea of perfection, of not ever being confused at all. Such perfection is a misleading, inhuman ideal. As a great American yogi said, with one of my favorite Dharma utterances, "If the world were perfect, it wouldn't be."[98]

I instead aspire simply to "I'm almost not confused by self."

THE PECKING OF TEACHER AND STUDENT

A couple of other stories about Jingqing are interestingly relevant to this story. One is about a Zen image invented by Jingqing, the common metaphor for teacher and student depicted as hen and chick. The teacher is like the hen pecking on the outside of the shell, and the chick is pecking from the inside of the shell. I do not believe this actually happens when chickens hatch. But Jingqing presented this image for how student and teacher work together. As cited in the *Blue Cliff Record* case 16, he said once, "In general, foot travelers must have simultaneously the breaking in and breaking out eye, and the breaking in and breaking out function. Only then can they be called patchrobed monks. It's like when the mother hen wants to break in, the chick must break out, and when the chick wants to break out, the mother hen must break in."[99]

"Foot travelers" refers to the monks who wandered around China checking out different teachers and trying to see for themselves, without being confused by self. Jingqing cites this simultaneous breaking in and breaking out action as an image for breaking through the shell of self, of delusion and grasping after things. The chick and the mother hen both peck, peck, peck. After pecking at the shell, when the chick is ready, suddenly the shell cracks opens and the chick pops out. Jingqing originated this image, still mentioned in Zen.

After this teaching, a monk approached Jingqing and said, "After the chick breaks out, from the standpoint of the teacher, what does this amount to?" Jingqing said, "Good news." The monk then asked, "When the chick breaks out and the mother hen breaks in, from the standpoint of the student, what does this amount to?" Jingqing said "Revealing your face." The koan commentary adds, "From this we can see that they did have the device of 'simultaneous breaking in and breaking out' in Jingqing's school." Jingqing was a Dharma brother of the great Yunmen (864–949; Jpn.: Unmon), founder of one of the Chan five houses.

Consider again from this perspective of pecking the main story. Jingqing asked, "What is the sound outside the gate?" and the monk answered, "The sound of raindrops." Jingqing pecked a little by saying, "Living beings are upside down, chasing after things." This monk was able to peck back, saying, "How about you?" Pecking further, Jingqing replied, "I'm almost not confused by self."

If my teacher had said that to me, I might have stopped speechless and just sat with it for a while. But the monk in the story was ready to continue the pecking process, and he said, "What does that mean, to be almost not confused by self?" Jingqing replied, "It is most easy to be released from the self, but expressing this dropped off body is very difficult." Our practice includes both sides, each revealing our face, whether teacher or student. As a teacher I am learning again and again how to break through and reveal my face. For each of us in practice we are always pecking, sometimes pecking out, maybe sometimes pecking in at ourselves. How do we just let go of chasing after things and being deluded by self?

THE WATERWAY ENTRY

The story about the sound outside the gate also relates to the story about Jingqing's own awakening. Jingqing went to study with Xuansha (835–

908: Jpn.: Gensha), a great teacher, though, like Xuansha, Jingqing later became a successor of Xuefeng (822–908; Jpn.: Seppō). Xuansha is the teacher who said, "The entire universe is one bright pearl," the topic of one of Dōgen's *Shōbōgenzō* essays.[100] Upon arrival, Jingqing said to Xuansha, "As a student just entering the monastery, I implore you to instruct me about the path of entry." A good question, how do we find the path to enter the gate? How do we see our breathing, posture, confusion, and grasping at things and thus find an entryway?

Xuansha replied, "Do you hear the sound of water flowing downstream over the weir?" A weir is a little dam that slows down the river. The temple must have been near a stream and a sound of flowing. Jingqing said, "I hear it." Xuansha replied, "Enter through this," and Jingqing realized some entrance.

The sound of water and sounds themselves are traditionally recommended objects of meditation, even the flow of traffic, although conversation or any overheard discussion is usually too distracting. Later Fayan (885–958; Jpn.: Hōgen) said about this dialogue between Jingqing and Xuansha, "As a result of gaining entrance one can freely move in all directions. If you have not yet done so, don't carelessly leave here."

Perhaps the monk in the story first discussed had heard about this story of his teacher, so when Jingqing asked, "What is the sound outside the gate?" he replied, "The sound of raindrops." Maybe he had been practicing by listening to sounds. How do we find our way to enter, to see if we are deluded by self or grasping after things? What is our relationship to the sound of raindrops, the sound of the river flowing downstream? Is that sound inside or outside? Is it something to chase after? How do we use that as an opportunity to almost not be confused by self? Does "almost not confused by self" actually mean being a little bit confused by self? This is worth considering.

DECONSTRUCTING THE SELF

For Westerners, even if we cannot free ourselves from it, this idea of a constructed self is not so difficult. We know that the self is a construction, with habit patterns, family dynamics, cultural influences, and other ways in which all the other beings in our lives have collaborated to help create this self that we often hold on to very tightly. But sometimes we can let go a little bit. Even if we let go of this constructed self fairly well, if we break through the shell, not holding on to the sound of water as being outside nor as being inside either, still we can engage and breathe in this present situation. Our practice and the buddha work involves finding how to express dropped off body-mind. How do we share this, each in our own way? Maybe we can say there is no ultimate self, but it is difficult to say there is no person. Each of us has our own ways to express this dropped off self. Maybe we need to be a little confused by self. Total release is a little touchy, a little tender, and yet there is the buddha work to perform, each of us in our own way.

The dynamic that Jingqing discloses and Dōgen comments on is a way to do the work of studying the self, the heart of studying the way in zazen. We can take all these questions and give our attention to the sound outside the gate. How is it that we are grasping after things or not grasping after things? How is our confusion from the self upside down or not upside down? How is our being almost not confused by the self, if we come close to that, upside down or not?

People react differently to different sounds. The sound of traffic some people experience as harsh, while some people like it. For someone from the countryside not used to it, the sound of traffic might be annoying. For people used to cities and many people, perhaps it is reassuring. Letting the sounds just flow along provides the possibility not to react immediately to whether you like a sound or not. No one approach to sound is right. They may all be topsy-turvy; they may all be just right.

In all our reactions, though, how do we not grasp after things?

How are we almost not confused by self?

Readying the Ox

A TRANSMISSION STORY

DŌGEN COMMENTS in three different modes in *Eihei Kōroku* on a traditional koan about the nature of Zen teaching. This story involves two of the great masters of the ninth century: Baizhang Huaihai (749–814; Jpn.: Hyakujō Ekai), supposed to have founded the Zen monastic regulations, and his student Huangbo Xiyun (d. 850; Jpn.: Ōbaku Kiun), who in turn became the teacher of the great master Linji Yixuan (d. 867; Jpn.: Rinzai Gigen). This story occurred when Huangbo was studying with Baizhang.

Huangbo asked Baizhang, "How shall I instruct people about the essential vehicle from the ancients?" Baizhang sat still. Huangbo asked, "What will our descendents in later generations transmit?" Baizhang said, "I had thought you were that person," and then he returned to the abbot's quarters.[101]

That is the whole story. After Baizhang silently sat still, Huangbo asked, "What will our descendents in later generations transmit?" One way to hear this is Huangbo frustrated that Baizhang would not say anything. And then Baizhang did say, "I had thought that you were that person." Then Baizhang returned to the abbot's quarters.

Dōgen gave a few comments on this story. First is one that is part of his collection of ninety old teaching stories with his verse comments in volume nine of *Eihei Kōroku*, compiled early in Dōgen's career in Kyoto. His four-line verse celebrates this event.

Having been verified and transmitted by the previous ancestors,
How could the practice of a whole lifetime be in vain?
Long ago, his face broke into a smile on Vulture Peak,
Warmth arrived, and he attained the marrow on Shaoshi.

The third line is a reference to the story about Śākyamuni Buddha holding up a flower on Vulture Peak and Mahākāśyapa smiling. This is not an
historical story, with no written record of this legend appearing until the
eleventh century. But still, it is a good story. Śākyamuni held up a flower
on Vulture Peak and one disciple in the assembly smiled. Thereupon
Śākyamuni said to Mahākāśyapa, "You have received the true Dharma
eye treasury of the wondrous mind of nirvana." ("True Dharma eye treasury" is the meaning of "Shōbōgenzō," the name of Dōgen's other major
work.) This is supposedly the first instance of Dharma transmission and
is frequently cited in Zen literature starting in the twelfth century, partly
as a way of claiming authenticity for the tradition as going all the way
back to the Buddha. From a modern perspective, we can acknowledge
that the lineage of names of Indian ancestors usually chanted in Zen was
constructed later in China; even some of the early Chinese names in the
lineage have been questioned by historians. Nevertheless, we appreciate
that someone in each generation after the Buddha must have maintained
and conveyed the actual physical practice until it arrived in China and
eventually reached to us.

Dōgen says, "Warmth arrived, and he attained the marrow at Shaoshi."
This is a reference to the Second Chinese Ancestor, Dazu Huike (487–593;
Jpn.: Taiso Eka), with Shaoshi the place where Bodhidharma, the great
legendary founder of Chan who came to China from India, is said to have
"bestowed the marrow" of Dharma on Huike. Dōgen here seems to be
celebrating and praising both Baizhang and Huangbo. We are still talking
about this story today, and part of the point of these teaching stories is that
they have been studied for a thousand years.

Baizhang just sat still. "How can we instruct people about the essential vehicle from the ancients?" Yes, this is the challenge; my challenge in the teacher's seat, and the challenge for all of us. How do we receive and carry on this wonderful way of practice of zazen and its teaching of inner meaning? Baizhang simply said, "I thought you were that person," and then he returned to the abbot's quarters. Demonstrating how to just sit still, or remaining silent, are traditional Zen responses. Fundamentally all these teaching stories are simply commentaries on silence.

ZAZEN AS THE TEACHER OF WHOLENESS

Fortunately, we have a couple more commentaries by Dōgen about this story. Years after he wrote his verses on the ninety cases in volume 9 of *Eihei Kōroku*, late in his career in 1251 after he had moved away from the capital up into the mountains of Eiheiji in 1243, in a short Dharma hall discourse (423) Dōgen related the same story. Then he added:

> Suppose someone said to me, Eihei, "What Dharma did previous sages present to people?" I would simply say to him, "I show people my sitting cushion." So it is said, "I came to this land fundamentally to transmit the Dharma and save deluded people."[102]

The job of a Zen teacher is simply to show people how to sit zazen, to find their way to just sit uprightly, facing the wall and themselves, to not run away from this body and mind, here and now. So Dōgen said, "If someone would ask me what Dharma to present to people, I show people my sitting cushion." Then, "I came to this land fundamentally in order to transmit the Dharma and save deluded beings" is what Dōgen would say on behalf of Baizhang. This refers to the statement in the Lotus Sutra that all buddhas appear in the world simply for the single great cause of helping beings onto the path of awakening.[103] One traditional mode for teachers commenting on the stories is to say what they would have said themselves in the same situation.

FISTICUFFS AND GRANDMOTHER ZEN

Dōgen continues, "As to 'What will descendants of later generations transmit?' I would simply tell him: I transmit it with my fists. Therefore it is said, 'One blossom opens with five petals and naturally bears fruit.'" Why does Dōgen say, "I transmit it with my fists"? Some teachers in China used to strike their students to wake them up. One Chinese wild guy, the teacher Deshan Xuanjian (780–865; Jpn.: Tokusan Senkan), is famous for punching out his students. Perhaps he had some difficult disciples. Japanese monasteries have usually included mostly young men, who also may be used to this. But we do not do that in American Zen, and that is not what Dōgen meant either. Traditionally and now in America, Zen also includes Grandmother Zen. Some students need some tough father figure, and some people need grandmothers. Whatever you need is what Zen tries to give, whatever will help lead to just dropping body and mind.

When I lived in Japan bodhisattva spirit was most apparent in the old women, the grandmothers who would come out in the morning and hose down and sweep the street. Being out early they would say good morning to the kids and encourage them on their way to school. It was very sweet. But grandmothers can be tough too. One of the strictest teachers I ever had was Suzuki Roshi's widow, Suzuki Sensei, when I studied *chadō* (the way of tea) with her for a little while. She lived at the Zen Center for many years after Suzuki Roshi died, watching over us. She could be very gentle and considerate, and she would invite people in for tea and conversation, but when she was teaching tea, she could be fierce. A tiny bit of the wrong movement, and she would let you know very definitely. She was tough but a wonderful person, training people in the spirit of performing the simple act of making tea properly. But I do not know any stories of her actually hitting anyone. In Japanese training Zen is a performance art. Not just for Zen monks, but also in many of the art forms: tea, martial arts, flower arranging, calligraphy; the point is to perform each action beautifully. The teacher's job is to correct the students and stop them when they go off a tiny bit.

When Dōgen says, "I transmit it with my fists," what does he mean? Conveyed warm hand to warm hand; hands closed or hands open; just this round fist, or just this circle. How do we find our wholeness—each of us at our own seat, and together? Dōgen concludes this commentary, "Therefore it is said, 'One blossom opens with five petals and naturally bears fruit.'" This is an old phrase attributed to Bodhidharma, but it is actually from much later and is often taken as a reference to the single transmission from Bodhidharma to the Second Ancestor and all five subsequent ancestors up to the great Sixth Ancestor, Huineng, or else as a reference to the historical fact of the later five houses of Chan in China. But I believe there is a deeper meaning. If someone were to ask me, "One blossom opens into five petals and naturally bears fruit—how is that?" I would say, we inhale, we exhale. Naturally in our witnessing the wholeness of our open heart, something happens, something bears fruit. One fist opens with five fingers. Each in our own way, coming and going, we enter into our life, right here not turning away from our world and its suffering. Here we are. So Dōgen says, "I would simply say, I show people my sitting cushion."

BRUSHING OUT SLEEVES

This wonderful practice of just sitting facing the wall, facing ourselves, breathing in and out, finding our inner wholeness and inner uprightness, that is enough. But then how do we share it? There are many teaching stories, and it is not necessary to learn all of them, as Dōgen seems to have done himself when he went to China. How shall we create new stories of awakening? How shall we transform our own stories of difficulties and conflict into stories of everyday awakening? This is a great challenge. Still, in sitting practice awakening opens in its own way.

Dōgen gave another, somewhat longer and more elaborate commentary on this same story of Baizhang and Huangbo in Dharma hall discourse 131 in 1245, not so long after he moved from Kyoto. In this talk Dōgen offers a slightly varied version. After Huangbo asks, "What will our descendents in later generations transmit?" Baizhang brushed out his sleeves, stood up, and said, "I had thought you were that person."[104] Brushing out one's sleeves is traditionally a gesture of dismissal, but often in these old Zen stories much of what happens is ironic. What seems like praise or criticism might be the opposite. When Baizhang stood up and brushed out his sleeves I believe he was not dismissive of Huangbo but satisfied. Saying "I had thought you were that person" was in some way entrusting this to Huangbo.

TIGER'S STRIPES AND DRAGON MARKINGS

Dōgen has more to say, as usual. In his extended 1245 comments he adds:

> These two old men could only speak of a tiger's stripes, they could not speak of a person's stripes. Moreover, they could not speak of a tiger without stripes, a person without stripes, a phoenix without markings, or a dragon without markings. Why is this so? Great assembly, listen carefully. For the sake of people, the ancient ones just sat, without moving. For the sake of people, later generations just return back to the abbot's quarters. Although this is right, it is not yet fully completed. Where is it not complete? Great Assembly, you should know that if the question is not complete, the response is not complete. Why didn't Huangbo ask, "Ancient ones and those of later generations both receive the teacher [Baizhang's] instructions. What is the connecting pivot right now?"

This is what Dōgen would say:

> When it is asked like this, look, how will Baizhang instruct him?
> If someone would ask me, [Dōgen], "What Dharma did the ancient ones use long ago to instruct people?" then I would answer: Others put a rope through their own nostrils.

Can you do that for each other?

> If also asked, "What will our descendants in later generations trans-
> mit?" then I would tell him: I pull myself by my own nostrils.
>   If someone also asked, "What is the connecting pivot right
> now?" then I would say to him: One person transmits emptiness,
> and then ten thousand people transmit reality.

What is going on in this commentary? The point of these stories is
not to be mysterious or inscrutable. They are not nonsensical riddles that
require a lobotomy to answer. There is a logic to them, and it helps to know
what these images are about. "Putting a rope through my own nostrils"
is a reference to the ox-herding pictures and their motif of Zen training.
There are different versions of these pictures, sometimes six, sometimes
ten, but they are prominent images in Zen, depicting the training process
for becoming a whole person.[105] One set of ox-herding pictures begins
with a boy searching for the ox. Then he sees traces of the ox, then actually
glimpses the ox, and eventually he catches it and rides it home. Following this comes an image of nature, described as the ox forgotten. Then
is a blank full moon, and finally old Hotei, the jolly laughing buddha, is
portrayed "entering the marketplace with bliss-bestowing hands." These
images of the ox depict the process of training of this wild self, this conditioned, confused, deluded self that we all are, though not separate from the
self that is deeply interconnected and interwoven with all being.

PIERCING NOSTRILS

Zen is a practice for human beings, not for cows and cats, who already
know beyond discriminations. Baizhang's Dharma brother Nanquan
Puyuan (748–835; Jpn.: Nansen Fugan) once declared, "The buddhas of
past present and future do not know it is: cats and cows know it is."[106] But
the image of the ox as referenced indirectly by Dōgen is about willingness
to be trained. Dōgen uses the image of piercing one's nostrils several times

in *Eihei Kōroku*. When I was translating this with Shohaku Okumura, I first assumed this image had to do with breathing. I still believe that is relevant, inhaling and exhaling fully with nostrils open. But also piercing nostrils describes putting a nose ring through the ox's nose so that the ox can be led. We need to put ourselves in the position of being led, being trained, of serving Buddha.

Huangbo is asking Baizhang about the whole teacher and student process. Baizhang just sat still. Nothing to do. He does not go around punching out people. Dōgen says, "If I were asked what will our descendents in later generations transmit I would say, 'I pull myself by my own nostrils.'" In this ancient venerable tradition, no teacher can tell you how to be a buddha. I cannot—and even if I could, would not want to—do that. My teacher could not do that for me. How do we find our own way, our own way to be led? Dragons and tigers, how do we pierce our own nostrils? When asked, Dōgen said, "Others put a rope through their own nostrils."

It is up to each of us to find our way of being buddha. There is not one right way. In fact, there are many ways on each sitting cushion right now. The path is wild. The path is not a matter of a roadmap or a few rules and regulations. If it were that easy you could join Marine bootcamp and become a buddha. Not that you might not become a buddha by joining the Marines, but how do we allow ourselves to be led by Buddha? Returning to the first verse commentary by Dōgen:

> Having been verified and transmitted by the previous ancestors,
> How could the practice of a whole lifetime be in vain?

It is important to hear that this is the practice of a lifetime. However, a whole lifetime is right now. How can you appreciate your whole lifetime right now?

> Long ago his face broke into a smile on Vulture Peak,
> Warmth arrived and he attained the marrow on Shaoshi.

That person is here now. How do we find our way to appreciate the Buddha, and not just the Buddha represented on the altar? How do we bring our whole life to our whole life and sustain this? Dōgen talks often about buddha going beyond Buddha. You may show up and sit a period of zazen and feel wonderful, or feel lousy, either way appreciating just one period of zazen. Zen temples make this available to people. If someone comes and sits zazen once and never returns, still it is wonderful. Something about your whole lifetime is present now. Each of us also has various sanghas, many contexts, other realms. In those worlds as well, how do we put a rope through our own nostrils? How are we willing to be taken, or sometimes dragged, along the path? How do we allow the difficulties, conflicts, and challenges of our life to lead us on the way? What is the connecting pivot right now?

TEN THOUSAND SHOWING UP

There is more to Dōgen's reference to dragons and tigers. "These two old men could only speak of a tiger's stripes, they could not speak of a person's stripes. Moreover, they could not speak of a tiger without stripes, a person without stripes, a phoenix without markings, or a dragon without markings." How do we appreciate this training and conveyance, not needing markings, special robes or status, no fancy attitudes? He continues, "Why is this so? Great assembly, listen carefully. For the sake of people the ancients just sat, without moving. For the sake of people, later generations just return back to the abbot's quarters." Just to show up and sit, and to support each other to show up and sit, in the present, is where buddha appears, on each cushion. So we are still discussing this story.

Saying a little more about the noninscrutable, non-koan aspect of teaching, we might make a distinction between practice and training, although not a sharp distinction; they are not ultimately separate. People need a space where they can show up to practice, and just sit. Studying the teachings and listening to Dharma talks has an effect and may be very helpful, but zazen is what is essential.

Here is more about one line in Dōgen's commentaries: "If someone asked, 'What is the connecting pivot right now?' then I would say to him: One person transmits emptiness, and then ten thousand people transmit reality." As context, an old Chinese saying goes, "One dog howls meaninglessly, and ten thousand dogs follow." Dōgen might be implying that the teaching of emptiness is a mere provisional skillful means, although it does continue to manifest the true Dharma. But also, each person's practice can influence ten thousand. Supporting others to practice, slow down a little, and breathe and relax their minds a bit, the impact cannot be tracked or traced. People who experience zazen may go out into their lives and their jobs and be a little kinder or more generous, and ten thousand flowers bloom.

SPIRITUAL FRIENDS

That is the side of Zen "practice," and it is wonderful. But for those interested in piercing your nostrils and being guided, there are ways to give yourself to what might be called a training program. One training format involves formally receiving bodhisattva precepts as laypeople or as Zen priests. The precepts are guidelines on how to live in this world, and they are not only for people who have gone through the formal ceremony of lay ordination; actually we all receive them together. Zen teachers are also available to talk in individual practice interviews, if you want to try to do this training, putting a rope through your nostrils. Longer sittings and residential retreats are also helpful to training context. The tradition certainly recommends consulting with teachers about your practice. It is helpful to see Zen teachers simply as good spiritual friends (kalyāna mitra in Sanskrit). Idealizing teachers as exalted perfect masters has caused much damage in American Buddhism. As a teacher I just have considerable experience in this practice over decades, and my job and joy is to share that experience. Good training can be very flexible and informal. There is not one right way to be training in the path and the lineage of Dōgen and all the ancestors. Such training is an individual matter, worked out by agreement between teacher and student, and subject to continuous adjustment.

But it is fine if you do not want be an ox and pierce your nostrils. Some people like the piercing; some do not. Just to show up and sit still, quietly like Baizhang, is excellent and transformative practice, helpful to all beings. My job as a Zen priest is to keep this opportunity alive and available for later generations, and all who engage this practice are helping.

How do we see the dragons without markings? How do we see our way of aligning ourselves with wholeness? How do we find our way to oneness that includes everything? The point of Buddhism is to alleviate suffering. Period. How may we relieve the suffering of the world in all its varied forms? One way to understand the first Noble Truth of suffering is that everything is just a little off. It has always been that way and perhaps it always will. And yet there is a path to find a way to wholeness, openness, toward sharing this together. On this path we sometimes need to be willing to be led; led by ourselves, by Buddha, by a spiritual friend.

Please be willing to make mistakes. The way usually is not just one straight road. That would be too boring. Lose your way. Sometimes our practice is to wobble to one side, then return to upright. Wobble to the other side, then again return to upright. Allow yourself to lose your way, but do not forget where the nose rings are. This is a practice for human beings. When you do lose your way and make mistakes, try not to create harm for yourselves or others. One problem in reading these old stories is thinking the ancient masters were super-beings. They were just people. Lose your way, but then return. Do not forget the rest of us. The individual student holds a great deal of responsibility in Zen. There are teachers, many libraries of texts with sutras and commentaries, and there is sangha, perhaps the greatest teacher, as we try to find the way together. But each of us has to show up, to be willing to be a dragon with or without markings, to be willing to be part of the circle of uprightness. This is not easy. And yet it is a matter of just being willing to not run away from ourselves, to stay present. I believe it is helpful toward remaining present to smile just a bit during zazen, as Thich Nhat Hanh has suggested.

Over time training may shift or change. Yet we still have these old stories. We are making it up for our situation, but we also have patterns to follow. Gary Snyder says when making an axe handle, the pattern is right at hand. We must shift and adapt our training modes, because no matter how hard we might try to be in Kamakura Japan, or Song China, here we are, twenty-first-century United States. The practice and training manifest as a vital, living being. Just sitting still and silent is very helpful.

Dropping Body-Mind, and the Pregnant Temple Pillars

DROPPING OFF AS THE END AND THE BEGINNING

HERE IS A short Dharma hall discourse (501) from *Eihei Kōroku* from 1252 at Eiheiji, where Dōgen was training his monks, a year before he died. Dōgen says:

> Body and mind dropped off is the beginning of our effort, but when a temple pillar becomes pregnant, how do we discern their absence? The thick cloud matting spread over the mountain peaks is still, and above the heights the round moon shines in all directions. It stands alone, eminent, not relying on anything. The lofty buddha body does not fall into various kinds. Therefore, an ancient worthy said, "The sage empties out his heart. The ten thousand things are nothing other than my own production. Only a sage can understand the ten thousand things and make them into oneself." At this very moment how is it? Do you want to understand this clearly?
>
> After a pause Dōgen said: The moon moves following the boat, with the ocean vast. Spring turns following the sun, with the sunflowers red.[107]

Shohaku Okumura and I added names at the beginning of each Dharma hall discourse, calling this one "Moonlight Over the Pregnant Temple Pillars."

Dōgen starts by talking about body and mind dropped off, the subject of this short Dharma hall discourse. It is humorous that he says, "Body and mind dropped off is the beginning of our effort." Dropping off body and mind is an important technical term for Dōgen, in Japanese *shinjin datsuraku*. Body and mind dropped away is a name Dōgen uses for zazen, which he sees as simply dropping off body and mind. But it is also his name for *annuttara saṃyak saṃbodhi*, "Complete unsurpassed perfect enlightenment," and yet also he calls it the "beginning of our effort." "Body and mind dropped off" refers in part to the letting go of our ancient, twisted karmic attachment to this limited body and mind. We are conditioned to try to acquire objects to embellish, enhance, or improve this body and mind. Just dropping off body and mind is to abandon that effort of acquisitiveness, and it is a statement of the ultimate for Dōgen.

The traditional story behind this phrase is that when he was training with his teacher in a monastery in China in 1227, some twenty-five years before this talk, Dōgen was sitting in the monks' hall late one night and his teacher, Tiantong Rujing, walked behind the meditating monks while the person sitting next to Dōgen was sleeping. Rujing took off his slipper and hit the sleeping monk, saying, "You are supposed to be dropping off body and mind; why are you engaged in just sleeping instead of just sitting?" Supposedly Dōgen was greatly awakened upon hearing this. He thereupon went to Rujing's room and offered incense, saying that he had dropped body and mind. When Rujing immediately approved him, Dōgen is said to have asked that he not be confirmed so quickly. Rujing said that this was dropping off dropped off. If you drop off body and mind, please let go of that too.

Modern Sōtō scholars question whether this incident really happened, because they cannot find any record of Dōgen's teacher talking about "Body and mind dropped off." Certainly this does not refer to a dramatic *satori* or *kenshō* awakening experience, as sometimes claimed, since Dōgen never mentions this incident and clearly does not encourage seeking such experiences.[108] But an earlier teacher in his lineage, Hongzhi Zhengjue (some of whose writings I translated in *Cultivating the Empty Field*), does speak in some ways about dropping body-mind.[109] At any rate, this phrase, "Dropping away body and mind," is very important for Dōgen as the ultimate goal and the true essence of zazen practice.

Dōgen begins this Dharma hall discourse by saying, "Body and mind dropped off is the beginning of our effort." He is following the practice style of Sōtō Zen to start from the very top of the mountain. Then we have to spend years sometimes filling in the background. Here he is saying that the ultimate attainment is only the beginning of practice.

PILLARS ALIVE

"When a temple pillar becomes pregnant, how do we discern the absence of body and mind?" How can we see that body and mind have dropped off, are absent, when the temple pillars become pregnant? This phrase about the temple pillar getting pregnant sounds like an enigmatic Zen saying. Somebody once asked the great master Yunmen, "What is the meaning of the Buddha Dharma?" and he said to go ask the temple pillars.[110] I am sure those pillars had heard many Dharma talks.

There are many other phrases in Zen about the apparently inanimate coming alive, such as, "When the wooden man begins to sing, the stone woman gets up to dance," or, "A dragon howls in a withered tree." Deep in winter the first intimation of spring are the plums blossoming, so Dōgen also says, "The plum blossoms open afresh on the same withered branch as last year."[111] There was a famous teacher whose zendo was called the Dead Stump Hall, because his students sat still like dead tree stumps. Dōgen is talking here about body and mind dropped off as the beginning of our effort when he asks, "When the temple pillars get pregnant then how do we discern their absence?" Our practice is to sit facing the wall, inhaling, exhaling, still as a dead tree stump. We turn within, let go, and put aside worldly affairs and concerns for forty minutes, or for a day, or perhaps for a week, or a practice period. And of course these concerns may jump up behind us and chatter away. But when we really can just let go, in what is sometimes called the great death, then eventually deep life may emerge. The dragon howls in a withered tree. The stone woman gets up to dance. The temple pillars become pregnant. In spring the buds prepare an outburst, just like last year. So ultimately, beyond dropping body and mind, Zen is about finding and reclaiming true life, our true vitality and energy, which is not separate from anything, totally connected with the whole world. This is what we practice.

Body and mind may be dropped off, but that does not mean that we have no awareness; quite the opposite. When body and mind have dropped away, how do we discern their absence? This great death is sometimes confused with having no thoughts or feelings as the goal, and then we hear about the heretical school of Lobotomy Zen. That surgical operation is not recommended. You do not have to become stupid to be a Zen student, although it is all right if you happen to be stupid. You do not have to be smart either. But Zen is not about getting rid of your thoughts and feelings. It is simply about letting them totally drop away. Then how do we discern their absence? How can we know it if we have dropped body and mind?

CONNECTING TO CLOUDS BELOW AND THE SAGE'S SELF

Dōgen explains, saying, "The thick cloud matting spread over the mountain peaks is still, and above the heights the round moon shines in all directions." When high enough up in the mountains, you can look down and see the cloud covering below. Maybe the moon appears, shining, whether the moon is full or crescent. "It stands alone, eminent, not relying on anything. The lofty buddha body does not fall into various kinds." It is noteworthy that he does not call it the buddha mind or buddha awareness; it is the lofty buddha body. This is a kind of physical body, part of the world of form. Though entering into the world of form, yet it does not fall into the particularities of the phenomenal world, all the various kinds of things.

Then Dōgen quotes Sengzhao (374 or 385–414; Jpn.: Sōjō), whom he calls an ancient worthy. Sengzhao was a great early Chinese Buddhist scholar, teacher, and sage in the fifth century, before Bodhidharma. Sengzhao was a student and assistant of the great translator Kumārajīva (344–413), translator of most of the sutras studied in East Asia. There were other great translators, but Kumārajīva translated most of the Mahāyāna scriptures, including the Lotus Sutra, the Vimalakīrti Sutra, the Diamond Sutra, and other Perfection of Wisdom Sutras. Kumārajīva was from Central Asia and was brought to China, where the emperor made him translate all these sutras. In addition to supplying him with good Chinese scholars to help him produce fine Chinese translations of the Indian sutras, the emperor tried an experiment in eugenics, and he forced on Kumārajīva a harem to engage his superior genetic ability to produce other new translators. I do not know if any of his progeny ever produced any translations, but perhaps even the temple pillars in Kumārajīva's temple became pregnant. Sengzhao was one of Kumārajīva's assistants and himself a great scholar who later wrote important commentaries.

Dōgen quotes from Sengzhao, who said, "The sage empties out his heart." This character could be read as "mind" as well as "heart." It literally means "to cherish." It is the mind, but not like the head. We translated this as, "The sage empties out his heart. The ten thousand things are nothing other than my own production." In some ways we create the world, inhalation after exhalation after inhalation. How we see the world is our own production. But it is not that we create the world only by ourselves, because there is also the world that exists as a mutual coproduction of all beings. Maybe it would be more accurate to say, "The ten thousand things are nothing other than our own production." But here Sengzhao explicitly calls it "my" own production.

Then Sengzhao says, "Only a sage can understand the ten thousand things and bring them into the self." This is a famous quote in Sōtō Zen, as it was important to the great Chinese teacher Shitou Xiqian (700–790; Jpn.: Sekitō Kisen), the teacher who wrote "Harmony of Difference and Sameness" (Sandōkai) and "Song of the Grass Hut."[112] Case 91 in the Book of Serenity relates that Shitou was vastly awakened when he read this quote.

Thomas Cleary's translation of the entire Sengzhao passage goes: "The ultimate man is empty and hollow; he has no form, yet of the myriad things there is none that is not his own making. Who can understand myriad things as oneself? Only a sage." Shitou awakened as he read this, and his response to this quote was to say, "A sage has no self, yet there is nothing that is not himself."[113] It is said that thereupon Shitou wrote "Harmony of Difference and Sameness." What Dōgen and Sengzhao are talking about here is how we are related to the entire world. What is the relationship between ourselves and this lofty moon, which does not depend on anything? What is our relationship to this energy that springs forth in spring? When spring arises we feel it in everything, in the flowers, the animals, and the grasses, but also in ourselves.

When you feel that connection with all things, however we each may feel it, then let go of needing it to be outside. Be willing to come back into the temple, or into your house; to wash the dishes or go to your job. It is okay to dance wildly in the mountains. But then please come back and hang out with the rest of us.

THE ZEN SECRET

How do we see our connection to all beings? How do we see their connection to our own arising energy and vitality? How do we see the temple pillars getting pregnant in the light of all beings, under the light of the moon? Dōgen's image of the clouds covering the mountain peaks with the moon above reminds me of those wonderful Japanese rock gardens, "dry landscapes," with a simple bed of raked gravel and a few rocks in some wonderfully asymmetric, syncopated arrangement, arising out of the gravel. This is about form and emptiness. How do we find our own true form in the middle of emptiness? It is possible to find our true life and vitality in the middle of feeling deadness. When we just let go and feel there is nothing left, if we can stay present and keep breathing and sitting for the last five or ten minutes, when it is really difficult and the bell has not yet rung, if we just keep sitting, it is possible that the temple pillars may become pregnant.

"The sage has no self, yet there is nothing that is not himself." This is dropping body and mind. We do not try to change ourselves or the world to obtain some benefit. In fact, we are already deeply connected with everything, but that does not mean that we just kind of collapse. We can be quite lively in that situation, as an expression of the ten thousand things. If we are connected with all things, when there is nothing that is not ourself, then we actually are dancing with everything. Excuse me for saying it so blatantly. This is the great Zen secret. Please forget that you read that!

The entire quote from Sengzhao (in Thomas Cleary's translation) says:

> The mysterious Way is in ineffable enlightenment, enlightenment is in merging with reality, merging with reality involves seeing existence and non-existence as equal, and when you see them equally, then others and self are not two. Therefore, heaven, earth, and I have the same root; the myriad things and I are one body.

This is that buddha body, shining above, not relying on anything.

> Being the same as me, they are no longer existent or non-existent; if they were different from me, that would oppose communication. Therefore, neither going out nor being within, the Way subsists in between.

This is saying that the teaching, the Dharma, reality itself, is a relationship. We are not the same and not different. But the energy that flows between us and all things, and between each of us, is where the buddha body is, and where the Dharma is alive.

DREAM FLOWERS

Interestingly, the *Book of Serenity* case with this quote seems to criticizes Shitou, or at least Sengzhao. The passage from Sengzhao was quoted by a government official named Lugeng, who was a student of the great teacher Nanquan Puyuan (748–835: Jpn.: Nansen Fugan). The commentator to the *Book of Serenity* says, "Lugeng quoted these lines as being wonderful. He hardly realized that this indeed is talking about a dream. Even so, even someone as great as Master Shitou was vastly awakened to the Way while reading Sengzhao." Then he goes on to talk about the quote. The case or story to which this is a commentary is relevant, and it has a somewhat different fundamental interpretation from Dōgen's.

In the story that is the main case, Officer Lugeng said to Nanquan, "Teaching Master Sengzhao was quite extraordinary. He was able to say, 'Heaven and earth have the same root. Myriad things are one body.'" That is part of Sengzhao's long quote. Hearing this, Nanquan pointed to a peony in the garden where they were walking and said, "People today see this flower as in a dream."

Perhaps Nanquan was not criticizing Sengzhao, but still he questioned this lofty talk about only a sage understanding the ten thousand things and taking them into him- or herself. Nanquan wondered about how to actually smell the flowers. How do we not get caught in some dream of awakening or a mere dream of dropping off body and mind? Nanquan challenges us to really appreciate and engage this moment we inhabit and the fragrance of this very world. I like this story and I like this little talk by Dōgen, because they do not let us off the hook anywhere.

THE MOON MOVES AND SPRING RETURNS

After that quote from Sengzhao in Dharma hall discourse 501, Dōgen asks his monks, "At this very moment how is it? Do you want to understand this clearly?" Then after a pause, Dōgen said, "The moon moves following the boat, with the ocean vast. Spring turns following the sun, with the sunflowers red." It is not just that the moon shines over the ocean and we see the reflection of the moon everywhere, in the waves and in the stillness of the ocean, with the Pacific Ocean actually peaceful. But beyond that, the moon moves, following the boat. We can only see the moon depending on where we actually sit right now. Spring turns following the sun. It is early February now. Is it spring out? Here we have some wonderful flowers outside.

This talk by Dōgen is about how we find our deep life and vitality. If you try and grasp for it, that is not it. We have to be willing to just sit, right in the middle of this body, this mind, this life. And really let go. And then let go again. And when we drop off body and mind, this is the beginning of our effort, according to Dōgen. A charming aspect of Dōgen's Zen is his constant talking about going beyond. There is no end to it; you are never going to finally, completely understand or "get it." But don't worry; just let go of it. This is really wonderful, because Buddha is actually alive not static, extremely benevolent, and totally interconnected with all beings. The more different beings you happen to run into, the more it unfolds. It is not about getting something or understanding anything; it does not matter if you understand a word I have said or that Dōgen said.

But you should enjoy it, and play with it, and allow it to sing in your body and mind.

Practice-Realization-Expression

THE WONDER BEYOND WORDS

I WANT TO ACKNOWLEDGE THE truth of the Dharma that even were I to write a hundred pages about the following teaching, these words could not possibly come close to reaching the wonder of just sitting together on a beautiful spring morning. The wonder of just being present is beyond any words.

But I will comment on a teaching by Dōgen from *Dōgen's Extensive Record* from his earlier teaching in Kyoto. It is about the oneness of enlightenment, practice, and expression, from a *hōgo*, or Dharma words, which were letters he wrote to his Zen students. He starts:

> With the whole body just as it is, who would get stuck in any place? With the entire body familiar, how could we find our way back to a source? Already beyond the single phrase, how could we be troubled by the three vehicles? When you open your hand, it is just right; when your body is activated it immediately appears.[114]

The tradition of zazen, or sitting meditation, is about just being present in this life, this body and mind, and becoming very familiar with how it is to be this person in this reality just as it is, right now. "With the entire body familiar, how could we find our way back to a source?" The main practice in Dōgen's Zen is considered in other systems of Buddhist meditation and thought as the highest, most advanced, most developed kind of meditation. Our style is to just dive in at the top of the mountain. It may seem so simple that it feels difficult, or it may seem puzzling. Just become familiar with the entire body: This body on our cushion, this body in this sitting place, the body of the specific neighborhood around us as we sit.

A little further Dōgen says:

> Truly, the point of the singular transmission between buddha ancestors, the essential meaning of the direct understanding beyond words, does not adhere to the situation of the kōans of the previous wise ones, or the entryways to enlightenment.... It does not exist in the commentaries and assessments with words and phrases, in the exchange of questions and answers, in the understandings with intellectual views, in the mental calculations of thought, in conversations about mysteries and wonders, or in explanations of mind and nature.

Even though there may be many wonderful phrases and understandings expressed, the emphasis in this practice and teaching and expression is just how to take care of the present situation. How do we take care of our everyday activities? How do we allow this practice-realization-expression to find its voice and body and mind and its love in our everyday ordinary world?

THE FRIEND OF NOT KNOWING

Dōgen continues, "Only when one releases the handles [from all these teachings], without retaining what has been glimpsed, is it perfectly complete right here, and can fill the eyes. Behind the head, the path of genuine intimacy opens wide; in front of the face, not knowing is a good friend." We may have all kinds of wonderful understandings, but our best friend is just not knowing, the openness of not knowing how to proceed, not knowing exactly what the world is, not even knowing who we are. Many people yearn for some understanding. Being smart monkeys, we wish to understand. That is fine, but actually, the practice and expression of enlightenment, the enlightenment of practice and expression, is right here, before and after and outside of whatever we think we understand, no matter how good our understanding might be.

Dōgen says this even more strongly in a different place, in a letter to one of his nun disciples, Ryōnen. Dōgen had many women disciples, but he praised Ryōnen in particular, saying her practice was wonderful. He ends one of his letters to her by saying:

> Without begrudging any effort in nurturing the Way, for you I will demonstrate the precise meaning [of the ultimate truth of Buddha]. That is, if you do not hold on to a single phrase or half a verse, a bit of talk or a small expression, in this lump of red flesh you will have some accord with the clear, cool ground. If you hold on to a single word or half a phrase of the buddha ancestors' sayings or of the koans from the ancestral gate, they will become dangerous poisons. If you want to understand this mountain monk's activity, do not remember these comments. Truly avoid being caught up in thinking.[115]

Dōgen is disclosing that the ultimate teaching is not to remember what he is saying. This is pretty funny, I think.

Sometimes, as a sort of game, I have asked a Zen student who I know has gone to a Dharma talk, "What did the teacher talk about?" Many times even very good Zen students do not remember. Or they may remember something about the topic but not anything else. But it is also okay if you do happen to remember.

NOT REMEMBERING, INFORMED BY DHARMA

But actually Dōgen has given you a problem, and now I have as well. If you remember that you do not need to remember these words, then you are remembering these words. And if you do not remember that you do not need to remember these words, then you might remember them and make them into a poison. I am sorry to have to say it, but you have a problem...

But the point of this or any Dharma writing is not the words themselves. It is your paying attention and hearing. I remember many years ago a practice discussion I had with San Francisco Zen Center Abbess Linda Cutts, which was very helpful to me, and I confess that I do remember it. She said that you do not need to remember the insights or teachings arising in your zazen. When you are informed by the teaching it is in your form, and when you need it, it will be there. To be informed by this Dharma or any Dharma words, or Dōgen's words, is to allow this practice expression into your body and mind. It is not primarily about your thinking. Whether you remember some of it or do not remember any of it, that is fine. But when it is needed, this Dharma is here.

Dōgen says in the first letter, "Within this [true Dharma] there is practice, teaching, and enlightenment. This practice is the effort of our zazen." It does require some effort just to arrive at the meditation hall, to get to your cushion, to sit upright, to keep your eyes open, breathe, and return to being present and upright in this body and mind. This is the effort of zazen practice. The Chinese character Dōgen used in these passages for the word "enlightenment" from among the three commonly used characters means literally "verification" instead of "enlightenment" or "awakening," indicating the verification of enlightenment. The following quotes simply use "enlightenment." But Dōgen is emphasizing confirmed enlightenment.

CARRYING THE RAFT UP THE OTHER SHORE

Dōgen adds, "It is customary that such practice is not abandoned even after reaching buddhahood, so that it is still practiced by a buddha." Even after becoming Buddha, Śākyamuni Buddha continued to practice. When he became enlightened, that was not the end of Buddhism, but just the beginning.

Dōgen goes on to say:

> Teaching and enlightenment should be examined in the same
> way. This zazen was transmitted from Buddha to Buddha, directly
> pointed out by ancestors, and only transmitted by legitimate suc-
> cessors. Even when others hear of its name, it is not the same as
> the zazen of buddha ancestors. This is because the principle of
> zazen in other schools is to wait for enlightenment.

We easily tend to think of this practice that, if we wait long enough, we
will eventually be enlightened. We imagine if we put enough hours into
sitting on this cushion, or enough lifetimes, some day, somewhere, when
you least expect it, there it will be, the big Enlightenment.

Dōgen says, "The principle of zazen in other schools is to wait for
enlightenment." Many branches of Buddhism seem to encourage practicing to eventually reach enlightenment. Dōgen criticizes that perspective.
He says, for example, some people practice as having crossed over a great
ocean on a raft, "thinking that upon crossing the ocean one should discard
the raft." That notion is very sensible. This simile of the raft is common in
Buddhism, that once we have reached the other shore we do not need the
raft any more. But Dōgen implies that one should still carry the raft while
climbing up the mountains. The practice continues.

"The zazen of our buddha ancestors is not like [waiting for enlighten-
ment], but is simply Buddha's practice." Dōgen's practice is not practice
to acquire something, some so-called enlightenment somewhere else, in
some other time, or other state of mind. This is not practice to get high,
or reach some altered state of consciousness or being. This is actually the
practice of our enlightenment and realization expressed right now. Enlightenment and realization naturally lead to practice. There is no enlightenment that is not actually put into practice. That would just be some idea
of enlightenment, not true enlightenment. Each person is practicing their
realization right now and realizing their practice right now. This is simply
Buddha's practice.

ENACTING THE MEDITATION TECHNOLOGY

In many schools of Buddhism there are wonderful techniques, and a whole meditation technology, which is sometimes very helpful. It may help to know how to follow your breath, or count breaths, or settle your mind, even to recite mantras in zazen, or to sit in the middle of the ancient stories. Using such supports is fine, but those particular techniques may be enacted with this attitude of Buddha's practice, not about practicing such techniques in order to get something else. This is deeply counterintuitive. Almost everyone comes to practice because of some problem. We want to feel better, to reduce stress, or to learn how to deal with our loss, confusion, frustration, greed, rage, or sadness. Meditation does help those situations. But it is not that we meditate for the purpose of accomplishing that. Just your thought of practice already is Buddha's practice.

EXPRESSION AT THE HEART

Dōgen says:

> We could say that the situation of Buddha's house is the oneness in which the essence, practice, and expounding are one and the same. The essence is enlightenment; expounding is the teaching; and practice is cultivation. Even up to now, these have been studied together. We should know that practice is the practice of essence and expounding.

This Chinese character called "expounding" here also means simply "to express," and in the following I will sometimes use the word express where we used expound in the text. Speaking as a Dharma teacher I am officially and institutionally expounding the Dharma. But since the same character can be used for "expounding" and "expressing," each reader, right now, in the way you are sitting, in the way you are thinking, in your breathing as you read, is expressing your practice-realization. You are always doing

this. It is not that it is automatic, but, still, right now you are expressing your practice-realization. The enlightenment of your practice is being
expressed. This is actually the way it is, the reality of all things.

Dōgen then says, "The practice is the practice of the essence [or enlight-
enment] and expounding; and expounding [or expressing] is to expound the
enlightenment and the practice; and the essence is the enlightenment of
expounding and practice." There is no enlightenment that is not expressed.
This enlightenment that you are expressing, which is the enlightenment
of your practice right now, is not some idea about enlightenment that you
might have. Actually, if you have ideas about enlightenment, you should
realize and practice and express your ideas about enlightenment. But these
ideas are not the enlightenment that you are expressing and practicing. It
is very natural to have these ideas. It is okay to be a human being. Dōgen
is emphasizing that practice-enlightenment is a mode of expression, and
he requires that we express enlightened practice.

Dōgen then goes on:

> If practice is not the practice of expressing and is not the practice
> of enlightenment, how can we say that it is the practice of Bud-
> dha Dharma? If our expression is not the expression of practice
> and is not the expression of enlightenment, it is difficult to call
> it [true] expression of Buddha Dharma. If enlightenment is not
> the enlightenment of practice, and is not the enlightenment of
> expressing, how can we name it the enlightenment of the Bud-
> dha Dharma? Just know that Buddha Dharma is one in the begin-
> ning, middle, and end. It is good in the beginning, middle, and
> end; it is nothing in the beginning, middle, and end; and it is
> empty in the beginning, middle, and end.

Our expression as the expression of our practice-realization is always
occurring, but that does not mean just passive acceptance of whatever is
happening. We actually do have to express it in order to give expression.
This is the practice-realization, and the Buddha, that you are expressing

right now. How you are as you read, how your back is, your posture as you sit; all that is your expression now. We have the responsibility to actually express our practice and our awakening and realization.

Dōgen adds, "This single matter never comes from the forceful activity of people, but from the beginning is the expression and activity of Dharma [or of reality, or truth]." People's postures are always inevitably expressing their current realization. But the effort and enactment of the practice derives from the responsibility to ever more thoroughly enact that expression. "This single matter" refers to a line in the Lotus Sutra, which says that the single matter of buddhas appearing in the world, and we could say the single matter of a buddha's practice and expression appearing in the world, is simply to become aware of and assist suffering beings into their own path toward awakening. This means helping beings into their own path to helping others into their own path to helping others. This is the purpose of buddhas.

This practice-enlightenment-expression begins with our awareness of suffering, awakening to the first Noble Truth. The world is not the way we think it should be or see that it might be. Again and again we have to come back to recognizing the pain of the world and of ourselves and our friends, and listen to it, realize it. This is the starting point of this practice-expression-realization.

When we are aware, then we naturally respond. In Buddhism the name of the bodhisattva of compassion is "the one who hears the sounds and cries of the world." In Buddhism, compassion first of all means just to listen. We hear our own pain, our own weariness, confusion, or frustrations, and then see and hear pain in our friends and families and the people with whom we come in close contact. First, just listen. Then we hear it further in the world around us and open to this truth of the sadness and cruelty of the world. Out of this comes our responsibility. We do not know what to do. We do not know how to fix the world, and maybe that is not even the point. But just from listening we find a sense of this possibility of active compassion.

THE PASSION OF PRACTICE

When you enter a zendo and look at people sitting, you may think they are being very stoic or stern. But actually, to keep doing this practice, period after period, day after day, year after year, is a very passionate practice. It is passionate because it is compassionate. We are willing to be with our own passions and the passions of others, and this being together with the suffering and passion and confusion of others is a definition of compassion. We are willing to be with this suffering, willing to listen to each other, because we know how wonderful it feels to actually be heard ourselves. When we are willing to then also hear others, this is the response of compassion in Buddhism.

This expression is not passive. Presenting this practice-realization-expression is not automatic. We have a responsibility. Dōgen says, "This single matter never comes from the forceful activity of people." Our responsibility is not based on our ideas of how things should be. He says, "From the beginning it is the expression and activity of Dharma," of the teaching of the truth. When we are realizing and practicing and expressing this, we do offer some response, sometimes just being present and listening. With the songs of the birds or the cries of our friends, there is some way to respond.

Dōgen continues, "We already know that there is teaching, practice, and enlightenment within Buddha Dharma. A single moment in a cultivated field always includes many times." Literally Dōgen uses a double negative, saying: A single moment in a cultivated field never does not include every time. Just being present we are meeting all of our own past, and the past of our world and our friends, as well as our future. We are open to the processes of our response and expression and realization, and to our practice of this practice-realization-expression. Our response has an effect in the future, and in the present and the past, even though we do not understand that. But even if you do not understand it, still this is actually our responsibility. The expression is already just this. We are already expressing ourselves and our practice and our realization right now. The practice is also just this, right here. And enlightenment is also thus. This is the way it is. There is no other enlightenment somewhere else, over in India or Japan or Tibet. We are here, just sitting, right now.

THE RANGE OF PRACTICE EXPRESSION, BEYOND CONTROL

Dōgen adds, "As such, we cannot control whether or not we ourselves can control the teaching, the practice, and enlightenment." He does not merely say that we cannot control it, but that we cannot even control whether or not we control it. Maybe there are times when it is almost as if your practice-realization-expression is controlling and taking care of all of the suffering of the world, or at least some piece of the suffering. This might be so, we do not know. This is the range of this practice, the raft we carry as we walk in the mountains.

Dōgen ends by saying, "Wherever they [teaching, practice, and enlightenment] have penetrated, how could there not be Buddha Dharma?" Always there is some expounding, some expression that you are doing in all of your movements. Zen students are passionate about expressing their practice-realization, whether or not they know it. This practice-realization-expression responds to suffering, the pain of the world, but also enjoys the wonders of the world. We do not have to be gloomy and depressed. But if that is where you are, please express that, with realization and practice.

Responding to the sources of suffering in the world is our enlightenment-practice-expression. Through zazen and the bodhisattva precepts, we aim to benefit all beings, prevent harm while supporting life, to be generous, and speak truth. Our practice is to sit upright and study and awaken to our delusions, to be this person right here. When the bell rings, we get up from the cushion and go out and take care of our lives and relate to the people around us. And the bodhisattva precepts are guidelines to how we express our zazen mind, our expression of realization-practice in everyday activity.

PRACTICE-EXPRESSION "RESPONSE ABILITY"

This expression happens in three realms: within, just sitting on our cushion; in our personal relationships, our work life and family life and with friends; and also in relationship to the world around us, to our society. Just as we do not practice for some future enlightenment but as the expression of our enlightenment right now, similarly we do not wait for some future enlightenment to express actively our current practice and enlightenment. We always are responding in some way. We have some responsibility to say something as we meet and listen to the world around us. Our expression of our practice-realization, as Dōgen describes it, and our responding to conditions of suffering, even without knowing all the answers, has something to offer. Responding from this realization and practice is not about opinions. We all have opinions, likely not all the same. But how do we respond to the world around us from whatever we realize in our practice and from whatever we practice as our realization now?

I encourage everyone to develop awareness, to face the sufferings of the world and our society, not to turn away. Sometimes we need to take a break amid all the corruption, cruelty, and recklessness, but inasmuch as you can, work at paying attention to what is happening. In Buddhism we learn that awareness is transformative. How awareness is transformative does not occur based on our expectations or desired outcomes. Express something when you have something to express. Share information with friends; respond as best you can. There are many ways to respond, and no one right way to respond. Just sitting and wishing well to people in various parts of the world might have an effect.

You may read spiritual teachings as a way to escape from fears. But with awareness of fears, we can respond amid them. Whatever fears our society encourages, we can admit and acknowledge our fears. This is expression of our practice-realization. See what is happening, and consider how to share your truth with others. Also listen to others, so as not to get stuck with one particular opinion. There is no one right way to respond. We express our practice-realization however we can, not just for ourselves, but for the world around us.

My faith is that this practice and teaching of the buddhas is actually relevant to our world. This practice-awareness-expression has something to offer. Not needing to feel overwhelmed or despair, our willingness and responsibility to be present in our fear and continue to express practice-realization for the world has great power. We do not know if our awareness will stop new unnecessary wars. But not being afraid is actually more fun. Courage is not about being without any fears but is willingness to stay upright amid our fears, as the persons we are, in a damaged world. This is a wonderful opportunity to express our practice-realization in a way that can make a big difference.

PART 4

Zen Expressions

Rumi's Words of Love

ZEN USE OF IMAGERY

ZEN TEACHING often employs poetry, images, and metaphors as "fingers pointing to the moon," to cite one common Buddhist image. Zen appeals primarily to the imagination and senses, unlike the more philosophical discursive analysis of earlier Indian Mahāyāna teachings such as from Madhyāmika and Nagārjuna, in their own way extremely useful wisdom teaching. Chinese Huayan philosophical teaching, brilliant in its dialectical account of interconnectedness, is also more analytical than Chan or Zen. But Chan teaching absorbed largely from Daoism a poetic style of using evocative nature metaphors as well as colloquial stories. Although his poetry uses very different language than Zen poetry, Jalal ad-Din Rumi, eight hundred years ago in a completely different culture, offers poems that strike many of the same themes, with similar wisdom. Many American Zen teachers appreciate his lively metaphors.

Rumi was a Sufi poet, born seven years after Dōgen in 1207. Many religious geniuses appeared in the thirteenth century, including also Saint Francis and Thomas Aquinas. Rumi was born in what is now Tajikistan and then fled from a Mongol invasion to what is now Turkey. The Sufis are not considered Muslim by many Muslims, but they consider themselves Muslim.

MANIFOLD LOVES

Rumi talks explicitly about love and loving-kindness, and his love imagery already has affected American Zen teaching. Rumi offers to Buddhism helpful new ways of talking about love. In our society this word has so many connotations that we have difficulty understanding it. As Eskimos are said to have fifty words (more or less) for snow, a mature, emotionally sensitive culture would have a great many words for what we designate as love. Western culture does contain, derived from the Greek, a few varied contexts of love: *eros* for romantic and aesthetic love; *philia* for the intimate affection between friends; and *agape* for the creative, redemptive good will to all people (although the Buddhist context for *agape* would include all beings).[116] Rumi's poems encompass all these perspectives on love and offer expressive insights into the heart of love in its varied meanings.

I will discuss a few of my favorite Rumi poems.

Be Melting Snow

Totally conscious, and apropos of nothing, you come to see me.
Is someone here? I ask.
The moon. The full moon is inside your house.

My friends and I go running out into the street.
I'm in here, comes a voice from the house, but we aren't listening.
We're looking up at the sky.
My pet nightingale sobs like a drunk in the garden.
Ringdoves scatter with small cries, *Where, Where.*
It's midnight. The whole neighborhood is up and out in the street
thinking, *The cat-burglar has come back.*
The actual thief is there too, saying out loud,
Yes, the cat-burglar is somewhere in this crowd.
No one pays attention.

Lo, I am with you always, means when you look for God,
God is in the look of your eyes,
in the thought of looking, nearer to you than your self,
or things that have happened to you.
There's no need to go outside.
Be melting snow.
Wash yourself of yourself.

A white flower grows in the quietness.
Let your tongue become that flower.[117]

"Totally conscious, and apropos of nothing, you come to see me." A wonderful phrase! This is our zazen, Zen heart, totally conscious, but not caught on anything. "Is someone here, I ask?" And the next line is in italics like a whisper. *"The moon. The full moon is inside your house."* This is the truth always. This is what we start to see in zazen. In Zen poems, when they mention the moon the poets mean the full round moon. But either way, the moon is inside your house. We go outside looking for it, but the moon is right on your cushion. Rumi says, "My friends and I go running out into the street. *I'm in here*, comes a voice from the house, but we aren't listening." We sit, and often we are not listening to this whisper, this voice that calls us back to something deeper, something beyond the daily chatter. Instead we are looking elsewhere, up into the sky.

"The actual thief is there too, saying out loud, *Yes, the cat burglar is somewhere in this crowd*. No one pays attention." Our job as zazen people is just to pay attention. With all the hubbub happening on our cushions sometimes, our job is just to notice that no one is paying attention and then return to attention. The moon is right here on your cushion.

VALUE IN YEARNING

Then Rumi says, *"Lo, I am with you always*, means when you look for God, God is in the look of your eyes, in the thought of looking, nearer to you than yourself, or things that have happened to you." I could render that as when you look for buddha nature, or when you look for the heart of awakening, it is in the looking. There are many understandings of "God." When you look for the divine it is about the search itself. In Buddhism we talk about *bodhicitta*, the thought of awakening, this looking for something beyond. Even if we are not trying to acquire anything particular from our zazen, still we are all here because of this question. We wish to learn how to express our heart more fully, to find the deeper truth of our lives. There is some looking, some searching, some look in our eyes. Just in the thought of looking it is nearer to you than yourself, Rumi says. And then he says, "There's no need to go outside. Be melting snow. Wash yourself of yourself." Dōgen says, "Drop body and mind," or, "To study the Way is to study the self." Rumi says it, "Wash yourself of yourself." A lot of what we do in this practice is pay attention to ourselves and let go. Can we let go, and then let go of letting go, and keep paying attention?

The last two lines, "A white flower grows in quietness. Let your tongue become that flower," reminds me of a line about zazen, "Sitting quietly, a flower grows in the back." Let your tongue become that flower. How do we learn to express this possibility of the lotus growing out of the mud? How do we express this possibility of actually paying attention, with this desire to express our love of the world, even with its cruelty and difficulties? How can we let our tongue become this flower?

SINGING WITH THE ODD, LOST PEOPLE

Here is another Rumi poem:

The Whole Place Goes Up

Today with Spring here finally we ought to be living
outdoors with our friends.
Let's go to those strangers in the field
and dance around them like bees from flower to flower,

building in the beehive air
our true hexagonal homes.

Someone comes in from outside saying,
Don't play music just for yourselves,
Now we're tearing up the house like a drum,
collapsing walls with our pounding.
We hear a voice from the sky calling the lovers
and the odd, lost people. We scatter lives.
We break what holds us, each one a blacksmith
heating iron and walking to the anvil.
We blow on the inner fire.
With each striking we change.

The whole place goes up, all stability gone in smoke.
Sometimes high, sometimes low, we begin anywhere,
we have no method.
We're the bat swung by powerful arms.
Balls keep rolling from us, thousands of them underfoot.

Now we're still. Silence also is wisdom, a flame
hiding in cotton wool.[118]

I will focus on a few lines. "Someone comes in from outside saying,
Don't play music just for yourselves." When we sit and settle, and sometimes
deeply as in sesshin, still it is important to hear someone coming in from
outside saying, "don't play music just for yourselves." This is the bodhisattva path we follow. We accept that we are connected, that the music of
our sitting, and our heartbeat and breath, is not just for ourselves but also
for all of our friends practicing in other ways. It is also for people we have
not met.

"We hear a voice from the sky calling the lovers and the odd, lost people.
We scatter lives." You may not want to join the odd, lost people. But part

of the practice is admitting that there is a question sitting on your cushion right now, that we are all a little bit lost, a little bit damaged. We can be willing to be sad, willing to feel our anger when that arises. We can be willing to be ourselves. This practice that we do, which I feel Rumi talking about, is not about becoming some special great person but about becoming fully ourselves. Sometimes that is a little strange. Can you be the strange person you are? This is the challenge of our zazen. We must break through that which holds us back from ourselves. Can you be lost amid the thoughts and feelings and winds blowing through you? This practice is a cauldron, a practice in which something happens, and this alchemical process moves us beyond our calculations and discriminating consciousness. It is not that we should not use our intelligence, but that does not get to the heart, really.

Rumi says, "We break what holds us, each one a blacksmith, heating iron and walking to the anvil. We blow on the inner fire. With each striking we change." So there is this inner fire, a hot iron we are forged on. "And the whole place goes up, all stability gone in smoke." This world, this life, this sitting posture is all very fragile. Nothing to hold on to. Rumi says, "We begin anywhere, we have no method." In Sōtō Zen practice we are willing to try on all the methods, but really it is just about being here, being present, facing what comes up. You cannot do it wrong. You cannot succeed either. Just this is it; here we are. We begin anywhere. Whoever you are, today, however you are, in the next inhalation, this is your heart, this is the possibility of love in our life. Now we are still, and Rumi also invokes silence as wisdom, a flame hiding in cotton wool, a strange image. I would imagine that it is very difficult to have a flame in cotton wool. Compared with other substances, cotton wool would not burn very loudly, but silently. The smoke would be like clouds.

THE CURE FOR PAIN

Here is another of Rumi's poems with one line especially that always speaks to me.

There's Nothing Ahead

Lovers think they're looking for each other,
but there's only one search: Wandering
this world is wandering that, both inside one
transparent sky. In here
there is no dogma and no heresy.

The miracle of Jesus is himself, not what he said or did
about the future. Forget the future.
I'd worship someone who could do that!

On the way you may want to look back, or not,
but if you can say *There's nothing ahead,*
there will be nothing there.

Stretch your arms and take hold the cloth of your clothes
with both hands. The cure for pain is in the pain.
Good and bad are mixed. If you don't have both,
you don't belong with us.

When one of us gets lost, is not here, he must be inside us.
There's no place like that anywhere in the world.[119]

Particularly I appreciate "The cure for pain is in the pain." Can we be willing to feel what we feel? Tremendous power actually lies in sometimes being able to sit upright and be with the sadness and frustrations. The cure for pain is in the pain. This includes romantic love, but also the searching that implies the love for all beings and the widest aspect of healing.

Looking for the future, looking for enlightenment somewhere else, we may think that when we get this or have gotten rid of that, then all will be okay. Rumi talks about how it is right here, nothing is ahead. "On the way you may want to look back, or not." He does not say do not look back.

You may or may not, okay, but when you do look back you can say, "*There's nothing ahead, there will be nothing there.*" Here we can sit, and enjoy just paying attention.

He says, "Good and bad are mixed. If you don't have both, you don't belong with us." In some ways Buddhist practice is not about being good. It is not about being bad either, of course. But can we see the good and bad; can we realize all of it arising in us? Can we confess our confusion, greed, and ill-will and also confess our goodness and caring and kindness and our love for the world and ourselves and even particular beings? "Good and bad are mixed. If you don't have both, you don't belong with us. When one of us gets lost, is not here, he must be inside us." Can anyone really be lost? If someone gets lost, where does she go?

It is not that there is no future, but we are not here for that. Or we are here for that just like we are here for everything. Many spiritual practices fall for a trap of wanting to be good; if only I could become a good medi-tator and learn to sit really still. Back in the early days of "macho Zen," people seemed to think that whoever could sit in the hardest position for the longest without moving was the most enlightened. So silly! Our usual worldly way of thinking in our culture, but also with our human conscious-ness, leads us to think, If I do this, I will get that. We try to manipulate things, thinking, If I get a better job, or finish my degree, then everything I want will happen. But actually, can you just be here, enjoying this process, without needing validation from the future? When the future gets here, it will be here too.

The cure for the pain is in the pain. Or as Shitou's Zen poem "Song of the Grass Hut" concludes, "Do not separate from this skin bag here and now." Enjoy your misery, your confusion and frustration, your sadness, or your heartache. Can you just be here and be who you are? This is not easy. And yet I think Rumi, like Dōgen, is pointing to some deep satisfaction, even right in the pain, when we can "Wash yourself of yourself."

WORDS BLOWN INTO EMPTINESS

Here is one last poem, called "This World Which Is Made of Our Love for Emptiness." He does not describe emptiness in the way that Buddhism uses that term. But this love for emptiness encompasses the ultimate bodhisattva love for all beings and for the suchness of reality itself.

This World Which Is Made of Our Love for Emptiness

Praise to the emptiness that blanks out existence. Existence:
This place made from our love for that emptiness!
Yet somehow comes emptiness,
this existence goes.
Praise to that happening, over and over!

For years I pulled my own existence out of emptiness.
Then one swoop, one swing of the arm,
that work is over.
Free of who I was, free of presence, free of
dangerous fear, hope,
free of mountainous wanting.
The here-and-now mountain is a tiny piece of a piece
    of straw
blown off into emptiness.

These words I'm saying so much begin to lose meaning:
Existence, emptiness, mountain, straw:
Words and what they try to say swept
out the window, down the slant of the roof.[120]

That is a really Zen poem. This is the boredom of Zen, happening over and over and over again. All of existence arises out of emptiness; all of emptiness overcomes existence. Inhale and exhale. Ahh! It is wonderful, but in another mood it can be boring. Here is a poet who is willing to see how words lose meaning. And all of the words of the Buddha were just commentaries on silence. The point is, how can we be present and meet ourselves, be willing to be ourselves and share loving-kindness, and just sing to each other?

Bob Dylan's Visions of Zen Mind

S OMETIMES IN ZEN we sit for a day, or three, five, or seven days, in
what is called *sesshin*. *Sesshin* means to "gather or meet the mind," or
"to settle into Zen mind." During sesshin we may experience and become
intimate with a deeper awareness, going beyond our discriminations or
calculations and deliberations, though maybe it includes those. But such
settling reveals a wider panoramic awareness that is transformative. It can
change how we see our deep connection to the world.

In March 2007, I attended a symposium at the University of Minnesota
about Bob Dylan, my favorite American Dharma bard, whom I quote frequently. This was one of the more interesting academic conferences I have
attended, although it was not strictly academic. Spider John Koerner and
Tony Glover, distinctive blues singers who used to play with Dylan when he
lived in Minneapolis, performed. Anne Waldman, one of the Beat poets and
cofounder of the Jack Kerouac School of Disembodied Poetics at Naropa
University in Boulder, and who accompanied Dylan's Rolling Thunder tour,
offered a wonderful shamanic talk about Dylan as a shaman. A range of
stimulating presentations and discussions about Dylan were given. In such
an eclectic spirit I will consider a Bob Dylan song that I hear as being about
sesshin. When I say this is a song about sesshin, of course it also involves
many other things. The song is called "Visions of Johanna."[121]

Among other things, "Visions of Johanna" is about the feminine, or the narrator's relationship to women. The song also includes drug references. Some commentators claim it is about hell. This song is often considered gloomy and pessimistic by critics, but I do not feel that way about it at all.[122] "Visions of Johanna" reveals much about the experience of sesshin. This is not at all to claim that Bob Dylan's intention in writing this song was to speak about sesshin, or Zen, or that he even had Zen in mind while creating it. I am discussing what I hear in the text of the song about the work itself. As the Japanese philosopher and celebrator of folk art Yanagi Sōetsu (1889–1961) said, "The thing shines, not the maker."[123] Yanagi spoke of the aesthetics of folk art where the beauty of a piece of pottery, for example, was a function of the mutual influence of other, often unknown potters. In this sense Bob Dylan has been the consummate true folk singer throughout his career, including his work described as belonging to blues, rock, and gospel genres. Dylan has emphasized his songs themselves over speculations about his own life, for which he has tried to maintain privacy. Ample sanction allows presentation of a Zen view of "Visions of Johanna."

We do know that Bob Dylan has been greatly influenced by Judeo-Christian spiritual teachings, but he has obviously had some connection with Buddhism as well. He sang about Rubin Hurricane Carter, the falsely accused boxer, who "sits like Buddha in a ten-foot cell." The image of the ten-foot cell goes back to the size of the room of the legendary enlightened layman Vimalakīrti, in the sutra named after him.[124] The traditional size of the abbot's quarters in Zen monasteries is based on this, and "ten-foot" (Jpn.: Hōjō) is the honorary name given Zen abbots in China and Japan. Dylan had a close association with Allen Ginsberg and many other practicing Buddhists.[125]

NOTHING TO TURN OFF

I hear a turning line, sometimes two, in each verse, and then one turning line for the whole song. I will present each verse and then comment.

Ain't it just like the night to play tricks when you're tryin' to be so
   quiet?
We sit here stranded, though we're all doin' our best to deny it
And Louise holds a handful of rain, temptin' you to defy it
Lights flicker from the opposite loft
In this room the heat pipes just cough
The country music station plays soft
But there's nothing, really nothing to turn off
Just Louise and her lover so entwined
And these visions of Johanna that conquer my mind

"Ain't it just like the night to play tricks when you're trying to be so
quiet?" As we sit in sesshin, or even in one period of zazen, ain't it just like
your mind to play tricks when you're trying to be so quiet? Even in settled
sitting, unexpected thoughts may continue to arise. As for "night," in Zen
imagery, going back to Shitou's "Harmony of Difference and Sameness"
that is often chanted, light is an image for how we see with the lights on
all the different particular people.[126] The dark or night, when all light is
extinguished, is an image for oneness beyond any visible distinctions and
for the possibility of deep communion with wholeness and the fundamental mind.

Sometimes in sesshin we may feel that "We sit here stranded, though
we're all doin' our best to deny it." You may feel this in one period of
zazen, but particularly sitting period after period we realize that we are
stranded on our cushion. You may be doing your best to deny it, but you
are radically alone in zazen. This provides an opportunity to be radically
present with this body and mind, in a way that we do not have a chance
to experience in our ordinary everyday activities. Of course, that is not the
whole story. We are also doing it together and supporting each other in
community, but initially at least it may feel like we sit here stranded. And
yes, we all have various patterns of resistance and ways in which we are
tempted to deny it.

Key lines in this stanza are, "In this room the heat pipes just cough"—during the relative quiet of sesshin we hear the sounds of the building—and "The country music station plays soft." Country songs could be an apt metaphor for all the melodramas possibly going through our thought streams during zazen. Then Dylan, or the singer of the song, says this amazing thing: "There's nothing, really nothing to turn off." This is a basic fundamental statement of Zen truth, core to the Platform Sutra, for example. There is nothing to turn off, really. We see all the forms of the world, yet in our sitting we may realize that they are all constructions or fabrications. Our mind, even as we do our best to deny this reality, is busy creating all the melodramas they sigh about on the country music stations; but there's nothing, really nothing to turn off. Actually, for each situation, each problem in our life, each itch, each pain in our knees, ache in our shoulders, there is nothing, really nothing to turn off or evade. What you learn in sitting, eventually, is that it is okay to be the person sitting on your cushion right now, with the problems that you have. Then the buddha work is about how we meet our situation. We do not need to turn it off, to destroy our thoughts, or to crush or deny our humanity. There's nothing, really nothing to turn off.

I will not attempt to say who Johanna is or was or what she represents. Johanna could represent many things. One pessimistic suggestion from commentators is that "Johanna" is Hebrew for Armageddon, or that "Gehenna" is Greek and Latin for hell or future torture.[127] We all have negative, fearful visions or positive ones, including visions of awakening, or of the perfect being we could be, or could be relating with.

ELECTRIC GHOSTS HOWL

The next verse goes:

> In the empty lot where the ladies play blindman's bluff with
>   the key chain
> And the all-night girls they whisper of escapades out on the
>   "D" train

We can hear the night watchman click his flashlight
Ask himself if it's him or them that's really insane
Louise, she's all right, she's just near
She's delicate and seems like the mirror
But she just makes it all too concise and too clear
That Johanna's not here
The ghost of 'lectricity howls in the bones of her face
Where these visions of Johanna have now taken my place

In the beginning of this verse Dylan mentions the "empty lot." This may refer to the previous verse where there is "nothing, really nothing to turn off." Our whole world and all its stuff may be an empty lot, the myriad forms of emptiness. Notice the night watchman who clicks his flashlight so the light comes on and off. We see the particulars of our situation, and then we have glimpses of something deeper, of some communion with wholeness. As he clicks his flashlight he asks himself if it is him or them who's really insane. This is part of sesshin. Is it me or are these visions insane? What is really going on here? Part of opening the mind of sesshin and really meeting the wholeness of mind is being willing to expand our capacities and our sense of reality. This conjures up the fourth of the classic five fears of Buddhism: fear of death, fear of loss of reputation, fear of loss of livelihood, and then this fear of weird mental states. What is sanity? It might be good to ask whether it is me or these visions who is really insane. By the way, the fifth fear is of public speaking, seemingly trivial compared to the others. Yet we all may have some of that, and perhaps the night watchman is afraid to speak out, or even Johanna.

This verse includes one of Dylan's greatest lines, "The ghost of 'lectricity howls in the bones of her face." When we sit facing the wall, the wall seems like a mirror. Indeed this is delicate. Whatever we are is projected on that wall. The wall is ourselves, and the wall of the world is what we meet. And we also meet face to face between teacher and student. I do not think it only Johanna for whom the ghost of electricity howls in the bones of her face. For all of us, especially in sesshin, this shadow ghost of vitality, of electricity, of energy howls in the bones of our face. Dōgen talked about face-to-face practice. Usually we recognize people by their faces rather than other body parts. And always, if you look in a mirror, the ghost of electricity may be howling there.

MUTTERING AT THE WALL

> Now, little boy lost, he takes himself so seriously
> He brags of his misery, he likes to live dangerously
> And when bringing her name up
> He speaks of a farewell kiss to me
> He's sure got a lotta gall to be so useless and all
> Muttering small talk at the wall while I'm in the hall
> How can I explain?
> Oh, it's so hard to get on
> And these visions of Johanna, they kept me up past the dawn

"Little boy lost" is a reference to William Blake's "Songs of Innocence and Experience," where there is a little boy lost and a little girl lost.[128] For most Zen practitioners, when you first attend sesshin and sit facing the wall all day, somehow this little boy lost or little girl lost appears. In this practice we must engage our little boy or little girl, and we often get lost in them. Sometimes students come with these very serious questions and take themselves so seriously and brag of their misery. This happens, and I remember that I sometimes did that, too. Buddhist practice involves letting go of the self. But we do that by studying the self. How do we take care of this part of us that feels lost, that takes very seriously all of the stories of our personal history, the constructed self that we grasp so tightly, and even after we let go, it persists so subtly. Dylan sings, "He's sure got a lotta gall to be so useless and all." All this self-concern arises amid the pain and sadness of the rest of the world and does nothing to abet the suffering.

The next line is how I first came to see this song as about sesshin, "Muttering small talk at the wall while I'm in the hall." I have long witnessed this in the halls of meditation. Perhaps we have all at times muttered small talk at the wall in the hall. Dylan here does not offer any assistance. You might even see this line as somewhat cruel, a kind of put down, but we must face this little boy lost or little girl lost, holding on tight to our constructed self so seriously, bragging of our misery. The first Noble Truth of suffering brings us into this practice of sitting and facing ourselves, and sometimes it feels so overwhelming that all we can do is just brag of our misery.

The key line in this verse is "How can I explain?" It is difficult to say anything to the one who brags of their misery. How can one explain the whole world that goes beyond this little boy or girl lost? We must each of us and together be kind when we see this little boy or little girl lost, in ourselves or in another. Practice involves not just seeing through, and Dylan is a great example of penetrating wisdom, but there is also the question of how we take care. There is no way to explain, but can you befriend and be kind with this little lost child? Sometimes such kindness might take the form of a put-down, or a sharp "Wake Up." Beyond any particular situation of misery, "How can I explain?" is an incisive utterance of the ultimate. Explanations tend toward sterile shutting down of discussion and inquiry. Explanations can become slogans or dogmas to inflict on others or to fight wars for. More vital and inspiring than explanations are the visions that sometimes keep us up past the dawn.

VERDICTS OF INFINITY

Here comes what I hear as the pivotal line in the whole song:

> Inside the museums, Infinity goes up on trial
> Voices echo this is what salvation must be like after a while
> But Mona Lisa musta had the highway blues
> You can tell by the way she smiles
> See the primitive wallflower freeze
> When the jelly-faced women all sneeze

Hear the one with the mustache say, "Jeeze
I can't find my knees"
Oh, jewels and binoculars hang from the head of the mule
But these visions of Johanna, they make it all seem so cruel

I feel the crux of the whole song with "Inside the museums, Infinity goes up on trial." Then follows, "Voices echo this is what salvation must be like after a while." Several members of my sangha work in museums, and I enjoy regularly visiting museums. I think of this line more for art museums, but it is also true of natural history museums and science museums. The Dylan conference I mentioned at the University of Minnesota had in conjunction an exhibit on Dylan at the Weisman Museum, part of the University. And this song was one of those you could hear at the museum. So "inside the museums, infinity goes up on trial," as did the very notion of infinity on trial at that museum.

A while ago there was an exhibit at the Chicago Art Institute called "From Cézanne to Picasso," which I liked quite a bit. This exhibit not only had paintings by Cézanne and Picasso, but many other great works of art collected by a dealer who befriended many artists. Included were works by Gauguin, Monet, and Renoir, and two rooms of paintings by Vincent Van Gogh. Inside a great museum, if we look patiently, "after a while" we can see infinity go on trial, as the ultimate worth of all humanity, perhaps at its best, is subjected to the visitors' verdicts. Amid great beauty or visual insight we might feel, "this is what salvation must be like." We see exquisite beauty, and can feel the value of all human endeavor, or perhaps put it on trial with our evaluations.

VAN GOGH AND SLAVERY ON TRIAL

I am particularly fond of Vincent Van Gogh's paintings—each one of them is a kind of a miracle, his landscapes are so vibrantly alive, as are even his brushstrokes. People commonly think of Van Gogh as a tortured artist, and we know he expressed deep loneliness in his letters to his brother Theo, his best friend and patron, and that Vincent finally committed suicide. But when I look at his paintings I do not see torture but astonishing vitality and a sense of wonder illuminating and enlivening the earth itself. Recent interpretations or historical suggestions claim that he had some chemical imbalance that gave him terrible headaches and drove him to suicide. Other recent speculation, based on Vincent's letters, concern Theo's family. Theo and his wife were about to have a baby, and shortly before his death Vincent felt that he was a financial burden to them.[129] Theo's wife, whose name happened to be Johanna, is the one who later protected Vincent's paintings and dedicated herself to getting them exhibited, so that eventually the world could appreciate them. But I do not know if Dylan might have been thinking of Theo's Johanna.

The American Zen teacher Bernie Glassman from the Maezumi Roshi lineage has led sesshins at Auschwitz with Jewish and German participants, including descendants of holocaust survivors and descendants of camp guards. I have never attended one of them, but I have heard from people who have done so that they are extremely powerful. They sit for seven days with the ghosts of a different kind of electricity—present with mind open in a place where such a horror has occurred. For a number of years I annually visited a Zen group in Richmond, Virginia, leading sittings there. Sangha members took me to visit local historic sites, such as where Patrick Henry said, "Give me liberty or give me death," or where Edgar Allan Poe gave his last reading of "The Raven." Richmond also contains the site of slave auction houses used from before the eighteenth century. This place was the center of all American slavery for over a fifty-year period in the first half of the nineteenth century, when hundreds of thousands of Virginian home-grown African-American slaves were literally sold down the river, shipped to cotton plantations in the deep South. In 2007 the state of Virginia formally expressed its regret about this history. Inspired by Glassman's sittings at Auschwitz, in April 2008 I led a sitting at the Richmond slave auction house site. We started by walking the trail from the dock where the slaves were deposited along the riverbank, and then across the bridge to the auction site where we did zazen, the site now below a large freeway. It was indeed an intense experience for all, and this place remains a power spot critical to all our ongoing American history and karma.

But at the Chicago Art Institute exhibit, inside the two rooms with beautiful Van Gogh paintings, I had a vision of a different kind of impactful sitting, to do a sesshin for a day, or five or seven, performing zazen in one of those rooms with this sacred art. Just sitting amid Van Gogh's luminous brushstrokes, then we would stand up and do walking meditation seeing these miraculous visions from Vincent on the walls. I would gladly have them "conquer my mind."

In such a setting, as well as at Auschwitz or the auction houses at Richmond, infinity does go up on trial. Each of us and our karmic lives on this planet go up on trial. And that is what sesshin is like also. Inside the meditation hall infinity goes up on trial. Instead of paintings on the wall there are people sitting facing the wall. Each one is a miracle. Can we sit long enough to put infinity up on trial, to feel our connection with wholeness and all time?

The verdict is still out on humanity. Do the creative spirits and works of Van Gogh, Johann Sebastian Bach, Gandhi, Shakespeare, Coltrane, Laozi, Homer, and, yes, Dōgen and Dylan himself somehow outweigh the Nazis, the long histories of slavery, our current systematic torture of innocents, and massive environmental devastation for personal profit? As to infinity itself, from whence could there ever come judge and jury to adjudicate that ruling?

Dylan sings, "Voices echo this is what salvation must be like after a while. But Mona Lisa musta had the highway blues, you can tell by the way she smiles." Actually we cannot "explain" that smile, or the highway blues. Perhaps even Vincent Van Gogh in one of his amazing paintings of wheat fields or cypress trees could not totally capture the full reality or the life and the vitality of the ghost of electricity howling through those scenes.

Sometimes Zen students try to figure it all out. Or they have some experience of wholeness and believe they can put a frame around it and put it up on the wall so they can bow down to that, or sell museum tickets to see it. That certainly is not the point either. Dylan sings, "See the primitive wallflower freeze." There are various ways to interpret this line. But as a frieze of figures face the wall, a flower blossoms in the back of each, as we sit, quietly. Then of course we also hear many exclamations, "Jeeze I can't find my knees!" This is a common utterance during sesshin.

EVERYTHING RETURNED

Finishing with the final verse:

> The peddler now speaks to the countess who's pretending to
>   care for him
> Sayin', "Name me someone that's not a parasite and I'll go out
>   and say a prayer for him"
> But like Louise always says,
> "Ya can't look at much, can ya man?"
> As she, herself, prepares for him
> And Madonna, she still has not showed
> We see this empty cage now corrode
> Where her cape of the stage once had flowed
> The fiddler, he now steps to the road
> He writes ev'rything's been returned which was owed
> On the back of the fish truck that loads
> While my conscience explodes
> The harmonicas play the skeleton keys and the rain
> And these visions of Johanna are now all that remain

A lot is happening in this last verse, and as I said at the outset, this song is about much more than sesshin. I will discuss a few lines in this verse. The second lines goes, "Name me someone that's not a parasite and I'll go out and say a prayer for him." This is one aspect of our interconnectedness and a part of what needs accepting. We are all part of the food chain. We cannot claim any perfect image, of Johanna or of whomever we have a vision. Is there anyone who is not a parasite, not dependent on others? We can see this as parasitical or turn it over and see how we might become symbiotic. How do we cooperate together, but also how do we realize that we all are already totally interconnected? The Madonna, an image of perfect woman, still has not showed, and "We see this empty cage now corrode." The self we construct is a kind of empty cage. As we take up this practice our conditioned habits start to corrode.

The key line in this verse seems to me, "The fiddler, he now steps to the road. He writes everything's been returned which was owed." I recall one *shuso* ceremony at Tassajara monastery. The shuso is the head monk for a monastic practice period, and at this ceremony near the end of the three months all of the students and many former head monks who visit for the day in turn ask the head monk questions about practice and the teaching, a sort of rapid-fire Dharma combat. This is the first time a monk is publicly questioned like that, a potentially frightening but also exhilarating experience. At the end after all the questions and the head monk's responses, the former head monks each make congratulatory statements. On this occasion Rev. Lou Hartman, a longtime monk at Zen Center and close friend whom I highly esteemed, just said to the shuso, "Everything's been returned that was owed."[130]

All infinity is on trial, and yet we each owe something. We have some responsibility; we have Buddha's work to perform. And yet it is possible for everything to be returned that was owed. It is possible to give ourselves fully to being ourselves, not merely to becoming or clutching on to some magical Johanna, however we see her.

STRENGTHEN WHAT REMAINS

Dylan adds, "On the back of the fish truck that loads while my conscience explodes." Many commentaries have seen this line as very negative, as the death of conscience. But I hear it otherwise as somehow exploding the whole world into conscientiously taking care of all beings, a very positive image. Either way, "The harmonicas play the skeleton keys and the rain, and these visions of Johanna are now all that remain." We might feel the singer sadly missing Johanna, some lost or regretted love, and it is "all too concise and too clear that Johanna's not here." But something about those visions of Johanna still remain. In another song Dylan sings, "Strengthen the things that remain,"[131] and in many ways I feel that as our practice. Taking care of whatever remains that may help all beings is Buddha's work. Dōgen says to express the dream within the dream. Perhaps these visions of Johanna are more important than Johanna herself, if there even is a Johanna

At the end of one of his more recent songs Dylan sings, "My heart's in the Highlands" and "there's a way to get there and I'll figure it out somehow. But I'm already there in my mind. And that's good enough for now."[132] How can we open our minds, for now, to seeing infinity up on trial, to envisioning and connecting with the wholeness of the highlands?

Making Yourself into a Light

FLYING HOME

ONE OF MY FAVORITE contemporary American poets is Mary Oliver. I will discuss briefly a few of her poems. First is "Wild Geese," a poem that a number of American Zen teachers have commented on.

Wild Geese

You do not have to be good.
You do not have to walk on your knees
for a hundred miles through the desert, repenting.
You only have to let the soft animal of your body
    love what it loves.
Tell me about despair, yours, and I will tell you mine.
Meanwhile the world goes on.
Meanwhile the sun and the clear pebbles of the rain
are moving across the landscapes,
over the prairies and the deep trees,
the mountains and the rivers.
Meanwhile the wild geese, high in the clean blue air,
are heading home again.
Whoever you are, no matter how lonely,
the world offers itself to your imagination,
calls to you like the wild geese, harsh and exciting—

over and over announcing your place
in the family of things.[133]

The poet starts by saying you do not have to be good. A kind of trap
or problem that any spiritual practitioner can fall for is feeling they have
to be good, be perfect, or match some ideal. Mary Oliver says, "You do
not have to walk on your knees for a hundred miles through the desert,
repenting." Some people feel that to be spiritually worthy they must go to
such extremes. Sometimes people do go walk in the desert, maybe just for
fun, but you do not need to walk on your knees repenting. The Buddha
proclaimed the Middle Way, not to be indulgent, but also one need not
perform austerities to prove oneself.

Mary Oliver says, "You only have to let the soft animal of your body love
what it loves." This wonderful line relates to trusting buddha nature, trusting something deeper than our usual perspectives and conceptualizations
about what is spiritual practice, what is good, what it means to be enlightened, all these ideas people have. When we settle, when we are willing to
sit and face the wall and ourselves and breathe, this is what faith is about in
Buddhism, learning to trust the process of being ourselves. Be the animal
creatures we are. We can actually study what it is we love, what goes deeper
than our ideas of who we think we are or should be. Just "let the soft animal of your body love what it loves." This is reminiscent of Suzuki Roshi
encouraging students to find what is the most important thing. Whatever
nourishes you, whatever you can give yourself to, trust that.

At the end of the poem, she says:

the world offers itself to your imagination,
calls to you like the wild geese, harsh and exciting—
over and over announcing your place
in the family of things.

Mary Oliver is a nature poet. In many ways she is similar to Daoists.
When we stop and see the world of nature within us as well as without us,

it calls to us. This call to our imagination is important, allowing us to let go of ideals of perfection.

FINDING THE BIRD'S PATH

Geese and other birds have flight patterns as soon as they are born. Going home is in them from the beginning, and they do not have a problem knowing where they belong. We have to trust the soft animal body, but here is the fire also. We have to make peace with what comes from our greed, hate, and delusion. Such homecoming underlies Mary Oliver's poems. The wild geese returning home is like our taking refuge in Buddha. Whether we do that in a formal ceremony or just come and sit upright, we turn toward something deeper. It is not our ideas of what home is, or what we should do, or our desires or impulses, but more profound. It is as deep as the birds, over many centuries, keeping the same migratory patterns as if they see road signs in the sky. In the vital process of practice we sit with similarly deep patterns, including the fundamental ignorance that allows us to objectify things out there for us to grab or to destroy. The Chinese Caodong/Sōtō founder Dongshan Liangjie (807–869; Jpn.: Tōzan Ryōkai) talks about the bird's path in the sky as a metaphor for our practice. Mary Oliver's poems offer guidance for the bird's path.

In a later poem, "Snow Geese," Mary Oliver describes hearing the startling sound of snow geese "winging it faster than the ones we usually see." They passed quickly, and she never saw them again. But she declares:

> It doesn't matter.
> What matters
> is that, when I saw them,
> I saw them
> as through the veil, secretly, joyfully, clearly.[134]

Each of us has our place in the family of things and in the phenomenal world. Dōgen describes this as taking our Dharma position, being willing to be in the situation of this mind, this body, this life. How do we take responsibility for our place in the family of things? "Wild Geese" speaks to settling into something that is wild, unexpected, calling us. Over and over, the world announces your place in the family of things. Each of us in some way expresses all of it. Dōgen's recommendation to abide in one's Dharma position is about trusting karma. In the monastic context abiding in one's Dharma position involves your position in the sangha. But each of us also has our place in the sangha of the world and in our efforts to express something in the world. Each of us has our own unique vantage point. Can we enjoy seeing from there, "as through the veil, secretly, joyfully, clearly"?

THE BUDDHA'S BEQUEST

I do not know if Mary Oliver considers herself a Buddhist, but she has a powerful poem called "The Buddha's Last Instruction."

The Buddha's Last Instruction

"Make of yourself a light,"
said the Buddha,
before he died.
I think of this every morning
as the east begins
to tear off its many clouds
of darkness, to send up the first
signal—a white fan
streaked with pink and violet,
even green.
An old man, he lay down
between two sala trees,
and he might have said anything,
knowing it was his final hour.

The light burns upward,
it thickens and settles over the fields.
Around him, the villagers gathered
and stretched forward to listen.
Even before the sun itself
hangs, disattached, in the blue air,
I am touched everywhere
by its ocean of yellow waves.
No doubt he thought of everything
that had happened in his difficult life.
And then I feel the sun itself
as it blazes over the hills,
like a million flowers on fire—
clearly I'm not needed,
yet I feel myself turning
into something of inexplicable value.
Slowly, beneath the branches,
he raised his head.
He looked into the faces of that frightened crowd.[135]

There are numbers of interesting aspects to this poem. Often the last instruction of the Buddha is translated as, "Be a light unto yourself," which has a little different meaning, something like, "Trust yourself. Find your own way to clarify your practice, now that the Buddha is gone." But this reading by Mary Oliver is more stimulating, "Make of yourself a light." How does each of us, in our own way, make ourselves into a light? How do we find our way to be a beacon to help others to enter into the path to then find their own way to make themselves into a light? Reading it as "Make of yourself a light" has a different feeling from "Be a light unto yourself," maybe with more Mahāyāna spirit.

Mary Oliver interestingly takes this last instruction and mixes in a scene of Buddha going to this place, laying down, and people gathering. Then she herself sees this scene around the Buddha. "Even before the sun itself hangs, disattached, in the blue air, I am touched everywhere by its ocean of yellow waves.... And then I feel the sun itself as it blazes over the hills, like a million flowers on fire." This image of the sun and the flowers on fire is very striking. Mary Oliver seems to be not only calling on the historical Buddha, who passed away sometime in the fifth century B.C.E., but on the roaring of the Dharmakāya Buddha, the ultimate body of Buddha, that is the whole phenomenal world. The different bodies of Buddha promote the primary question, What is Buddha? Along with the historical Buddha, the Mahāyāna includes a great panoply of buddha figures, such as Amida Buddha, who is venerated in Japanese Pure Land Buddhism, a kind of meditation body buddha. Then there is Buddha, the Awakened One, as the nature of all things, or all phenomena seen in this awakened way. This is called the Dharmakāya in Sanskrit, the reality body of Buddha. In Japanese this Buddha is called Dainichi Nyōrai, the great sun Buddha. The sun is the great source of light and energy for us, and Mary Oliver talks about the sun in this poetic way.

SITTING AMID FIRE

The Buddha spoke of the world of samsāra and all the senses being on fire, the fire of our greed, passions, hatred, and our confusion.[136] In early Buddhism the idea of nirvāna was to cool and let go of all the passions, and to be free of the fires of this world. An old Zen saying goes, "Practice like your hair is on fire," with such intensity. But here Mary Oliver talks about a million flowers on fire, and it turns the image in some ways, showing our place in the family of things. She says, "Clearly I'm not needed, yet I feel myself turning into something of inexplicable value." We all have our place in the family of things. We each may evoke the soft animal body of ourselves. Oliver sees the million flowers on fire, the world as illuminated, "yet I feel myself turning into something inexplicable," what Buddhism often calls the "inconceivable." And she ends her poem, "He looked into the faces of that frightened crowd." This precedes the Buddha's utterance from the poem's outset, "Make of yourself a light."

This is a beautiful turning of this image of the fire of saṃsāra. In Zen there are various sayings about how all buddhas must sit in the middle of fire. Xuefeng Yicun (822–908; Jpn.: Seppō Gison) said, "Buddhas in the past, present, and future abide in flames and turn the great Dharma wheel."[137] Buddhas and bodhisattvas are willing to enter into the fires of suffering of the world again and again. This invokes the alchemical line from "Wild Geese," "You only have to let the soft animal of your body love what it loves." Sitting in the middle of fire is part of that process. Mary Oliver presents the soft, gentle side but also the intense call to Buddha's successors to make yourself into a light. Practice calls for this, both in zazen and the practice after arising, turning yourself into a light for the world. For each of us, when we are willing to sit through the fire of being ourselves, when we are willing actually to do this noble practice of sitting down and being ourselves amid all of our confusion, habits, grasping, and aversion, all the varied parts of being this soft animal body, something can happen. She describes what happens as making yourself a light. Maybe all of the precepts are just about how we may become a light. How do we bring forth Buddha's light in the world today, in this time, in twenty-first-century America?

A DEATH AND LIFE OF AMAZEMENT

I feel something very positive, encouraging, and challenging in this poem about the Buddha's last moments, and in the next one maybe even more so. This one is called, "When Death Comes." We had two members of our small sangha pass away in the year I talked about Mary Oliver. The odds are exceedingly high that each of you reading this, as well, will someday face this death. Mary Oliver turns our understanding of it.

When Death Comes

When death comes
like the hungry bear in autumn;

when death comes and takes all the bright coins from
   his purse

to buy me, and snaps the purse shut;
when death comes
like the measles-pox;

when death comes
like an iceberg between the shoulder blades,

I want to step through the door full of curiosity, wondering:
what is it going to be like, that cottage of darkness?

And therefore I look upon everything
as a brotherhood and a sisterhood,
and I look upon time as no more than an idea,
and I consider eternity as another possibility,

and I think of each life as a flower, as common
as a field daisy, and as singular,

and each name a comfortable music in the mouth,
tending, as all music does, toward silence,

and each body a lion of courage, and something
precious to the earth.

When it's over, I want to say: all my life
I was a bride married to amazement.
I was the bridegroom, taking the world into my arms.
When it's over, I don't want to wonder
if I have made of my life something particular, and real.

I don't want to find myself sighing and frightened,
or full of argument.

I don't want to end up simply having visited this world.[138]

This poem is powerful. It feels like the other side of "you don't have to walk on your knees, repenting." Something positive and beautiful is found in death. "I want to step through the door full of curiosity, wondering: what is it going to be like, that cottage of darkness?" The British poet William Blake spoke about death as like a door through which one walks from one room to another. This was how he envisioned it, and he died singing.[139] In some ways our meditation is like a doorway. Suzuki Roshi talked about the swinging door of inhalation and exhalation.[140] Walking through the door even into a small room and sitting down, perhaps we may enter a cottage of darkness. In each period of zazen there is some possibility, some doorway. Then Mary Oliver says:

And therefore I look upon everything
as a brotherhood and a sisterhood,

Here again is the idea of the whole world as Buddha's body, as a flower of fire.

and I look upon time as no more than an idea,
and I consider eternity as another possibility,

and I think of each life as a flower, as common
as a field daisy, and as singular.

Something about those last two lines, each life both as common and also as singular, extraordinary, magnificent, speaks to the way in which we may sense something deeper, some possibility of wholeness that we glimpse when we engage this practice. Each event, and each one of us

in the wholeness of sangha, each one of us as an expression of buddha
nature, is singular, particular.

> When it's over, I want to say: all my life
> I was a bride married to amazement.

That line calls to the crucial sense of wonder of our life and how we
might appreciate all the challenges of our life. Considering death allows
us to wonder at the awesome glory of life.

Gary Snyder and Wild Practice

PRACTICE IN HARMONY WITH NATURE

THE AMERICAN ZEN PIONEER Gary Snyder provided my introduction to Zen Buddhism in the mid-60s through his starring role in Jack Kerouac's *Dharma Bums*.[141] In his own inspiring books of poetry and prose since then, Snyder has remained a monumental figure in American Zen and one of my esteemed influences.[142] In this essay I will comment on just a few elements of the deeply stimulating material in Snyder's *The Practice of the Wild*, a most valuable Dharma text. This brilliant book presents a rich context for the organic process of Zen questioning and practice through appreciating the wildness of nature, of language, and of the path of practice itself.

Snyder clarifies that spiritual training or cultivation is not a matter of fighting or overcoming nature and the wild. Often Western spiritual discipline is viewed as conflicting with our innate human "natures," seen as malevolent. However, he goes on to say, "There is learning and training that goes *with* the grain of things as well as against it. In early Chinese Daoism, 'training' did not mean to cultivate the wildness out of oneself, but to do away with arbitrary and delusive thinking." Snyder paints the wild more sympathetically as part of an organized pattern, "Nature is orderly. That which appears to be chaotic in nature is only a more complex kind of order."[143]

WILD LANGUAGE

The wilderness of nature is not separate from our own human biology and culture. We are creatures of nature and the wilderness. An accomplished poet, Snyder reveals how language itself is a wilderness system. Our language and its channeling of our thought process and cultural forms is not some simulated, artificial product. Snyder says:

> It would be a mistake to think that human beings got "smarter" at some point and invented first language and then society. Language and culture emerge from our biological-social natural existence, animals that we were/are. Language is a mind-body system that coevolved with our nerves and needs.

Humans did not create our own language or its grammar as a rational, discursive mechanism. Language is an organic, "wild" expression.

> Like imagination and the body, language rises unbidden.... All attempts at scientific description of natural languages have fallen short of completeness,... yet the child learns the mother tongue early and has virtually mastered it by six.... Without having ever been taught formal grammar we utter syntactically correct sentences, one after another.[144]

Perhaps the evocative poetry and images of Zen discourse point back to the natural quality of language and mind itself. Snyder wonders if society "might stay on better terms with nature," and he cites Thoreau discussing "tawny grammar," from a Spanish phrase that invokes the wildness of the leopard. We are embedded with the markings of wild predators, but also, "the grammar not only of language, but of culture and civilization itself, is of the same order as this mossy little forest creek, this desert cobble."

DWELLING IN BEGINNINGLESS LANDSCAPES

How do we reclaim the fresh, raw quality of our own wild awareness? Snyder suggests exploration and recovery of this undomesticated natural order, referred to in East Asia and Zen as "landscape" or in Japanese *sansui* (literally "mountains and water"), the context for fine East Asian painting, poetry, and garden art. In the chapter "Blue Mountains Constantly Walking," Snyder points out, "One does not need to be a specialist to observe that landforms are a play of stream-cutting and ridge-resistance and that waters and hills interpenetrate in endlessly branching rhythms."[145] These branching rhythms provide the natural topography, mysteriously echoing our internal topographies. Snyder starts this chapter with a translation from "The Mountains and Water Sutra," an essay from Dōgen's *Shōbōgenzō*, which begins:

> The mountains and rivers of this moment are the actualization of the way of the ancient buddhas. Each, abiding in its own phenomenal expression, realizes completeness. Because mountains and waters have been active since before the eon of emptiness, they are alive at this moment. Because they have been the self since before form arose, they are liberated and realized.

Dōgen sees the landscape itself, the world of what we call nature, as the vital primal form of entirety and its awareness. "Mountains and waters" is a way to refer to the totality of the process of nature. We are each a vital portion of such a landscape.

Snyder talks about how Dōgen left home to become a monk by climbing Mount Hiei northeast of Kyoto. "This three-thousand-foot range at the northeast corner of the Kamo River basin, the broad valley now occupied by the huge city of Kyoto, was the Japanese headquarters mountain of the Tendai sect of Buddhism." The two years or so I lived in Kyoto, traveling regularly to translate Dōgen with Shohaku Okumura at his temple west of Kyoto, I enjoyed living surrounded by temples in the foothills at the edge of Mount Hiei, one of the many Japanese mountains covered with ancient temples. Snyder clarifies:

> Sacred mountains and pilgrimage to them is a deeply established feature of the popular religions of Asia. When Dōgen speaks of

mountains he is well aware of these prior traditions. There are hundreds of famous Daoist and Buddhist peaks in China and similar Buddhist and Shinto-associated mountains in Japan.

Hiking the steep trails around Tassajara monastery in the mountains of Monterey County, after my earlier visit to Japanese mountains, I imagined many little shrines or sub-temples emerging there in years to come, as in East Asian sacred mountains.

The guts of Dōgen's "Mountains and Water Sutra" plays with a saying by a Chinese Sōtō teacher, Furong Daokai (1043–1118; Jpn.: Fuyo Dōkai), who proclaimed, "The blue mountains are constantly walking." At first blush this may seem like some strange, nonsensical Zen enigma. But in actuality, this is simply the everyday activity of mountains, for those who live in mountains. Dōgen affirms, "Mountains belong to the people who love them." When we are truly alive, so are the coursing mountains and rivers. When the mountains and rivers are all destroyed, clear-cut, or mountaintops removed for coal, our own lives will end. Mountains fully express the life of mountains. Snyder notes Dōgen's comment, "The path of water is not noticed by water, but it is realized by water." Water naturally flows and finds its way, as water.

SPACE WALKERS

In *The Practice of the Wild* Gary Snyder masterfully weaves together the reality of mountains and water, the nature of walking, and the wild path we walk. He reminds us that when Dōgen studied in China and traveled around to visit various teachers at different mountain monasteries, like the other foot-traveler Zen monks who wandered around China, he traversed many mountains and rivers. There was no guide-bus available. Walking is the traditional mode for learning a space and the true reaches of that space. As Snyder says, "We learn a place and how to visualize spatial relationships, as children, on foot and with imagination. Place and the scale of space must be measured against our bodies and their capabilities." I recall my own one-mile stroll home from high school every day where I grew up in Pittsburgh, enjoying explorations of slightly alternate routes through alleys and different cross streets, learning my space. Walking meditation is a natural extension of the awareness of zazen, or sitting meditation, how we find our path of practice, or way, for this life. As zazen is a physical, yogic practice for locating our inner dignity, walking is how we harmonize our inner and outer landscapes, whether in the meditation hall or the wider, everyday location we inhabit.

The poetic language of mountains and rivers marches through most Zen discourse, metaphor, and teaching stories. As zazen helps us find inner upright posture, the interplay of flowing mountains and waters expresses the inner dignity of our world, and our place and responsibilities to the earth. We are called to express this sacred space in the context of our everyday lives. The realm of spirit is not confined to the meditation hall or temple. As Snyder says:

> Inspiration, exaltation, and insight do not end when one steps outside the door of the church. The wilderness as a temple is only the beginning. One should not dwell in the specialness of the extraordinary experience nor hope to leave the political quagg behind to enter a perpetual state of heightened insight.

The bodhisattva path of universal awakening expresses insight and kindness right outdoors in the particular mountains and waters in which we walk.

LANDSCAPE DIVERSITY

East Asian Zen poetry and its discourse of mountains and rivers is well suited to China, Japan, and also California, where I used to live. However, practicing now in Chicago I look to find expression for this vital wildness that reflects the mountainless heartlands. How may we express the dynamic strolling of the wilderness in the interplay of Midwestern prairies and lakes? Looking at Frank Lloyd Wright's architecture or listening to

Carl Sandburg's poetry, rather than Asian Zen poetry, may help with this landscape.

How do we see the wilderness amid big cities? Urban landscapes are not other than nature. We may see the interplay of skyscrapers walking with the flowing of riverbed boulevards and notice how grass shoots up through broken concrete. As Gary Snyder colorfully describes it:

> As for towns and cities—they are (to those who can see) old tree trunks, riverbed gravels, oil seeps, landslide scrapes, blowdowns and burns, the leavings after floods, coral colonies, paper-wasp nests, beehives, rotting logs, watercourses, rock-cleavage lines, ledge strata layers, guano heaps, feeding frenzies, courting and strutting bowers, lookout rocks, and ground-squirrel apartments.

We cannot ultimately disconnect ourselves from the dynamics of the wilderness through the mere distractions and intoxications of modern technology. We remain mammalian expressions of our world.

Gary Snyder, erudite as well as poetic, informs us about the city of Hangzhou in Song China, which Dōgen very probably passed through on his journeys between mountain monasteries. It was then one of the largest and most affluent cities in the world. It is curious that the same society bequeathed to the world both Zen love of nature and the ideal of cultured, cosmopolitan cities, "both brimming with energy and life." As Snyder divulges:

> The South China of that era sent landscape painting, calligraphy, both the Sōtō and Rinzai schools of Zen, and the vision of that great southern capital to Japan. The memory of Hang-zhou shaped both Osaka and Tokyo in their Tokugawa-era evolution. These two positions—one the austere Zen practice with its spare, clean halls, the other the possibility of a convivial urban life rich in festivals and theaters and restaurants—are two potent legacies of East Asia to the world.

Zen awareness and expression need not be restricted to the beauty of the deep mountains.

PLAYING OFF THE PATH

How can these reflections on the landscapes of our world inform our sense of path and practice? The Buddhist model of "the path," the progression of practice toward awakening, intertwined happily in Chan/Zen discourse with the expressions of the Chinese *Dao*, the model of "the way" from the great Chinese Daoist tradition. Paraphrasing Laozi's Daoist classic, the Dao De Jing, Snyder says, "'A path that can be followed is not a spiritual path.' The actuality of things cannot be confined within so linear an image as a road."[146]

Snyder proposes a model of the path, and of our practice, that embraces the wildness of our lives and is not caught by ruts, routines, or literalist instruction manuals. The true way cannot be tread through systems of stages or through our imagined attainments. As Snyder states, "The 'perfect way' is not a path that leads somewhere easily defined, to some goal that is at the end of a progression." Our living way is followed through listening to our inner wildness, by sauntering beyond proscribed walkways. "The relentless complexity of the world is off to the side of the trail."

Practice and awakening is a matter of play and liveliness. Play is the enjoyment of meeting our situation, including its problems, and enjoying playfulness with our life. There is also a "play" in our life inasmuch as it gives, shifts, loosens, or wavers as we actually engage reality and its impermanence. Snyder says, "The real *play* is in the act of going totally off the trail—away from any trace of human or animal regularity aimed at some practical or spiritual purpose." This is how we meet what is authentic. "All of us are apprenticed to the same teacher that the religious institutions originally worked with: reality." We may learn most deeply by accident, by making mistakes that reveal creative possibilities or alternative modes.

The forms of spiritual practice are a valuable legacy we receive from our lineage, from our Zen ancestors. But following the rules and performing ritual forms perfectly are not the point of the Zen bodhisattva tradition. In Dōgen's monastic standards he cherishes as his exemplars teachers who as monks expressed kindness and dedication to the practice, often while seriously violating the regulations.[147] We find our real heart by meeting the realities and problems of our lives and worlds. As Snyder says, "There have always been countless unacknowledged Bodhisattvas who did not go through any formal spiritual training or philosophical quest. They were seasoned and shaped in the confusion, suffering, injustice, promise, and contradictions of life." The way is a matter of staying open to the sadness of the world and not running away from ourselves or our situation.

Snyder says it this way:

> "Off the trail" is another name for the Way, and sauntering off the trail is the practice of the wild. This is also where—paradoxically— we do our best work. But we need paths and trails and will always be maintaining them. You first must be on the path, before you can turn and walk into the wild.

The point of Zen forms and guidelines is not to follow them slavishly, but to use them as lattices around which to entwine our wild true hearts, love, and creativity, at the service of the world of which we are expressions. Such a path is available to each of us.

PART 5

American Zen Engagement

Liberation and Eternal Vigilance

VARIETIES OF LIBERATION

I N VARIOUS WAYS Buddhist practice and Buddhist ritual forms are fairly strange to most Americans. But many aspects of our culture are congenial and receptive to Buddhism, and they serve as gateways to enter this spiritual practice. For example, our interest and sophistication in psychology is an entry for many people interested in various Buddhist therapeutic techniques and psychological insights. Also our culture has a deep yearning for community, so the Buddhist experience of twenty-five hundred years of spiritual community is attractive. People interested in science, such as the cutting edge of the new physics and neurobiology, find that Buddhist cosmology, philosophy, and meditative practices resonate with new scientific discoveries. In many ways aspects of our culture offer openings to Buddhism.

One of the potentially strongest and most synchronistic American interfaces with Buddhist perspectives is the ideal of freedom, of liberty and justice for all, enshrined in the Declaration of Independence and in its celebrated opening line, "We hold these truths to be self-evident, that all men are created equal, that they are endowed by their Creator with certain inalienable rights, that among these are life, liberty, and the pursuit of happiness."

The goal of Buddhist practice is universal liberation, which bears a strong relationship to this Declaration. One account is that when the historical

Buddha Śākyamuni was awakened and became the Buddha, he said, "Now I see that all sentient beings without exception have buddha nature, and it is only because of their conditioning and confusion and ignorance that they do not realize it."[148] In the thirteenth century Eihei Dōgen expressed that idea as, "All sentient beings' wholeness is buddha nature."[149] This is a kind of Buddhist declaration of independence, a proclamation of the liberated quality of totality. Various meanings of freedom and liberation appear in the interface between the American ideal of freedom and liberty and the Buddhist goal of liberation.

ONGOING VIGILANCE

One of my favorite American Dharma utterances, "The price of liberation is eternal vigilance," is from Thomas Jefferson, the primary author of the Declaration of Independence. Jefferson's rendition is, "The price of liberty is eternal vigilance." This applies to our political liberty, as Jefferson was thinking of the corruption of governments and the need for sustained public oversight. We certainly need to watch for and respond to oppression in our society. But ongoing vigilance is also critical for Buddhist liberation. One must continually attend to inner intentions and habitual patterns. Insights into our habit patterns may be transformative, but are not usually sufficient to eradicate them. Our humanity includes the recurrence of personal shortcomings. When the Buddha was liberated it did not mean that he could check out and go back to the palace, live a life of privilege, and take it easy. And when American Zen students get some taste of Buddhist liberation, it does not mean they are finished and should go home and become unaware couch potatoes; or, for that matter, that they should stay in the zendo, close their eyes, and doze off to become zafu potatoes.

Both liberty and liberation require maintaining ongoing vigilance. Whether for freedom from social oppression or from personal oppression, freedom from corrupt corporations running our government or from our own corrupted psyches, the price of liberation is eternal vigilance. Awakened wisdom and compassion apply to our efforts to bring awareness and forgiveness to the confusion, fear, and sorrow inside our own conditioned skin bag. We are similarly challenged to express dignified, helpful responsiveness with the sufferings that arise among our friends, family, coworkers, and neighbors. Bodhisattva precepts and compassion further require our attention to our society and the environment at large, remaining open to hear and respond as beneficially as possible to the suffering of the world and all beings.

INDEPENDENCE IN INTERDEPENDENCE

The dynamic of self and society is evident in the relationship between independence and interdependence. Buddhist teaching starts from the insight into the interdependence of all things. Actually each of us is totally interconnected with the whole universe. Each piece of wood or floorboard is totally connected to the sky and the clouds and the rain that nourished the tree, the logger who cut down the tree, the trucker who drove the lumber to the mill, and the mill workers who milled the tree. And what did those workers have for breakfast, and where did that come from? Take any one item and trace it back and it connects with everything. And because everything is totally interdependent we have independence. In Buddhist teaching we might call this *non*dependence. Nondependence means that there is not a single thing to depend on. When we face any one thing we face everything, all together, all at once. We can express the whole each in our own unique fashion. The image of this in Buddhism traditionally, from Chinese Huayan teaching, is the jeweled net of Indra. The whole universe is a vast net, and at every interstice, every place where the meshes meet, there is a little jewel. Each jewel reflects the jewels around it. And each of those jewels reflects all the jewels around them and so forth. So that actually each jewel reflects everything, every jewel in the whole net. Now we might call it the jeweled *inter*net.

Any one thing, any particular teaching, or any particular person, job, or relationship, any one thing that we wish to hold on to, or that we think exists separately, also depends on all things. There is nothing that is separate. It becomes a form of slavery to feel you are depending on some one thing, whatever it is. Actually, each of us has access to vast resources, because we are all interconnected. By not depending on any single thing, by acknowledging interdependence with all things, we see our connection to all beings. That is how we find our innate independence. We are actually all free individuals because we are connected up with everything.

Eternal vigilance could be described as heightened, constant attention. Attention is the cost required for this liberation. We must continue to pay attention. When the Buddha awakened, he paid a great deal of attention to how he could share this with all beings. In Buddhism, with such eternal vigilance, "eternal" means right now, not some abstraction of infinite time. Every moment includes all times. Right now our liberation is a matter of vigilantly paying attention to what is in front of us, including paying attention to the ways we imagine we can depend on some one particular thing as if it were fixed and reliable. Of course things we imagine we can depend on may be provisionally dependable to some extent. That is how we get up in the morning, get out the door, and into our car and on our way. We depend on many things, but we also must be ready to let go of things we deem as dependable, separate entities.

One side of this freedom is nonattachment, as described in Buddhism. As the American song by Kris Kristofferen goes, "Freedom's just another word for nothing left to lose." The Japanese Zen master Uchiyama Roshi said, "Gain is delusion, loss is enlightenment." Thinking we have got hold of something is a delusion. When we can let it go or lose it, and are willing to surrender that to the vast jeweled internet, that is awakening, or liberation. This is not easy.

The American ideal of democracy, of liberty and justice for all, particularly resonates with the teaching of Universal Vehicle Buddhism, or Mahāyāna, of which Zen is a part. Early Buddhism promoted the ideal of personal liberation; if one purified one's own attachments and were free from desires, that would be liberation. Then Buddhism evolved and the universal vehicle developed. But it still includes this sense of personal liberation, which requires study of our own perceptions and what arises in our own body and mind just sitting on our cushions. We study this closely, continuingly vigilant right now. Thereby we come to see how we concoct this process of alienation from the world, estranging ourselves by solidifying our sense of self and other, and we study this process closely. This is the intimate work of eternal vigilance and freedom from fundamental ignorance, the underlying confusion that Buddha spoke of as he awakened.

The universal vehicle goes further to see that we cannot be truly liberated if others down the road are suffering. It is not just a matter of clearing up your own psyche and then you will be happy and free, with everything resolved. We see that others around us actually affect us and that ultimately we are completely connected with them. It must be liberty and justice for all, or, we might say, justice and liberation for everyone.

When the Declaration of Independence was written during the war to free the colonies from King George and British oppression, Benjamin Franklin said, "We must all hang together, else we shall all hang separately." He saw that all the colonies had to come together and stand together for their liberty. Similarly, Buddhist practitioners come together to sit upright, facing the whole universe, facing the fact that we create suffering by imagining ourselves separate from someone else. We have imagined we are hanging separately.

POSITIVE FREEDOM AND KARMIC LIMITATIONS

There is freedom *from*—freedom from colonization by governments or by our own confusion and ignorance, from our own psychology. And there is also freedom *to*—freedom to do something positive to help others, to help all beings, to share and develop whatever qualities we have that are satisfying for ourselves and for everyone.

However, freedom is not escape. We cannot escape from our situation. A popular idea of freedom when I grew up back in the sixties was freedom as running away from problems, escaping into some other way of being. Such escape does not really work. We have to acknowledge our karma and our Dharma position, which is to say that we have to accept who and where we are, and what we are doing. Then we remain present, with eternal vigilance. Liberty and liberation do not happen in some ideal place, somewhere up in the sky. We are always in some particular time and place, and we have to see ourselves and others in this context. The Buddha lived in a particular time and place; Thomas Jefferson lived in a particular time and place. Now most of us are aware that Thomas Jefferson owned slaves and probably fathered children with one of his slaves. This is an interesting problem. It is hard not to make judgments about that, and it is appropriate that we do have some judgments.

When the American founding fathers said that all men are created equal, women were not included. They could not vote, and also not all men were included. There was slavery, and even free men were not all included; one had to own a certain amount of property or land before one was included in the rights of the Constitution or in the right to vote. Supposedly the group drafting the Declaration originally had written, "Life, liberty, and the pursuit of *property*," and Thomas Jefferson insisted on changing it to the pursuit of happiness. I bow deeply to Thomas Jefferson or whomever made that change. Events have a particular context. We cannot escape from but must face the consequences of a particular time and place. Freedom is not a matter of escaping responsibilities.

THOMAS JEFFERSON AND THE VOWS OF FREEDOM

The United States Constitution was based in some large part on the confederation of the Iroquois nation. Benjamin Franklin and some others studied and used parts of this Iroquois political system to draft our Constitution. Yet Benjamin Franklin himself later considered the Native Americans an obstacle to the progress of the United States. Thomas Jefferson spoke highly of Native Americans, actually studied about the different tribes where information was available, and even wrote dictionaries of some of their languages. He was quite interested in their cultures, yet he arranged the Louisiana Purchase and spread the United States westward. Jefferson believed the Native Americans needed to learn agriculture rather than nomadic hunting, that they would be better off that way, and so was somewhat responsible for the destruction of native cultures, although perhaps this was historically inevitable. But while recognizing the serious shortcomings of Jefferson and many of his contemporaries, in some ways I celebrate Thomas Jefferson and other of our American forefathers, some of whose writings, at least, still represent something that resonates with Buddhist practice.

In addition to his statement about eternal vigilance, Jefferson vowed eternal hostility against every form of tyranny over the human mind. This was his personal vow. It feels very close to the traditional bodhisattva four vows, to save all sentient beings, to cut through all delusive afflictions, to enter all pathways to Dharma, and to realize the Buddha Way. These inconceivable vows are supported by vigilant attention to conduct and awareness, and steadfast helpfulness. Jefferson had a suitably dedicated and quite active mind, with interests in many realms, and significant accomplishments in many of them. His letters are very insightful. He was an architect, a painstaking agriculturist, a scientist, and wrote informatively about religion. As a Zen practitioner I feel related to him through his inquiry into the sacred and his questions and concerns. Some of these can be found in the wonderful collection of correspondence with his former rival John Adams later in their lives. Jefferson's powerful writings include prescient, currently relevant utterances such as, "If there be one principle more deeply rooted than any other in the mind of every American it is that we should have nothing to do with conquest," and "I hope we crush in its birth the aristocracy of our monied corporations which dare already to challenge our government to a trial by strength, and bid defiance to the laws of our country."[150] Sadly, it is his hopes that seem crushed in our current situation.

Jefferson was very insistent on religious freedom and tolerance, and on accepting all forms of religion. In the epitaph he wrote for his own tombstone he did not mention being president of the United States. Instead he noted writing the Declaration of Independence, founding the University of Virginia, and writing the Article of Religious Tolerance for the state of Virginia. This was important to him. Jefferson initiated the principle of separation of church and state in our country, but he never intended that we should not apply true spiritual values to public life. Jefferson used his own religious principles to consider what was happening in his world. But he insisted that no one person, not even the president, should be empowered to speak for everyone to or about God.

Jefferson's home at Monticello is still quite impressive. Jefferson invented many intriguing contraptions one can view there. Some of the Mahāyāna sutras talk about bodhisattva activity as including creating inventions and whatever mechanisms may help people. All of this said, still, Jefferson was a slaveholder. He thought it was an evil that should be eradicated, and he actually worked unsuccessfully to accomplish that in his early career. Yet he succumbed to the conditioning and economic imperatives of the slave plantation culture in which he was raised and did not free his own slaves until his will, on his deathbed.

ACKNOWLEDGING OUR OWN TIME

Looking back for inspiration in spiritual practice from those who have gone before, we have to acknowledge their particular time and place. Today some people criticize Śākyamuni Buddha also because he only reluctantly founded an order of nuns to go along with his order of monks, after quite a bit of persistent pressuring from his stepmother, Mahāprajāpati, who became the first leader of the order of nuns. The nuns were completely subordinate to the monks in the original Buddhist order, and they still are in many Buddhist countries. American Buddhists today often condemn that, and from our modern perspective, rightly so. But then we have to see the context of where the Buddha lived, and the society in northern India at that time, twenty-five hundred years ago. It was quite radical to start a Buddhist order and accept women at all. He accepted outcastes also, and he stated unequivocally that it was equally possible for women, outcastes, and everybody to awaken. This was extremely radical at that time.

Still we may have some criticism. But I wonder how we ourselves will be judged in two hundred years, or in twenty-five hundred years. We live in a very violent, militaristic society. That is the consequence of our collective karma, this particular history of slavery and of the near genocide of the Native American people who lived here before the colonies. What things that we take for granted today, or things that we protest against today, will people look back and wonder, "How could they have done that?" We create pollution, many problems with the environment, many wars. We watch people on television butcher each other and do not know what to do. The planet's climate has been damaged by human consumption and massive corporate corruption, and the extreme disparity in resources between the extremely wealthy and most human beings accelerates. We should be pretty humble in looking back and judging others.

Returning to this pursuit of happiness, or "life, liberty, and the pursuit of happiness," concerning this idea of freedom and the Buddhist sense of liberation, what does Buddhism have to offer to Americans today? Buddhism encourages sympathetic joy, to appreciate the virtues of others, and also to feel happy when somebody else finds good fortune. That is not always easy, to really be joyful and sympathetic. When something you want and do not have comes to somebody else, can you actually feel sympathetically joyful? Basic to happiness in Buddhism is to have gratitude for the everyday wonders around us, whatever our situation. We can be grateful just to be alive. In Zen practice happiness has to do with uprightly facing our own life. Whatever arises, you need not be shaken or reactive to that situation, and we can respond uprightly. This upright posture is the gateway of repose and bliss, the gateway of peace and freedom.

With this eternal vigilance, this attentiveness right now, we can give ourselves the time and space to be at liberty, to enjoy our lives, to appreciate what we have before us, and to see how to be helpful for the world. I value the following writing about liberation by another great American patriot who was also a great yogi. Henry David Thoreau wrote about leaving his hermitage at Walden Pond to reenter the marketplace:

I left the woods for as good a reason as I went there. Perhaps it seemed to me that I had several more lives to live, and could not spare any more time for that one. It is remarkable how easily and insensibly we fall into a particular route, and make a beaten track for ourselves. I had not lived there a week before my feet wore a path from my door to the pond side; and though it is five or six years since I trod it, it is still quite distinct. It is true, I fear that others may have fallen into it, and so helped to keep it open. The surface of the earth is soft and impressible by the feet of men; and so, with the paths which the mind travels. How worn and dusty, then, must be the highways of the world, how deep the ruts of tradition and conformity! I did not wish to take a cabin passage, but rather to go before the mast and on the deck of the world, for there I could best see the moonlight amid the mountains.[151]

As Thoreau suggests, liberation and true happiness has to do with vigilantly going beyond our mental ruts and being willing to share ourselves out in the world, enjoying the moonlight and mountains.

Consumerism and
the Bodhisattva Precepts

THE INTERACTIVE EVOLUTION OF BUDDHISM

D HARMA TEACHERS in the United States, and all the people who practice here, are involved in the project of bringing Buddhist practice
and teaching into our lives in twenty-first-century America. Throughout
the history of Buddhism in Asia, Buddhism has adapted, developed, and
grown as it has moved into different countries and different cultures and
interacted with native religions and traditions. In China with Daoism and
ancestor veneration, in Japan with native Shinto spiritual ways, and in
various different countries (including Tibet, Korea, and Southeast Asia),
Buddhism has been a living tradition, which developed and interacted with
the culture and has itself been transformed. This has been happening in
America over the last fifty years as well.

I have been very involved in Buddhist-Christian dialogue through various Buddhist-Christian conferences and dialogue workshops, and teaching
Buddhist studies at Berkeley Graduate Theological Union, where many of
my students have been Christian seminarians, and at Loyola University
Chicago, a Jesuit school. From the point of view of Buddhism, studying different religious traditions is very informative in learning what is important
in Buddhist practice. Many American Buddhists now are also very involved
in interactions with Judaism, with Native American religions, with science,
for example with modern physics and neurobiology, and very much with
Western psychology. Many former students at San Francisco Zen Center,

where I was mostly trained, are now therapists, and I sometimes speak of Northern California Zen as Jungian Buddhism.

Interfaith dialogue has great value. As we find our own seat as American Buddhists, we bring our experience and our awareness of American traditions and culture to Buddhism, and Buddhism is naturally transformed. I have taught college courses in world religion and enjoy studying comparative religion, finding something of value in every religious tradition. This is all background to the following discussion about the one major American religion whose fundamental values are in conflict with Buddhism: the religion of consumerism.

CONSUMERIST RELIGION AND HUNGRY GHOSTS

Consumerism has been described as a religion by the Buddhist scholar David Loy.[152] David Loy discusses the function of religions as teaching what the world is and our place in it. In this way consumerism functions as a religion, just like Buddhism and Christianity, grounding their followers in basic assumptions about themselves and the world around them. Religions teach how to live, what to do, and how to find fulfillment. David Loy describes two tenets or unquestioned items of faith for consumerism. One is that growth and subsidized world trade will benefit everyone. The second is that growth need not be constrained or curtailed by the limited resources of this finite planet. The economy can just keep growing indefinitely. In consumerism self-fulfillment and self-realization depend on how much we consume. This basic philosophy or goal, expressed by the bumper sticker "Whoever dies with the most toys wins," is an unquestioned, often unconscious value of our society.

The ramifications of consumerism can be clarified through the viewpoint of bodhisattva precepts, which are guidelines for how to express Buddhist awareness in everyday activity. Much of Buddhist practice is about balancing wisdom and compassion. In zazen we get a taste of wisdom through touching the possibility of wholeness, and seeing deeply our interconnectedness with all being and the fundamental emptiness of all

distinctions. On the side of compassion we use the precepts not as commandments but as guidelines to help express Buddha's awareness in the
various difficulties that arise in our ordinary everyday activity.

Trying to lead compassionate lives informed by the precepts brings fundamental conflict with some basic values in our society. In the mainstream
media, especially due to the religion of consumerism, the fundamental
values are greed, material acquisition, and even vengeance. All the television commercials and the other ads we see are designed very skillfully to
create more needs and more desires. The three thousand or more ads that
the average American is exposed to each day create desires that can never
be fully satisfied.

In Buddhism, beings who are never satisfied are called hungry ghosts,
depicted with tiny throats and huge stomachs that can never be filled. No
matter how hard they try they can never satisfy their desires—a very sad
situation. The hungry ghost realm is one of the six levels of existence into
which a being can be born. The other realms include human, animal, the
heavenly realms, and the hell realms. These are also considered as psychological descriptions of different potential aspects of our inner life. One
of the more ornate and important ceremonies done in American Zen is
Segaki, which means feeding the hungry ghosts, done with offerings piled
on the altar. We usually perform this in America around Halloween, which
traditionally has a similar function to the European "All Hallows Eve."
This ceremony is performed in Japan around August, during the Ōbon
time when restless spirits are invited to return to this world. Offerings are
made to appease the hungry ghosts and help them find some peace and
satisfaction. Eventually they will hopefully find their way to rebirth back
in the human realm.

Aiding hungry ghosts is important in Buddhist practice, but on the other
hand, in American society people are trained by advertising to become
hungry ghosts. The major holiday in the religion of consumerism has been
appropriated from Christianity. It is called Christmas, and its purpose is
to create hungry ghosts who are obliged to buy more, bigger, and more
expensive gifts.

CONTENTMENT AND THE MIDDLE WAY

A basic Buddhist value is contentment with what we have, and enjoying this world as it is. We are grateful for the ocean, the birds in the trees, and our friends and family. This gratitude does not mean being passive and accepting everything without question. The precepts encourage response to suffering. We try not to harm but to benefit all beings, to see our lives in the context of all beings, benefiting not solely our own profit margin but working to foster awakening and awareness. Satisfaction comes from dynamic and responsive activity, not through creating or indulging craving for more material wealth.

In the Zen and Buddhist traditions are many examples of characters who are nonconsumer extremists. It is possible to be extremist about not having desires, property, or needs. A wonderful Japanese Sōtō Zen monk and poet named Ryōkan (1758–1831) is still very popular in Japan. After finishing his training, instead of becoming the abbot of a temple or a formal Zen teacher, he went back to his hometown and lived in a tiny hut outside the town. He made his living by doing begging rounds, traditional in Asian Buddhism. He took as his name Daigu, "Great Fool," and many stories tell of his foolishness, forgetfulness, and his frequent play with children. One well-known story describes Ryōkan sitting in his hut looking through the window or perhaps the holes in his roof at the full moon, an image of wholeness, perfection, and peacefulness in Zen. A thief entered the hut, but could find nothing to steal. Ryōkan, thinking the fellow must be really needy, gave the thief his only thin blanket. The thief took it (somewhat embarrassed) and left. Then Ryōkan wrote a poem about wishing he could give this person the moon.

Ryōkan wrote many wonderful poems, one of which speaks to this issue of consumerism in terms of the values of Buddhism.

> Without desire everything is sufficient.
> With seeking myriad things are impoverished.
> Plain vegetables can soothe hunger.
> A patched robe is enough to cover this bent old body.

Alone I hike with a deer.

Cheerfully I sing with village children.

The stream beneath the cliff cleanses my ears;

The pine on the mountain top fits my heart.[153]

In Zen history are many examples of people who similarly went to extremes to not need any toys and just live simply, open-heartedly appreciating the world of nature and meditation. Buddhists, however, practice the Middle Way. The alternative to consumerism is not necessarily to give away all your property, or enter a residential center and support the Dharma as monks offering your labor to the community.

Consumerism goes back a while in world history. Ryōkan was, along with everything else, a great calligrapher, whose work was quite valuable even during his own lifetime. Among many stories of people trying to trick him into writing calligraphy, some children asked Ryōkan to write something on their kites to help them fly. He wrote "Heaven-Up-Great-Wind," and the kids were very happy. But their parents had put them up to it since they wanted to acquire the hot commodity of Ryōkan calligraphy.

Wealth actually offers an opportunity, and a responsibility, to find the "middle way" between extremes of consumerism and asceticism. In Buddhism are many examples of wealthy "nonconsumers" who have used their material resources and power to help the poor and needy, to help develop culture and the arts, and even to foster awakening in others. One famous example in Buddhist literature is Vimalakīrti, the legendary laymen who supposedly lived during Śākyamuni Buddha's lifetime, twenty-five hundred years ago.[154] He had great business skill and vast resources. But he used his wealth to benefit beings and help lead them toward the path to finding their true self. He expressed the middle way between not needing, like Ryōkan, and acquisitiveness, using his resources beneficially while not being consumed by them. Similarly, there are people with significant resources in our world today who use them wisely and help many. Buddhism does not require abandoning all material goods but uses the phenomenal world to help support awakening.

The gravest danger to Buddhism from consumerism is seeing spiritual practice as yet another commodity to consume. We have been trained by advertising and media to want the best, quickest, and fanciest of everything. Some people travel around visiting different Buddhist centers and teachers seeking the quickest path or the best teacher, the fast track to enlightenment. The consumerist approach to Buddhism is not so helpful. This practice is about expressing our deepest self and deepest truth. That takes some time, some settling in, and the willingness to be present in this body and mind. Zazen is not about gaining something we do not already have; it requires patience and a willingness to be present, fully inhabiting our body and mind, not trying to acquire some fancy new state of consciousness.

NOT KILLING THE WORLD

Returning to the question of precepts and ethics, the root of the problem of consumerism is the nature of basic values. Happiness need not involve wealth and property. We have a right to be happy just as Ryōkan was happy, walking on his begging rounds, playing with children, meditating, and looking at the moon. The sixteen bodhisattva precepts used in the Sōtō Zen tradition are not seen as commandments but as expressions of how awakened awareness acts in the world. Each of the precepts is a kind of problem or a question; each has many aspects. The first of the ten grave precepts is, "A disciple of the Buddha does not kill." Consumerism can kill the life of the world by making things into dead commodities. Do we see the world and each other as alive, or instead see the world, each other, and even ourselves as just commodities to be consumed? Is the world an array of dead objects, or is it alive, dynamic, and interactive as Buddhism teaches?

How we respond to these questions has effects both for our society and for our own hearts and minds. People in positions of power, believing the world just a commodity to be consumed, feel entitled to cut down old-growth forests or drill for oil recklessly without safety precautions along the shores of California or the Gulf Coast. They are just liquidating their assets, without concern for environmental consequences. Based on the values of consumerism, organizations like NAFTA and the World Trade Organization, controlled by massive multinational corporations, have arranged treaties and laws for globalization that make the corporate right to profits legally supersede human rights, labor rights, or reasonable environmental protections. These organizations treat the ecosystems of our world as a bunch of dead commodities to exploit.

The precept of not killing asks whether we see our world as alive. Do we see each other as alive? Do we see ourselves as separate from the world, from the oceans, from nature preserves, birds and trees, separate from each other? If so, then nature and people and everything we see are all just dead objects that can be manipulated to get the most out of them for our own profit. We consume everything, even people. This is the logic of consumerism.

A line from Bob Dylan says that people sometimes do what they do just to be "Nothing more than something they invest in."[155] When we follow the tenets of consumerism, we invest in ourselves. We are all familiar with this process of marketing ourselves as mere commodities in our resumes. But we may lose the other joy, not happiness based on the pursuit of property, but the happiness to enjoy responding positively and constructively to the situations in our world and our everyday activities, to enjoy what is already present.

CONSUMERIST INTOXICATION

The fifth grave precept is that a disciple of Buddha does not intoxicate mind or body of self or others. In some Asian countries it is rendered, "A disciple of the Buddha does not sell wine or alcohol," but this involves more than just alcohol or drugs. This precept refers to the basic practice of awareness, paying attention to the situation right now, which is the opposite of intoxication. Whether or not you have had a glass of wine, the important practice is to be present in the midst of this life.

On the other hand, based on the values of consumerism, advertising and entertainment industries very skillfully distract us from being present in our body and mind. They aim to increase our desires and cravings, in effect making us hungry ghosts. This is a kind of intoxication. It may be nice to have shiny new toys and keep up with the latest technological wonders. But we can get carried away. Paraphrasing Descartes' "I think, therefore I am," consumerism proclaims, "I shop, therefore I am." The middle way considers how we take care of what we have and the tools we use, without ourselves being consumed by the drive to have more and bigger and better. Are we avoiding our lives with addiction to acquiring material objects?

The founder of Sōtō Zen, Eihei Dōgen, in his noted writing "Genjōkōan," says, "When Dharma does not fill our body and mind we think it is already sufficient. When Dharma fills our body and mind we realize that something is missing."[156] This something missing is exactly our life problem, our sadness and frustration. In Zen practice we sit facing the reality that something is missing, as Dharma fills our body and mind. The problem with consumerism is that it attempts to fill this "something is missing" with new toys, to distract us from our own fears, sadness, and frustrations, and thus to take us away from our life.

Most people are not soaked in the Dharma like Ryōkan. Feeling a little frustration, instead of facing who we are and settling into that, we may attempt to feel better by buying new toys. This is very tempting. Sitting upright in the middle of our world and our situation is often very painful. Sometimes we need to take a break, to go enjoy a movie or even enjoy a new toy. But in the middle way we do not intoxicate ourselves such that we are not aware of "something missing," that sense of lack. Dylan has another line, "All of us, at times, we might work too hard, To have it too fast and too much. And anyone can fill his life up, With things he can see but he just cannot touch."[157] In consumerism we fill our life up with things that actually do not touch the reality of our lives. In Buddhism we do not need to possess everything. We can recall Ryōkan's happiness and enjoy the moon. We need not conquer the moon.

Buddhist practice is about learning not to be addicted, not to consume our world. We can appreciate the forest, wildlife, and our lives as they are without needing to accumulate more toys. If we do have a lot of toys, how can we use them beneficially? We can enjoy the toys we have, following the middle way, and not be consumed by needing more, bigger, and better.

GUIDANCE FOR CONTENTMENT

There is no "Buddhist policy" about how to deal with the damage being caused by consumerism all around the world. But practice does emphasize the basic value of awareness in our lives and encourages paying attention. Consider, "Do I really need this? How can I most beneficially use that?" With attention, aware of these values as they impact our society and our own lives, then eventually these patterns of addiction may change and consumerism stop harming the world. Ryōkan really was a fool in terms of consumerist values, but his poems offer guidance:

> All my life, too lackadaisical to stand up for myself;
> Buoyantly, I leave everything to the harmony of reality
> In my sack, three scoops of rice;
> Beside the fire, a bundle of firewood;
> Who would ask about traces of delusion and enlightenment?
> How could you know the dusts of name and gain?
> Evening rain; in my thatched hut
> I casually stretch out my legs.

Ryōkan's simple lifestyle of voluntary poverty and extensive meditation was obviously grounded in a sincere dedication to awakening. The integrity of Ryōkan's awareness is apparent in the following poem about his begging practice.

> Ringing a monk's staff, I enter the eastern town.
> So green, willows in the garden;
> So restless, floating grass over the pond;
> My bowl is fragrant with rice from a thousand homes.

My heart has abandoned splendor of ten thousand vehicles.
Yearning for traces of ancient buddhas,
Step by step I walk, begging.[158]

We can hear Ryōkan's joyful appreciation of a life of simple, unpretentious caring.

Meeting Our Ancestors of the Future

HONORING ANCESTORS IN DEEP TIME

WHEN WE CAN fully see our own time in the dynamic fullness of all time, without being blind to cause and effect, without being caught by limiting views of time itself, we can begin to be the present time in the depths of time, to presence the deep time that includes and honors the presence right now of our ancestors.

Those of us who have connected to a spiritual tradition have a natural inclination to appreciate and venerate our ancestors, the persons we look back to as having blazed the way for us. Thus these reflections include the past, honoring the ancestors whom I recall for enduring inspiration, whose wisdom and insight, efforts and generosity, help show me how to be more human and more fully myself.

But how can we also include the future, embodying faith that there is a future, and respecting the persons out there in the future who are also our ancestors? Although I do not know their names, and might find their worlds as unimaginable as our own modern world would be to venerable ancestors from distant past centuries, still I trust that these persons of the future will find their own appropriate ways to carry forth the principles and livelihood that motivate me. Inasmuch as they recognize the dynamic and total interconnectedness of all being, and act accordingly with kindness and clarity, these future beings are also our ancestors and actually support us now.

I feel responsibility to acknowledge, honor, and in some way represent, a great many specific beings and groups of beings. Speaking from my own personal truth and karma, I hear the chords that unite all those of good will, bringing together the web of past and future.

THE THREAT TO TIME ITSELF

These reflections on temporality and future generations were sparked by the work on the issue of nuclear waste by American Buddhist scholar, teacher, and activist Joanna Macy and by my participation in the Nuclear Guardianship Project that she initiated.[159] In the wake of the destruction now being unleashed around the world by global climate change, and the catastrophic BP oil spew off the United States Gulf Coast, nuclear waste had seemed a minor concern before the earthquake and nuclear disaster at Fukushima in northern Japan. Some are even still misguidedly advocating renewal of dangerous nuclear power technology as a substitute for the damages of fossil fuel energy.[160] The realities of the massive climate damage unleashed in our time, along with the deadly poison of nuclear waste our species has left on the earth, will be our most significant physical legacy to distant future generations. The nearly inconceivable extent of time in which nuclear waste materials will remain toxic (dozens and even hundreds of millennia) necessitates our rethinking our awareness of temporality. Our ancestors of the future are looking back on us, waiting for us to act and take up safekeeping and protection of the planet they will inherit. And our own mental health requires our concern and caring for future generations. We require some future for our present to be meaningful.

Our faith that there will be a future is vital. As Joanna Macy and others have pointed out, the great unrecognized disease of our time is the real possibility of the end of our species, the end of time itself, as we know it. The potential perils of nuclear catastrophe, along with other threats such as the effects of deforestation, pollution of land and oceans, massive global climate damage, and the Gulf oil disaster, all exact a devastating and often hidden psychic toll. Further, there are very strong indications that the current rate of species extinctions far exceeds anything in the fossil record.[161] The age-old apocalyptic fears are now rampant, reinforced by scientific evidence of the destruction of our environment, and our consciousness is impaired by hopelessness with this dull awareness. We must open to the meaning of our suppressed despair and find ways to recognize and act in concert with the people of the future, to imagine the continuation of our best efforts.

CHANGING THE PAST WHILE BEING TIME

To fully meet our ancestors of both future and past, we must envision a new dynamic relationship to time itself. The eighth-century Chinese Zen master Shitou (700–790; Jpn.: Sekitō) said, "I humbly say to those who study the mystery: Don't waste time."[162] A century later, the great master Zhaozhou (778–897; Jpn.: Jōshu) said to a monk, "I use the hours of the day, you are used by the hours of the day."[163] This not wasting time, or using time's hours, is not a matter of efficiency or productivity indices. Zhaozhou used time by being fully present, by fully sensing the immediate intimacy of his present being with all other beings in space and time. Not wasting time is to take care of the one who is not busy, who uprightly faces the present with steadiness right in the midst of the whirling sands of time.

The Huayan School of Buddhism in China, based on the Flower Orna-ment/Avataṃsaka Sutra, gives a rich depiction of the multidimensional quality of time. It speaks of ten times: the past, present, and future of the past, of the present, and of the future, respectively, and finally the combina-tion of all these nine times.[164] The past of the present may also be the past of a future. The present of the future will be intimately connected to the future of our present, yet is not necessarily predetermined or limited by our present future. We can reclaim the past in the present and thus actually change our past, as well as our present, for the sake of the future. History is the changing process of defining the past for the present, and the stories we tell about the past in the present change the meaning of past events.

Even if we cannot bring back extinct species or detoxify nuclear poisons, seeing those events as opportunities to change how we care for the world may change the meaning of this past. We can rewrite the history of the future in the present as well as in the future.

In the realm of "being time" elaborated in Dōgen's writing, time does not only flow from past to present to future.[165] Time moves in mysterious ways, passing dynamically between all ten times and beyond. Time is not some intractable external container we are caught in. We are time. When we fully express ourselves right now, that is time. We cannot help but fully express our deepest truth right now. We cannot avoid being time. Even a partial, half-hearted exertion of our being time is completely a partial being time.

When we realize that we are ineluctably being time in this very body and mind, we can choose to be and act from our deepest and noblest intention. We can choose to express our being of time in a way that connects with all beings here now and also connects with all beings, all of our ancestors, throughout the generations of past and future. We can intend to be a time that accepts the support and guidance of all beings of all times.

Having a wide, inclusive view of time deepens our appreciation of this present time. Such a range of time is expressed by Dōgen's twelfth-century Chinese predecessor, Chan Master Hongzhi, "This is the time and place to leap beyond the ten thousand emotional entanglements of innumerable eons. One contemplation of ten thousand years finally goes beyond all the transitory, and you emerge with spontaneity."[166] When we emerge from denial of the vast depths of time and are willing to contemplate the whole ten thousand years, then finally we can dynamically and freely exert and inhabit our present being time.

REINHABITING ANCESTRAL TIME

However, it is not that we should exclude the common, linear view of time. This being time in congress with all time does not at all deny or violate our conventional truths, our everyday notion of time being hours, minutes, and seconds. We must see how, right in the middle of our ordinary time of walking down the path, the ancestors of past and future walk together with us. Reenvisioning time, we can reinhabit time. Reinhabiting time we enrich our lives by reclaiming our intimate relationship and connection to beings of the past and beings of the future.

We have a rich multiplicity of ancestors to recognize, including our spiritual lineage and our diverse cultural heritage. As a Zen Buddhist priest, I represent and revere a particular lineage of practitioners and ancestors reaching back through Japan and China to Śākyamuni Buddha, twenty-five hundred years ago in India. Being in the first generation of American Zen priests, I clarify that situation to my Japanese counterparts, many of them the offspring of generations of temple priests, by pointing out that there are not yet American Buddhist priests who are sons or daughters of priests.

Contemplating the connections of generations, I also esteem and feel indebted to many Western cultural ancestors. Many people of fine spirit and dedication have strived to express the divine wonder of our human life. As just a tip of the iceberg, I personally venerate Bach, William Blake, Van Gogh, Rumi, Dostoevsky, Coltrane, and Rilke for such expression. From our American homeland we can recall those who have cared and acted for the planet and for human liberty, for example: Thomas Paine, Tecumseh, Henry David Thoreau, Harriet Tubman, Dorothy Day, John Muir, Jackie Robinson. Readers will have their own lists of culture figures who act as inspirational ancestors, from literature and legend as well as history.

Americans also all have particular, dramatically diverse genetic, ethnic backgrounds, whether from Native Americans, Europeans, Africans, or Asians. We may also imagine more arcane and subtle heritages, for example those derived from our past lifetimes. Just as we have this multiplicity of past ancestors, lurking in the future and connected to us are members of our spiritual, cultural, and genetic lineages, whom we may meet as future ancestors.

When I lived in Kyoto for two years in the early nineties, collaborating on translations of Dōgen and immersing myself in the ambience and practice life of ancient Buddhist temples and artifacts, I learned the Japanese word *keikō*. Signifying diligent practice or training, *keikō* literally means "to search out, study, and contemplate the way of the ancients." In modern Japanese it is a common term for "practice" while training in arts and sports, as in practicing tea ceremony, the piano, or karate. This was also an important term for Dōgen, referring to practice modeled on penetrating study of and reflection on the ancient sages and their standards. Respecting the ancestors, we learn to respect ourselves and more thoroughly become ourselves, more fully connected to our place in the web of time. Slavishly following the exact traditions and forms of the past is not the point. Rather, we learn from the spirit of the ancestors qualities of attention and caring, of awareness and steadfastness. In his "Writing on Arousing the Vow," Dōgen said, "Ancient buddhas and ancestors were as we; we shall come to be buddhas and ancestors. Venerating buddhas and ancestors, we are one with buddhas and ancestors; contemplating awakening mind, we are one with awakened mind."[167] Thus we join the ancestors.

MEETING FUTURE BEINGS

Might we also apply keikō, the enactment of appreciation of the ancients, not only to respect for past ancestors, but also to our respect for our ancestors of the future? How can we search for and study the examples and spirit of our future ancestors? I sense they are watching us now, looking back hopefully at our responses to the dreadful dangers of the present era.

During my two years living in Kyoto, I imagined another young American Buddhist, five hundred years hence, on her own pilgrimage to Kyoto to connect with our common roots. I saw her wandering like me between the thousand-year-old temples, pagodas, and cemeteries on Mount Yoshida, and wondered which old buildings would be left to see, what bits of human civilization would remain, what would be recognizable in the twenty-fifth century.

Any of our present humble efforts to care for the planet were vitally important to her. I felt her request to us. We have such a relationship and responsibility to all beings of the future, to all creation. As humans we now wield a powerful sword that can destroy or give life to many other species of life and to many rich forms of expression. Our ancestors expect something of us. It is not enough for us to know of our connectedness. We can honor the ancestors by giving immediate attention to educating the current generation and the next generation about the richness of time. We must encourage ourselves to see time as alive and multifaceted, not merely as dead, objectified clock-time.

DEEP EARTH TIME

Our connection to all time is also our connection to the earth. The ground of our being is the same ancestral ground that plants us in time. We uncover our ancestors in the earth we inhabit. This truth is strikingly depicted in a story in the Lotus Sutra. Myriad bodhisattvas, enlightening beings who have arrived from other dimensions or distant solar systems to hear Śākyamuni Buddha's teaching, ask if he needs their help to maintain this teaching in the future evil age. From our vantage point, twenty-five hundred years later, I imagine the question from Buddha they are responding to as: "In the distant age of television, automobiles, global climate damage, and nuclear waste, how will those people hear the true teaching of universal awakening?"

The Buddha tells them not to fear, and suddenly, from out of the empty, open space under the ground, spring vast multitudes of noble, gentle beings, dedicated to the emancipation of all creation.[168] The Buddha declares that these bodhisattvas practice diligently within the earth, forever guiding confused, worldly people. Moreover, they have all trained intently with him, even though many apparently are ages older than the Buddha himself. He is the ancestor even of those from his past.

Our ancestors awakening us to important realities are always nearby, coming from strange unexpected realms. In an apocryphal but useful story, Chief Seattle of the Duwamish people, in 1854 in what is now Washington State, supposedly issued a prophecy that resonates remarkably with the story of bodhisattvas emerging from the earth in the Lotus Sutra. Although not historically accurate, the essence of Seattle's reported message is reliable and congruent with the spiritual vision of indigenous peoples.[169] Purportedly Seattle eloquently described his people's intimate relationship with the land, seeing each feature of the earth as sacred and wondrous, especially venerating the resting places of their ancestors. Seattle marveled that the white men uncaringly wandered far from their ancestors' graves. We have forgotten and neglected our ancestors. But the spirits of departed native braves, maidens, mothers, and children still love the beautiful land, and Seattle predicted that in the future, when the white men's grandchildren walk their city streets, the native spirits would return, emerging from the ground to exert their influence.

Even today, the answers to our dilemmas might still be found in the open earth right beneath our feet. This requires our respecting the earth and its sensitivity as an organic biosystem. When we dig deeply, metaphorically, rather than to plunder the earth, this very ground can support us and awakened ones from future and past generations, forgotten or not yet conceived, can become our teachers and ancestors. The answers to our questions, our natural vitality, and our self-realization are all here in this place and life, not in some fantasy world in some other realm. What is needed is present and available. Our essential transformation is a matter of becoming more fully true to ourselves, rather than in becoming something other.

PROTECTING THE RHYTHMS OF TIME

In time, our connection to earth is the connection to its natural rhythms. With patience we can find our own expression of these rhythms. Despite all of our tantalizing technologies, we cannot control or manipulate the deeper rhythms of the earth. Human efforts to garner corporate profits from the earth's deep resources are now instead reaping disastrous consequences for all life. In a popular phrase, the earth does not belong to us, but we are part of the earth; we move to its rhythms. Attuned to these rhythms, appropriate actions may become clear and we may become ready to do what is needed. Our multiplicity of ancestors has bequeathed us valuable guidance in finding our footing in this ancestral time-ground. For example, the Iroquois people of America's past enacted all policies and programs only after considering their impact for the next seven generations. How can we also learn to proceed with such a range of vision, rather than operating only on quarterly profit margins?

The American Zen pioneer Gary Snyder has said that Zen practice comes down to sitting and sweeping the temple, and it is up to us to decide the boundaries of our temple. As in space, so in time. Gary Snyder also has said we must act immediately with full urgency, knowing how critical are the threats to our planet; and simultaneously, we must act as if we have all the time in the world, moving with dignity, care, and patience.[170] We must be determined to sustain our gaze and our response to the challenges before us.

How shall we apply our spiritual or philosophical insights to the concrete realities at hand? Many crises and dilemmas face our world and its ecosystems, and these will require spiritual as well as technological responses. We must halt the many scourges to the earth: mountaintop removal for the sake of climate endangering coal, massive deforestation harming our atmosphere and the balance of oxygen and carbon dioxide, oil drilling destroying our oceans, and the continuing production of lethal nuclear waste. Climate damage has arrived, and it is harming people and cultures all around the world. The BP oil bled into the Gulf continues to damage many eco-systems and species, a wounding of the earth whose full impact we cannot yet imagine. We must now find the fortitude to endure severe changes to our lifestyles and also to exert strong pressure on the corporate and political powers that be to create needed changes in how our societies are organized. Corporate profiteering that seriously endangers future generations, our ancestors of the future, is no longer morally acceptable.

But the dangers to our world are actually a wonderful opportunity to enrich our relationship to time and to beings of the future, to deepen the experience and worthiness of being human by taking on guardianship of our world. From the perspective of bodhisattva practice, living in challenging times is a bounteous gift. Everything we do now to add insight, caring, and beneficial activity to our world can actually make a huge difference to the planet's environment and to future generations of humans and other beings, all under threat in the current situation.

We have a responsibility to take care of our own garbage. The almost inconceivable time-frame of nuclear waste forces us to envision a new model of guardianship. Joanna Macy's Nuclear Guardianship Project realized that the current international nuclear policy makers seem unable to grapple with the time spans involved, as they plan burial of nuclear waste deep within the earth in containers that will inevitably leak and release their contents into the biosphere, long before the poisons have become neutralized. Responsible nuclear guardianship requires, instead, that nuclear waste be contained in retrievable, monitorable storage, so that leaks can be repaired and so that any possibly relevant future technologies might be applied to reducing and containing their radioactivity. Further, the nuclear disaster in northern Japan is evidence of the failure of regulatory systems to protect the public from this deadly technology. Such highly inadequate safety regulations, implemented with industry influence, have been documented elsewhere as well, resulting in so far less dangerous nuclear accidents, including in the United States. Even if no new nuclear power is utilized, the poison of the current wastes will be unimaginably persistent.

Similar considerations apply to our current use of fossil fuels. When the serious environmental costs are factored in, and the massive subsidies given to these industries by corrupted politicians are discounted, these energy sources are not at all economically sound, despite the claims of the corporate mass media. We require a strong international effort and investment to develop and implement sustainable, renewable energy technologies such as solar, wind, geothermal, and biomass, all feasible.

Apart from the need to transform global energy policies, in our everyday lives we can find ways to include and relate to friends in future generations. Meeting our ancestors of the future involves appreciating our multiple lineages and deciding how to act intentionally to strengthen the things that remain, to convey the heart of worthy traditions to their future ancestors. We also can envision, dream, and send messages to our future ancestors, recognizing the support they give us now, as they look back at us and consider our lives. We may imagine and forge personal bonds to particular future ancestors. As we take responsibility to do whatever we each can to make the world a more welcoming place for those who follow, they are watching us.

Our ancestors of the future are waiting to give us their gratitude.

Collective Karma and Systemic Responses to Climate Disruption

For Buddhists to respond appropriately to the calamities that have only started to befall us all from global climate disruption caused by human activities, we will need to rethink the common misunderstandings of karma that have prevailed in Buddhist Asia. The teaching of karma has been frequently misused in Asian history to rationalize injustice and blame the victims of societal oppression. The popular version of this includes that people born into poverty or disability deserve their situation because of misdeeds in past lives. Such views have themselves caused great harm.

This ignorance has also arisen in the face of human atrocities, the equivalent of saying that people in the World Trade Towers on 9/11 deserved to die because their previous karma brought them to be there that day, or victims of Hurricane Katrina deserved their fate because their past lives led them to live near failing levees. If we look fully at causes and conditions, the events of 9/11 cannot be separated from the unfortunate history of the Middle East and the complexities of the United States' and other nations' roles therein. The damage done by Hurricane Katrina cannot be separated from such factors as hurricanes intensifying due to climate change, the long history of American slavery and racism, and the complicated conditions through which the federal government in place at the time willfully disregarded warnings about the inadequacy of the levees.

THE KARMA OF INTERCONNECTED NONSELF

Inflation of the effects of individual karma and lack of acknowledgment of collective karma ignore the basic Buddhist teachings of nonself and interconnectedness. *Anātman* (nonself) is axiomatic to Buddhism, that all merely individual selves are empty and lack inherent, substantial existence. True "Self" is the whole interconnected web of phenomena, depicted in the seventh-century Chinese Huayan Buddhist school with the image of Indra's net, an intricate weave of connected interstices, each particular point of which completely reflects the totality of the vast network of being.[171] The application of Huayan thought to our environmental context has been clear to many modern Buddhists. Buddhist and environmental scholar Stephanie Kaza, for instance, extends the metaphor of this jeweled net:

> If you tug on any one of the lines of the net—for example through loss of species or habitat—it affects all the other lines.... If clouded jewels are cleared up (rivers cleaned, wetlands restored), life across the web is enhanced. Because the web of interdependence includes not only the actions of all beings but also their thoughts, the intention of the actor becomes a critical factor in determining what happens.[172]

Thus karma cannot be merely individual when our actions and intentions are so thoroughly connected with the whole environment. And our efforts toward collective, systemic responses have positive effects we cannot clearly measure or anticipate.

Going back to the thirteenth century, Dōgen described the mutually beneficial impact of one person engaged in Buddha's meditation interacting with all phenomenal objects: grasses and trees, fences and walls, tiles and pebbles. Each element offers spiritual guidance for all others. He went so far as to say that with one person's sitting, "all space in the universe completely becomes enlightenment."[173] Clearly the karmic impact of the individual expressed in such teachings is not separate from a whole range of collective events. The dependent arising of each phenomenal event is due to a complex web of causes and conditions. Collective entities, such as a nation or a culture or a species, no less than individual human beings, have patterns of conditioned activities based on prior group actions. Multitudes of layers and levels of such communities are always involved.

MODERN BUDDHISM AND REJECTION OF THE FOUR NOBLE TRUTHS

The failure of the teaching of individual karma was recognized by the great leader of the Untouchables, Bhimrao Ambedkar, when he led the mass conversion to Buddhism of over three million Indian "Untouchables" starting in 1956. Ambedkar chose Buddhism for his fellow Untouchables after his careful study of world religions, but he rejected the Four Noble Truths. He felt that this teaching blamed individuals for suffering and ignored "the heartless action of others and the systemic injustice of such social arrangements as the caste system. The idea of karma, he believed, would only accentuate the self-blame of the Untouchables instead of placing the blame on the caste system itself."[174] The second Noble Truth says that suffering has a cause, which is grasping based on desire, with resulting harmful karma. But this pattern of grasping and attachment is not necessarily, or even primarily, a simply individual matter.

Unfortunately, Ambedkar died less than two months after this mass conversion, but the Untouchables, now sometimes called Dalit, remain strong, constituting more than 90 percent of India's eight million Buddhists (as of the 2001 census). Today the Dalit Buddhists maintain vital teaching and organizations, and a robust socially engaged practice.[175] Other modern Asian Buddhists have also seen the necessity of responding collectively to sources of suffering. For example, the Sarvodaya Shramadana movement in Sri Lanka has benefited villagers and reduced suffering by seeing the need to inquire into collective needs in the villages and mobilizing a communal response through appropriate work projects and ongoing communication.[176]

Responding coherently to global climate change requires our recognition of the reality of collective karma, not seeing karma as merely individual. Individuals who practice recycling and modest use of resources contribute to helping the situation, but no matter how many individuals do so personally, the wider systemic causes also demand collective action to produce any significant effect. Without major development of sustainable mass energy sources and governmental regulation of industrial and energy corporations to lessen their negative impact on the environment, the climate disruption will worsen, despite the personal practices of well-meaning individuals. Just as the causes for the situation are collective, a cooperative, systemic response is required, addressing the societal as well as individual karmic conditions for pollution and excessive carbon emissions. A Buddhist response now must involve study of systemic conditions for damage. In the case of climate change, this may include a wide range of practical study, along with traditional Buddhist environmental perspectives.

DISASTER CAPITALISM AND SYSTEMIC CHANGE

Many current works may serve as resources for raising awareness and responding to systemic causes. Information on the scientific realities and also suggestions for solutions are available on the website "Ecological Buddhism: A Buddhist Response to Global Warming."[177] Other examples include Al Gore's film *An Inconvenient Truth*, with its vivid depictions of the scientific facts about climate change. Another perspective is offered by Naomi Klein's *The Shock Doctrine*, with its analysis of the workings of what she calls "disaster capitalism," in which corporate profiteers enrich themselves in the midst of disasters, which they sometimes encourage as well as exploit. She discusses how this applies to environmental as well as political crises, including the nonresponse to those endangered by Hurricane Katrina.[178] A rethinking of our current economic systems may be necessary for addressing global climate issues, which are not separate from the current global economic crisis. From the perspective of Buddhist "right view," no single ideological explanation by itself can encompass the total range of causes from many realms. Still, Buddhist practice confirms that awareness is transformative, both individually and collectively. Raising awareness, our own as well as that of all around us, will help make possible the larger changes that are needed.

As Al Gore among others has clarified, the situation of global climate change is urgent. Rapid systemic changes to use sustainable energy sources and stop emitting carbon are critical. Writings by the great American Zen thinker and poet Gary Snyder have illuminated the plight of our environment and an approach to response. He clarifies the need for a wide perspective, "The larger view is one that can acknowledge the pain and beauty of this complexly interrelated world."[179] Snyder addresses the harm to the planet from "the highly organized societies and corporate economies of the world. Thousands of species of animals, and tens of thousands of species of plants, may become extinct in the next century. To nourish living beings we must not be content simply to have a virtuous diet." Collective, systemic response is vital.

PERSONAL RESPONSE TO SYSTEMIC KARMA

Buddhist teaching, with its cosmological view of many arrays of buddha fields throughout vast reaches of time, may also provide us a wider, useful temporal horizon now. Buddhist cosmology suggests beginningless and endless cycles of kalpas or ages, perhaps even translatable as many cycles of Big Bangs, past and future. Snyder has employed the standard Zen image of our heads on fire, the "great matter of life and death," used commonly as a challenge to individual Zen students. Now the whole planet has its head on fire. Going back to the sixties, Snyder has been saying that we need to act in the current situation as if our heads are on fire, but also we need to respond with care, without feeling frantic or frenzied.[180] Even amid an urgent crisis, it is most effective to act in a calm, deliberate manner. The systemic social changes that will help mitigate the worst effects of climate change will require persistent attention and response to be realized.

Returning to the individual level, Buddhist practice is excellent preparation for the inevitable damage likely to occur around us. The harm already triggered may at least be lessened by systemic responses, as well as by our own immediate response to the suffering involved. Meditative practice helps individuals to develop more calm and patience, a wider capacity to be helpful in the face of distress. In the midst of the immediacy of the next Hurricane Katrina or Gulf oil spew, the specifics of which will likely not be apparent beforehand, the resource of our practice experience will allow each of us to be more skillful and flexible in responding to the suffering around us. And individual responses will be more helpful as we are willing to face our connection with the collective nature of the problem and its creation. We can respond individually to crises, but we must also work together to create societal responses to all the systemic factors that have brought trouble to this world.

Enlightened Patriotism and
Right Livelihood

NONSEPARATION AND PATRIOTISM

WE MAY FULLY celebrate and proclaim the merits of our own traditions, our own nation, or any of the various groups with which we identify, while still appreciating the positive qualities in others. One of the most fundamental principles of Buddhism is nonseparation. We are in reality deeply interconnected with all beings in ways we cannot perceive or imagine. It is possible to fully appreciate diversity and differences, while at the same time seeing how all beings function within a deeper sameness. All people in the world are the same in having needs and feelings, in wanting to love and be loved. We can learn deep respect for the special qualities of others and share together with them what is worthy of mutual appreciation.

Born and raised in the United States, I love many facets of my country, such as awe-inspiring mountains, rugged shorelines, and vibrant, culturally rich and ethnically diverse cities. I love rock and roll, jazz, baseball, and many Hollywood movies. Interestingly, these are the products of American culture that are prized in foreign countries as well.

The Buddhist ideal of universal awakening is supported by the American democratic principles of liberty and justice for all, equal justice under the law, and the unalienable right to life, liberty, and the pursuit of happiness. These American values are illuminated, in turn, by the Buddhist wish: May all beings be happy. True peace and justice, or happiness, needs to be shared with all people. Genuine national security cannot forever be maintained through the oppression of peoples we denigrate as "other." Enlightened patriotism depends on including all beings and on fearless openness to truth. We can stand for our own truth with dignified calm and wholeness and without stridency, while listening and learning from others. Truly inclusive patriotism, dedicated to universal freedom, would not make anybody into some evil other to subjugate.

RIGHT LIVELIHOOD AS AN ETHICAL VALUE

One of the most relevant Buddhist teachings for our modern situation is right livelihood. This early Buddhist value has strong implications for enhancing the implementation of ideals of freedom and liberation, and for truly providing that all beings may be happy. Right livelihood was taught by the Buddha as part of the eightfold path, which offers practical guidance in how to live with awareness and compassion, so as to fulfill the third Noble Truth of the end of suffering. Along with right livelihood, these eight are right view, thought, speech, action, effort, mindfulness, and concentration. These eight "rights" do not emphasize right as opposed to wrong views, wrong speech, and so on, but a spirit of uprightness and truth around studying and asking questions about each of these issues. Right livelihood in early Buddhist teaching referred to not pursuing harmful occupations, such as trading in weapons or intoxicants, or killing animals, or making a living through deception or cheating others.[181]

The spirit of right livelihood is to support oneself and one's family by honorable means that are not harmful but helpful to others and oneself. Right livelihood requires an activity in accord with the criteria of precepts, thereby supporting life rather than killing, generosity rather than theft, truthfulness instead of lies, awareness over intoxication, and hopefully that reflects respect for all beings. Right livelihood is supported by some knowledge of the consequences of one's work, to know whether the product at the end of one's assembly line will be used constructively or otherwise. Another criteria would be the pace of the work, whether the activity allows us the space to be mindful as we work. Even if the work involves the complexities of multitasking, can we still fully engage with awareness each of the shifting activites involved?

From the fundamental perspective of right livelihood, people should have some means to support themselves through meaningful activity that allows them the human integrity and dignity to employ their interests and express their abilities with vitality and creative energy. Right livelihood work would contribute constructively to people's communities. Even for so-called menial or unglamorous service jobs, workers have the right to make a living through dignified, constructive work. I have heard anecdotes and also witnessed kindly bus drivers, grocery cashiers, or shop clerks who through attentiveness and everyday kindness have inspired bodhisattva-like awareness in those they engage, and thus modeled right livelihood for all. In whatever job we are doing now in the world, even with its imperfections, we can bring our kindness, uprightness, and attentiveness to that situation.

RIGHT LIVELIHOOD AS A SOCIETAL CRITERIA

Right livelihood can be applied on a societal as well as personal level to examine systemic and economic organization. People who work with diligence and honesty should be able to support themselves and their families through their work. The "living wage" movement is an attempt to support this ideal, asking that all who work wholeheartedly be supported at a minimal level sufficient to insure livelihood. This reasonable standard has become more difficult in our current economy, when the interests of corporate profits have been given legal and electoral precedence over the well-being of the citizenry. How will our society respond to the extreme and increasing disparity between the income of corporate CEOs and the masses of working people?[182] Right livelihood and the opportunities for dignified, productive, and sustaining employment would seem one appropriate assessment of a healthy society's ethical standards. How can our society develop jobs that help support constructive development and necessary awareness for the future of the world?

The original Buddhist right livelihood standard implies strong disapproval of all war and violence, with its sanction against work involving

weaponry. Buddhist teachings certainly indicate a preference for nonvio-
lence and resolving international conflicts through diplomatic mediation
rather than aggression. But in the realities of the modern, post-Nazi Holocaust world, no less than the "post-9/11 world," contemporary Buddhists
may well acknowledge the necessity for military forces to be used for genuine self-defense, to resist terrorist attacks and hostile occupations, and as
peace-keeping forces in situations where genocide or other major harm
is being committed. Many people become soldiers through a genuine,
self-sacrificing desire to serve their country. While I deeply wish for complete nuclear disarmament, in the meantime I am very glad that there is a
meditation group at the Air Force Academy and that our Air Force pilots
have training in meditative calm.[183] Further, professional soldiers trained
in self-reflection and insight practices are more likely to have the spiritual
fortitude to resist if ordered to commit acts contrary to international conventions about war and war crimes.

American president Dwight Eisenhower uttered an eerily prescient
warning in his farewell address in January 1961, concerning the then new
"conjunction of an immense military establishment and a large arms
industry. The total influence—economic, political, even spiritual—is felt
in every city, every State house, every office of the Federal government." In
the spirit of Jefferson's eternal vigilance, Eisenhower cautioned that:

> Our toil, resources and livelihood are all involved; so is the very
> structure of our society. In the councils of government, we must
> guard against the acquisition of unwarranted influence, whether
> sought or unsought, by the military industrial complex. The
> potential for the disastrous rise of misplaced power exists and
> will persist."[184]

The point of this warning concerning right livelihood was not merely
that a weapons industry exists. But the current domination over the American economy and government by arms corporations and their overwhelming lobbying of legislators, as warned against by Eisenhower, has resulted

in a situation where policy is made at the service of military might, rather than vice versa.

With all congressional districts impacted by potential base closures, all are dependent on military spending and the missile economy, like Jefferson was dependent on slavery. The waging of preemptive wars of aggression and proliferation of dangerous weaponry all go unchecked as weapons manufacturing gains dominance, and much other more constructive American manufacturing is shipped overseas to sites of cheap and often slave labor. In this situation right livelihood is an ethical and moral model for assessing a society's livelihood as well as an individual's, and it may serve as a principle for the renewal of foundational American ideals.

Many military people have demonstrated that soldiers can express right livelihood and noble self-sacrifice. The honorable service of soldiers has included speaking out, as Eisenhower did, against misuse of the military by politicians and via corruption from corporate arms merchants. Good soldiers have expressed the folly of the American systemic torture program, ineffective for intelligence gathering, and also constituting war crimes according to global and American law. On the other hand, many generals now are corrupted by taking positions with weapons contractors soon after retirement and exerting self-interested influence on policy.[185]

ENACTING RIGHT LIVELIHOOD

How will principles of right livelihood come to be respected and enacted in the current situation? Buddhist teaching and experience demonstrates that awareness has transformative power. The founding of the Buddhist order of monks and nuns by the historical Buddha in fifth-century B.C.E. India included an intention to reform society over time by providing an ongoing countercultural alternative to the usual worldly greed, hatred, and confusion of societal systems. The example of sangha has indeed helped at times to reduce suffering and inform human societies historically.

How do we bring compassionate and clear awareness to the frustration and greed of our modern world? There is never only one right response.

Rather, awareness informed by concern for nonharming and the benefit of all beings can allow readiness to express creative and helpful individual responses, which may be different for each person. Hopelessness, though readily available amid the current human confusion and massive corruption, is not an appropriate or accurate response. All actions have consequences, everything changes, and none can foretell how transformation will arise, either personally or societally. After much effort, South African apartheid ended, seemingly suddenly and relatively nonviolently; similarly the Berlin Wall fell; and massive nonviolent demonstrations in Egypt unseated a dictator and offered the possibility of true democracy. Modern corporate corruption, exploitation, and militarism shall also pass, unfortunately with much devastation likely in its wake. Responsive concern for right livelihood, on all levels, will certainly help.

Chapter Sources

"Zazen as Inquiry" is adapted from a Dharma talk at Mountain Source Sangha, Bolinas, January 11, 2003.

"Zazen Mind and Transformative Function" is adapted from talks given at Ancient Dragon Zen Gate, Chicago, March 12 and May 6, 2007.

"Hongzhi, Dōgen, and the Background of Shikan Taza" is adapted from the preface to John Daido Loori, ed., *The Art of Just Sitting* (Boston: Wisdom Publications, 2002).

"Zazen as Enactment Ritual" is adapted from my article in Steven Heine and Dale Wright, eds., *Zen Ritual: Studies of Zen Theory in Practice* (New York: Oxford University Press, 2007), 167–184.

"The Gateway to Repose and Joy" is adapted from a talk at Ancient Dragon Zen Gate, Chicago, May 18, 2009.

"Reflections on Translating Dōgen" is adapted from an article published in "Dharma Eye," Journal of the Sōtō Zen Education Center, 2000.

"The Practice of Genjōkōan" is adapted from a Dharma talk given at Clouds in Water Zen Center, St. Paul, Minnesota, January 8, 2006.

"Practicing the Awesome Presence of Active Buddhas" is adapted from a Sunday morning Dharma talk at Clouds in Water Zen Center, St. Paul, Minnesota, November 4, 2007; supplemented with material from a talk at Udumbara Sangha, Evanston, Illinois, May 30, 2004.

"Expressing the Dream within the Dream" is adapted from a Dharma talk at Ancient Dragon Zen Gate, Chicago, January 25, 2010.

"Zen Rule-Bending and the Training of Pure Hearts" is adapted from portions of my article "Sacred Fools and Monastic Rules: Zen Rule-

Bending and the Training for Pure Hearts" in Bruno Barnhart and Joseph Wong, eds., *Purity of Heart and Contemplation: A Monastic Dialogue between Christian and Asian Traditions* (New York: Continuum, 2001), pp. 151–164. This article was based on a paper presented at a highly stimulating and inspiring week-long interfaith dialogue held at New Camaldoli Hermitage, Big Sur, California, in June 2000.

"Speak Softly, Speak Softly" is adapted from a Dharma talk given at Green Gulch Farm, July 20, 2003.

"Dōgen's Five-Part Approach to Zazen" is adapted from a Dharma talk at Ancient Dragon Zen Gate, Chicago, May 13, 2008. Portions of this chapter also appear in my article "Dōgen's Approach to Training in *Eihei Kōroku*" in Steven Heine, ed., *Dōgen: Textual And Historical Studies* (New York: Oxford University Press, 2011).

"Almost Not Confused by Self" is adapted from a Dharma talk at Ancient Dragon Zen Gate, Chicago, March 15, 2009.

"Readying the Ox" is adapted from a Dharma talk at Ancient Dragon Zen Gate, Chicago, April 6, 2009.

"Dropping Body-Mind, and the Pregnant Temple Pillars" is adapted from a Dharma talk given at Mountain Source Sangha, Bolinas, February 9, 2002.

"Practice-Realization-Expression" is adapted from a Dharma talk given at Green Gulch Farm, May 18, 2003.

"Rumi's Words of Love" is adapted from a Dharma talk given at Ancient Dragon Zen Gate, Chicago, October 1, 2007, the day after Rumi's 800th birthday.

"Bob Dylan's Visions of Zen Mind" is adapted from a Dharma talk at Ancient Dragon Zen Gate, Chicago, April 2, 2007, a week after the Minneapolis conference I mention.

"Mary Oliver: Making Yourself into a Light" is adapted from a Dharma talk given at Ancient Dragon Zen Gate, Chicago, August 4, 2008.

"Gary Snyder and Wild Practice" is adapted from notes from Dharma talks given at Ancient Dragon Zen Gate, Chicago, in August and September 2008.

"Liberation and Eternal Vigilance" is adapted from a Dharma talk given at Green Gulch Farm, July 3, 1994, in celebration of the Fourth of July.

"Consumerism and the Precepts" is adapted from a Dharma talk given at Green Gulch Farm, September 9, 2001. This talk was given two days before the September 11 attack in 2001. What I said still applies in the post-9/11 world, and perhaps more so.

"Meeting Our Ancestors of the Future" is adapted and updated from an article published in *Shambhala Sun*, September 1996, as "Now is the Past of the Future," which was based on a paper presented at the Future Generations Forum in Kyoto, Japan, 1994.

"Collective Karma and Systemic Responses to Climate Disruption" is adapted from an article in the book *A Buddhist Response to the Climate Emergency*, edited by John Stanley, David Loy, and Gyurme Dorje (Boston: Wisdom Publications, 2009), pp. 187–193.

"Enlightened Patriotism and Right Livelihood" includes some material from previously published articles. These include my article "American Buddhist Values and the Practice of Enlightened Patriotism" in the Fall 2004 issue of *Turning Wheel*, the journal of the Buddhist Peace Fellowship (which in turn was an expanded version of a talk I gave June 5, 2004, at *Tricycle*'s "Change Your Mind Day," at the Ellipse in front of the White House, Washington, D.C.). Another is "Unalienable Rights, Mahāyāna Inclusivity, and Right Livelihood," from the issue "The Value of Buddhism for Contemporary Western Society" of the journal *Bridges: An Interdisciplinary Journal of Theology, Philosophy, History, and Science*, Volume 13, number 3/4; Fall/Winter 2006.

REPRINT PERMISSIONS

Endnotes

1   Bob Dylan, "It's Alright Ma (I'm Only Bleeding)" www.bobdylan.com/songs ©
    1965 by Warner Bros. Inc.; renewed 1993 by Special Rider Music.
2   Wallace Stevens, *The Collected Poems* (New York: Vintage Books, 1990), pp. 462–
    463; originally published by Knopf, 1954.
3   "A Vision of the Last Judgment," written 1810, in Geoffrey Keynes, ed., *Blake Com-
    plete Writings* (London: Oxford University Press, 1966), p. 617.
4   Dōgen comments on this story in "The Acupuncture Needle of Zazen" (Zazen-
    shin) in *Shōbōgenzō*. See Carl Bielefeldt, *Dōgen's Manuals of Zen Meditation* (Berke-
    ley: University of California Press, 1988), pp. 190–200; or "The Point of Zazen," in
    Kazuaki Tanahashi, ed., *Treasury of the True Dharma Eye: Zen Master Dogen's Shobo
    Genzo*, vol. 1 (Boston: Shambhala, 2010), pp. 303–314. The story also appears in
    "Kōkyō" (Ancient Mirror); see Tanahashi, *Treasury of the True Dharma Eye*, vol. 1,
    pp. 205–221; and with Dōgen's verse comments in Taigen Dan Leighton and Sho-
    haku Okumura, trans., *Dōgen's Extensive Record: A Translation of the Eihei Kōroku*
    (Boston: Wisdom Publications, 2004), pp. 561–562. However, the quotations from
    this "Zazenshin" text that follow are based on a draft translation, not yet published,
    by Shohaku Okumura.
5   Leighton and Okumura, *Dōgen's Extensive Record*, p. 533.
6   See Kōshō Uchiyama, *Opening the Hand of Thought: Foundations of Zen Buddhist
    Practice* (Boston: Wisdom Publications, 2004).
7   For an accessible treatment of Yogācāra teaching, see Tagawa Shun'ei, *Living
    Yogācāra: An Introduction to Consciousness-Only Buddhism* (Boston: Wisdom Pub-
    lications, 2009).
8   For versions of this story with Dōgen's comment, see Leighton and Okumura,
    Dōgen's Extensive Record, pp. 327–328, 466–467.
9   Bob Dylan, "Stuck Inside of Mobile with the Memphis Blues Again" www.bobdylan
    .com/songs © 1966 by Dwarf Music; renewed 1994 by Dwarf Music.
10 See Shunryū Suzuki, *Branching Streams Flow in the Darkness: Zen Talks on the
    Sandokai* (Berkeley: University of California Press, 1999). See also Carl Bielefeldt,
    Griffith Foulk, Taigen Leighton, and Shohaku Okumura, trans., "Harmony of
    Difference and Equality," in Taigen Dan Leighton with Yi Wu, trans., *Cultivating*

the Empty Field: The Silent Illumination of Zen Master Hongzhi (Boston: Tuttle and Co., 2000), pp. 74–75.

11 Shitou does not use the Chinese characters for "shikan taza," but the reference to the iconic image of Bodhidharma just sitting, or "wall-gazing," in his cold cave with a quilt over his head is unquestionable. For "Soanka" see Leighton with Wu, *Cultivating the Empty Field*, pp. 72–73.

12 Leighton and Okumura, *Dōgen's Extensive Record*, p. 93.

13 In Dōgen's "Fukanzazengi"; see Leighton and Okumura, *Dōgen's Extensive Record*, pp. 532–535; or Kazuaki Tanahashi, ed., *Enlightenment Unfolds: The Essential Teachings of Zen Master Dōgen* (Boston: Shambhala, 1999), p. 55.

14 The Sōtō lineage almost died out in China a century before Hongzhi, but was revived by Touzi Yiqing (1032–1083; Jpn.: Tōsu Gisei), who brought a background in Huayan studies to enliven Sōtō philosophy. Touzi's successor, Furong Daokai (1043–1118; Jpn.: Fuyō Dōkai), was a model of integrity, and he solidified and developed the forms for the Sōtō monastic community. It remained for Hongzhi, two generations after Furong Daokai, to fully express Sōtō praxis.

15 Leighton with Wu, *Cultivating the Empty Field*, pp. 67–68. For more on Hongzhi and his meditation teaching, see also Morton Schlütter, "Silent Illumination, Kung-an Introspection, and the Competition for Lay Patronage in Sung Dynasty Ch'an" in Peter Gregory and Daniel Getz, eds., *Buddhism in the Sung* (Honolulu: University of Hawai'i Press, 1999), pp. 109–147.

16 Leighton with Wu, *Cultivating the Empty Field*, pp. 41–42.

17 Ibid., p. 31.

18 Ibid., p. 30

19 Ibid., p. 55.

20 Ibid., p. 68.

21 Ibid., p. 43.

22 Schlütter, "Silent Illumination, Kung-an Introspection" in Gregory and Getz, *Buddhism in the Sung*, pp. 109–110.

23 Leighton with Wu, *Cultivating the Empty Field*, p. 55.

24 Steven Heine, *Dōgen and the Kōan Tradition: A Tale of Two Shōbōgenzō Texts* (Albany: State University of New York Press, 1994).

25 Shohaku Okumura and Taigen Daniel Leighton, trans., *The Wholehearted Way: A Translation of Eihei Dōgen's "Bendōwa" with Commentary by Kōsho Uchiyama Roshi* (Boston: Charles Tuttle and Co., 1997), pp. 22–23.

26 Tanahashi, vol. 1, *Treasury of the True Dharma Eye*, p. 29.

27 Leighton and Okumura, *Dōgen's Extensive Record*, Dharma hall discourse 432, pp. 386–388.

28 Ibid., Dharma hall discourse 319, pp. 292–293.

29 Ibid., Dharma hall discourse 337, pp. 305.

30 See Leighton with Wu, *Cultivating the Empty Field*, pp. 20–23.

31 See, for example, Richard Payne, ed., *Tantric Buddhism in East Asia* (Boston: Wisdom Publications, 2006).

32 Robert Thurman, "Vajra Hermeneutics," in Donald Lopez, ed., *Buddhist Hermeneutics* (Honolulu: University of Hawai'i Press, 1988), p. 122.

33 Thomas Kasulis, "Truth Words: The Basis of Kūkai's Theory of Interpretation," in Lopez, ed., *Buddhist Hermeneutics*, pp. 260, 271.

34 Okumura and Leighton, *The Wholehearted Way*, pp. 26–27.

35 Foreword by Ikkō Narasaki Roshi in Taigen Daniel Leighton and Shohaku Okumura, trans., *Dōgen's Pure Standards for the Zen Community: A Translation of Eihei Shingi* (Albany: State University of New York Press, 1996), p. x.

36 For a full discussion of the textual variants of "Fukanzazengi," and its indebtedness to Chinese Chan sources, see Carl Bielefeldt, *Dōgen's Manuals of Zen Meditation*. All following quotes from "Fukanzazengi" are from Leighton and Okumura, *Dōgen's Extensive Record*, pp. 533–534.

37 Leighton and Okumura, *Dōgen's Pure Standards for the Zen Community*, pp. 63–64.

38 Carl Bielefeldt, *Dōgen's Manuals of Zen Meditation*, pp. 190–200. See also Tanahashi, *Treasury of the True Dharma Eye*, vol. 1, pp. 303–314.

39 See Leighton and Okumura, *Dōgen's Extensive Record*, pp. 19–25.

40 Ibid., p. 292.

41 Ibid., p. 404.

42 For Dōgen's attitude toward this element of the traditional Chan practice schedule, see Ibid., Dharma hall discourse 193, p. 210.

43 Ibid., p. 472.

44 Okumura and Leighton, *The Wholehearted Way*, pp. 30–31.

45 Tanahashi, *Treasury of the True Dharma Eye*, vol. 1, pp. 273–274. See the chapter "Practicing the Awesome Presence of Active Buddhas" later in this book.

46 Leighton and Okumura, *Dōgen's Extensive Record*, p. 124. For other examples of how Dōgen uses *jōdō* or Dharma hall discourses as enactment rituals, see Taigen Dan Leighton, "The *Lotus Sutra* as a Source for Dōgen's Discourse Style," in Richard Payne and Taigen Dan Leighton, eds., *Discourse and Ideology in Medieval Japanese Buddhism* (London: RoutledgeCurzon, 2006), pp. 195–217.

47 Dōgen recounts and comments on this story in Dharma hall discourses 8 and 319, and calls Mazu's teaching "most intimate." See Leighton and Okumura, *Dōgen's Extensive Record*, pp. 79, 292–293. Parts of this story are included in cases 30 and 33 of the koan anthology *Mumonkan* (Gateless Barrier). See Zenkei Shibayama, *The Gateless Barrier: Zen Comments on the Mumonkan* (Boston: Shambhala, 2000), pp. 214–222, 235–239.

48 This story is included as case 19 in the koan anthology *Mumonkan* (Gateless Barrier). See Shibayama, *The Gateless Barrier*, pp. 140–147. The story is also cited by Dōgen as case 19 in his collection of three hundred koans without any of his own commentary in his *Shinji* (or Mana, i.e. Chinese) *Shōbōgenzō*, not to be confused with the more noted work *Shōbōgenzō* with long essays, often commenting at length on koans. See Kazuaki Tanahashi and John Daido Loori, trans., *The True Dharma Eye: Zen Master Dōgen's Three Hundred Kōans*, with Commentary and Verse by John Daido Loori (Boston: Shambhala, 2005), pp. 26–27.

49   Leighton with Wu, *Cultivating the Empty Field*, p. 30.

50   Ibid., p. 37.

51   Thomas Cleary, ed. and trans., *Timeless Spring: A Soto Zen Anthology* (Tokyo: Weatherhill, 1980), pp. 112–119.

52   See Shohaku Okumura, trans., and ed., *Dōgen Zen* (Kyoto: Kyoto Soto Zen Center, 1988), pp. 43–135. For more on Menzan, see David Riggs, "The Zen of Books and Practice: The Life of Menzan Zuihō and His Reformation of Sōtō Zen," in Steven Heine and Dale Wright, eds., *Zen Masters* (New York: Oxford University Press, 2010), pp. 147–181.

53   Okumura, *Dōgen Zen*, pp. 51–73.

54   See the excellent, highly illuminating article by Victor Sōgen Hori, "Kōan and Kenshō in the Rinzai Zen Curriculum," in Steven Heine and Dale Wright, eds., *The Kōan: Texts and Contexts in Zen Buddhism* (New York: Oxford University Press, 2000), pp. 280–315.

55   For Dongshan's "Song of the Precious Mirror Samādhi," see Leighton with Wu, *Cultivating the Empty Field*, pp. 76–77.

56   See "Fukanzazengi," in Leighton and Okumura, *Dōgen's Extensive Record*, p. 534.

57   See Arthur Braverman, *Living and Dying in Zazen: Five Zen Masters of Modern Japan* (New York: Weatherhill, 2003), pp. 45–47.

58   Norman Waddell and Masao Abe, trans., *The Heart of Dōgen's Shōbōgenzō* (Albany: State University of New York Press, 2002), p. 46.

59   Leighton with Wu, *Cultivating the Empty Field*, p. 46.

60   Okumura and Leighton, *The Wholehearted Way*, p. 22.

61   Leighton and Okumura, *Dōgen's Extensive Record*, pp. 238–239.

62   The renditions of "Genjōkōan" in this chapter all are based on the translation in Tanahashi, *Treasury of the True Dharma Eye*, vol. 1, pp. 29–33. Other good translations include: Shohaku Okumura, *Realizing Genjōkōan* (Boston: Wisdom Publications, 2010), with extensive, very helpful commentary; Waddell and Abe, *The Heart of Dōgen's Shōbōgenzō*, pp. 39–45; Thomas Cleary, trans., *Shōbōgenzō: Zen Essays by Dōgen* (Honolulu: University of Hawaii Press, 1986), pp. 32–35; and Francis Cook. *Sounds of Valley Streams: Enlightenment in Dōgen's Zen* (Albany: State University of New York Press, 1989), pp. 65–69.

63   For all quotes from this text see, Tanahashi, *Treasury of the True Dharma Eye*, vol. 1, pp. 260–275.

64   See Gene Reeves, *The Lotus Sutra* (Boston: Wisdom Publications, 2008), pp. 279–281. See also Taigen Dan Leighton, *Visions of Awakening Space and Time: Dōgen and the Lotus Sutra* (New York: Oxford University Press, 2007).

65   Bob Dylan, "Dignity" www.bobdylan.com/songs © 1991 by Special Rider Music.

66   See the chapter "Practice-Realization-Expression" in this book.

67   Bob Dylan, "Like a Rolling Stone" www.bobdylan.com/songs © 1965 by Warner Bros. Inc.; renewed 1993 by Special Rider Music.

68   Leighton and Okumura, *Dōgen's Extensive Record*, p. 533.

69 Thomas Cleary and J.C. Cleary, trans., *The Blue Cliff Record* (Boulder: Shambhala, 1977), pp. 395, 397.

70 Tanahashi, *Treasury of the True Dharma Eye*, vol. 1, pp. 431–438. All the following quotes from this essay are from this translation.

71 See Bernard Faure, *Visions of Power: Imagining Medieval Japanese Buddhism* (Princeton: Princeton University Press, 1996).

72 Tanahashi, *Treasury of the True Dharma Eye*, vol. 1, p. 32.

73 Reeves, *The Lotus Sutra*, p. 83.

74 See Leighton and Okumura, *Dōgen's Pure Standards for the Zen Community.*

75 For full translation and comment see Steven Heine, *Shifting Shape, Shaping Text: Philosophy and Folklore in the Fox Kōan* (Honolulu: University of Hawaii Press, 1999), pp. 217–222.

76 Thomas Cleary, trans., *Sayings and Doings of Pai-Chang* (Los Angeles: Center Publications, 1978), p. 26.

77 See Yifa, *The Origins of Buddhist Monastic Codes in China: An Annotated Translation and Study of the Chanyuan Qinggui* (Honolulu: University of Hawaii Press, 2002).

78 For all citations to "The Pure Standards for the Temple Administrators," see Leighton and Okumura, *Dōgen's Pure Standards for the Zen Community*, pp. 139–147.

79 For a treatment of Maitreya and the six other major archetypal bodhisattvas of East Asian Buddhism, see Taigen Dan Leighton, *Faces of Compassion: Classic Bodhisattva Archetypes and Their Modern Expression* (Boston: Wisdom Publications, 2003). Maitreya was predicted by Śākyamuni to be the next, future Buddha, and exemplifies great patience and simple kindness. These bodhisattva figures are of questionable historicity, but they have pervaded Mahāyāna Buddhism as objects of veneration and also as archetypal models of approach to awakening practice to be incorporated and expressed by devotees.

80 Dōgen criticized, for example, the view that it is enough to understand about buddha nature without practice or observance of precepts in his writing "Bendōwa" in 1231. See Okumura and Leighton, *The Wholehearted Way*, pp. 32–34. Late in his career, Dōgen again emphasized the importance of ethics, for example in his essay "Jinshin Inga" (Deep Faith in Cause and Effect). See Francis Cook, *How to Raise an Ox: Zen Practice as Taught in Zen Master Dōgen's "Shobogenzo"* (Los Angeles: Center Publications, 1978), pp. 159–169.

81 Heine, *Dōgen and the Kōan Tradition.*

82 Leighton and Okumura, *Dōgen's Extensive Record*, pp. 215–216.

83 Yann Martell, *Life of Pi* (New York: Alfred A. Knopf, 2001).

84 See Leighton with Wu, *Cultivating the Empty Field*, pp. 76–77.

85 This story is recounted fully in several places by Dōgen, including the 1250 Dharma hall discourse 374 in *Eihei Kōroku*; see Leighton and Okumura, *Dōgen's Extensive Record*, pp. 328–329. It also appears as case 59 in Dōgen's collection of ninety kōans with his verse comments in volume nine of *Eihei Kōroku*, Ibid., pp. 575–576; in the *Shōbōgenzō* essay, "Henzan" (All-Inclusive Study), Tanahashi, *Treasury of the*

True Dharma Eye, vol. 2, p. 610; and in "Gyōbutsu Īgi" (The Awesome Presence of Active Buddhas), in Tanahashi, *Treasury of the True Dharma Eye*, vol. 1, pp. 261–262.

86   For a discussion of the bodhisattva of compassion, and her thousand hands and eyes, see Leighton, *Faces of Compassion*, pp. 167–209.

87   See case 54, Cleary, *The Book of Serenity* (Boston: Shambhala, 2005), pp. 229–232.

88   From "Like a Rolling Stone" in Dylan, *Lyrics, 1962–2001*, pp. 167–168.

89   Leighton and Okumura, *Dōgen's Extensive Record*, pp. 257–258.

90   See Leighton and Okumura, *Dōgen's Pure Standards for the Zen Community*.

91   Shunryu Suzuki, *Zen Mind, Beginner's Mind* (New York: Weatherhill, 1970), p. 32.

92   Leighton with Wu, *Cultivating the Empty Field*, pp. 72–73.

93   See Okumura and Leighton, *The Wholehearted Way*.

94   See Leighton, *Faces of Compassion*, pp. 167–204.

95   For translations of "Ūji," see Tanahashi, *Treasury of the True Dharma Eye*, vol. 1, pp. 104–111; Waddell and Abe, *Heart of Dōgen's Shōbōgenzō*, pp. 48–58; or Cleary, *Shōbōgenzō: Zen Essays by Dōgen*, pp. 102–110.

96   See Leighton with Wu, *Cultivating the Empty Field*, pp. 8–11, 62, 76–77; Alfonso Verdu, *Dialectical Aspects in Buddhist Thought: Studies in Sino-Japanese Mahāyāna Idealism* (Lawrence: Center for East Asian Studies, University of Kansas, 1974); and William Powell, trans., *The Record of Tung-shan* (Honolulu: University of Hawaii Press, 1986), pp. 61–65.

97   Leighton and Okumura, *Dōgen's Extensive Record*, pp. 105–106.

98   Yogi Berra, *The Yogi Book: "I Really Didn't Say Everything I Said!"* (New York: Workman Publishing, 1998), p. 52.

99   Cleary and Cleary, *The Blue Cliff Record*, case 16, p. 105.

100   See Waddell and Abe, *The Heart of Dōgen's Shōbōgenzō*, pp. 31–37; or Tanahashi, *Treasury of the True Dharma Eye*, vol. 1, pp. 34–38.

101   Leighton and Okumura, *Dōgen's Extensive Record*, pp. 565–566.

102   Ibid., pp. 377–378.

103   Reeves, *The Lotus Sutra*, p. 83.

104   Leighton and Okumura, *Dōgen's Extensive Record*, pp. 157–158.

105   See, for example, D. T. Suzuki, *Manual of Zen Buddhism* (New York: Grove Press, 1960), pp. 127–144.

106   See case 69, Thomas Cleary, trans., *The Book of Serenity*, pp. 290–294.

107   Leighton and Okumura, *Dōgen's Extensive Record*, p. 448.

108   See Okumura, *Realizing Genjōkōan*, pp. 86–88.

109   See Leighton with Wu, *Cultivating the Empty Field*, pp. 20–23.

110   See also case 31, Cleary, *The Book of Serenity*, pp. 137–139.

111   Leighton and Okumura, *Dōgen's Extensive Record*, p. 223.

112   Leighton with Wu, *Cultivating the Empty Field*, pp. 72–75.

113   Cleary, *The Book of Serenity*, pp. 390–393.

114   All excerpts from this teaching are from Leighton and Okumura, *Dōgen's Extensive Record*, pp. 519–522.

115   Ibid., p. 507.

116 For an insightful discussion of these aspects of love in Greek, see the inspiring sermon by Martin Luther King Jr, "Loving Your Enemies," November 17, 1957: http://www.mlkonline.net/enemies.html.

117 John Moyne and Coleman Barks, *Open Secret: Versions of Rumi* (Putney, Vt.: Threshold Books, 1984), p. 50.

118 Ibid., p. 36.

119 Ibid., p. 27.

120 Ibid., p. 31

121 Bob Dylan, "Visions of Johanna" www.bobdylan.com/songs © 1966 by Dwarf Music; renewed 1994 by Dwarf Music.

122 Apart from the many biographies, a number of useful critical studies of Dylan's work have been published. See, for example, Christopher Ricks, *Dylan's Visions of Sin* (New York: HarperCollins, 2003), an illuminating discussion of Dylan's poetics by a noted literature professor, but with only a few passing references to "Visions of Johanna." Stephen Scobie noticed the near-absence of comment on this song in his work, *Alias Bob Dylan* (Alberta: Red Deer College Press, 1991), so later self-published a useful short booklet, *Visions of Johanna;* see http://www.taxhelp.com/scobie-voj.html. Aidan Day, *Jokerman: Reading the Lyrics of Bob Dylan* (New York: Basil Blackwell, 1988), pp. 111–124, provides a critical analysis of the poetics of the song. Michael Gray, *Song & Dance Man III: The Art of Bob Dylan* (New York: Continuum, 2000), is a sometimes instructive tome of more than nine hundred pages with various scattered references to the song.

123 See Yanagi Sōetsu, *The Unknown Craftsman: A Japanese Insight into Beauty* (Tokyo, New York: Kodansha International, 1989).

124 See Robert Thurman, *The Holy Teaching of Vimalakīrti* (University Park, Pa.: Penn State University Press, 1976).

125 Bob Dylan, "Hurricane" www.bobdylan.com/songs © 1975 by Ram's Horn Music; renewed 2003 by Ram's Horn Music. I note that "Visions of Johanna," and most of Dylan's songs cited in this book, are from his work in the sixties, which is most commonly celebrated. However, I continue to appreciate Dylan's ongoing work, up through his fine CDs of the past decade. Eminent Dōgen and Zen scholar Steven Heine, in his book *Bargainin' For Salvation: Bob Dylan, A Zen Master?* (New York: Continuum, 2009), presents a Zen dialectical view of Dylan's famously shifting career. Heine sees Dylan's varying emphases as oscillating up through the nineties between prophetic moral certainty, as in both his protest and gospel periods, and on the other side periods of intense existential questioning. Heine sees Dylan's works from the mid-nineties on as representing a "Middle Way" synthesis including both questioning and conviction. This includes Dylan's *Time Out of Mind; Love and Theft; Modern Times;* and also *Together Through Life*, released after Heine's book was written.

126 See Suzuki, *Branching Streams Flow in the Darkness*. See also Bielefeldt, Foulk, Leighton, and Okumura, trans., "Harmony of Difference and Equality," in Leighton with Wu, *Cultivating the Empty Field*, pp. 74–75.

127 Gray, *Song & Dance Man III*, p. 154, and Scobie, *Visions of Johanna*, p. 12, respectively.

128 Keynes, *Blake Complete Writings*, pp. 112–115, 120–121, 218–219.

129 See Irving Stone, ed., *Dear Theo: The Autobiography of Vincent Van Gogh* (New York: Doubleday & Company, 1937), p. 478; and Cliff Edwards, *The Shoes of Van Gogh: A Spiritual and Artistic Journey to the Ordinary* (New York: The Crossroad Publishing Company, 2004), pp. 122, 133. Dr. Edwards is a Western theologian who also was a resident monk at the Rinzai Zen monastery Daitokuji in Kyoto. For his illuminating commentary on Van Gogh's spiritual art with comparisons to Zen Buddhist perspectives, in addition to *The Shoes of Van Gogh*, see also Cliff Edwards, *Van Gogh and God: A Creative Spiritual Quest* (Chicago: Loyola University Press, 1989).

130 In an early version of the song Dylan sang the line differently, and much more negatively, as "Knowing everything's gone which was owed," Gray, *Song & Dance Man III*, p. 489. But the version finally released on "Blonde on Blonde" in 1966 has "Everything's been returned," which also suggests the positive sense offered here.

131 Bob Dylan, "When You Gonna Wake Up?" www.bobdylan.com/songs © 1979 by Special Rider Music.

132 Bob Dylan, "Highlands" www.bobdylan.com/songs © 1997 by Special Rider Music.

133 Mary Oliver, *New and Selected Poems* (Boston: Beacon Press, 1992), p. 110.

134 Mary Oliver, *Why I Wake Early* (Boston: Beacon Press, 2004), pp. 34–35.

135 Oliver, *New and Selected Poems*, pp. 68–69.

136 See the "Fire Sermon," Ādittapariyāya-sutta, in Walpola Rahula, *What the Buddha Taught* (New York: Grove Press, 1959), pp. 95–97.

137 Tanahashi, *Treasury of the True Dharma Eye*, vol. 1, p. 270.

138 Oliver, *New and Selected Poems*, pp. 10–11.

139 Keynes, *Blake Complete Writings*, p. 442; and Peter Akroyd, *Blake: A Biography* (New York: Alfred A. Knopf, 1996), pp. 367–368.

140 Suzuki, *Zen Mind, Beginner's Mind*, pp. 29–31.

141 Jack Kerouac, *Dharma Bums* (New York: Grove Press, 1958).

142 Among Snyder's many works I especially admire Gary Snyder, *Earth House Hold: Technical Notes & Queries to Fellow Dharma Revolutionaries* (New York: A New Directions Book, 1969); and Gary Snyder, *The Real Work: Interviews & Talks 1964–1979* (New York: A New Directions Book, 1980). Other works I have greatly appreciated include: Gary Snyder, *Turtle Island* (New York: A New Directions Book, 1975); Gary Snyder, *Axe Handles* (San Francisco: North Point Press, 1983); Gary Snyder, *Left Out in the Rain: New Poems 1947–1985* (San Francisco: North Point Press, 1986); Gary Snyder, *A Place in Space: Ethics, Aesthetics, and Watersheds* (Washington, D.C.; Counterpoint, 1995); Gary Snyder, *Mountains and Rivers Without End* (Washington, D.C.; Counterpoint, 1996); and Gary Snyder, *Back on the Fire: Essays* (Berkeley: Counterpoint, 2007).

143 Gary Snyder, *The Practice of the Wild* (Berkeley: Counterpoint, 1990), pp. 99–100.

144 Ibid., p. 18. See also the chapter "Tawny Grammar," pp. 52–83.

145 Ibid., pp. 104–123. For Dōgen's "Mountains and Water Sutra," see Tanahashi, *Treasury of the True Dharma Eye*, vol. 1, pp. 154–164.

146 This and the remaining citations are from the chapter, "On the Path, Off the Trail," Snyder, *The Practice of the Wild*, pp. 154–165.

147 See Leighton and Okumura, *Dōgen's Pure Standards for the Zen Community;* and the chapter "Zen Rule-Bending and the Training for Pure Hearts" in this book.

148 See Cleary, *The Book of Serenity*, p. 281.

149 See Waddell and Abe, *Heart of Dōgen's Shōbōgenzō*, pp. 60–62.

150 Letters to William Short, 1791; and to George Logan, 1816. See Adrienne Koch and William Peden, eds., *The Life and Selected Writings of Thomas Jefferson* (New York: The Modern Library, 1944), p. 507.

151 Henry David Thoreau, *Walden: or, Life in the Woods* (New York: Vintage Books, 1991), p. 259. Originally published in 1854.

152 See David Loy, *The Great Awakening: A Buddhist Social Theory* (Boston: Wisdom Publications, 1983).

153 Translated by Taigen Dan Leighton and Kazuaki Tanahashi, in Kazuaki Tanahashi and Tensho David Schneider, eds., *Essential Zen* (HarperSanFrancisco, 1994), p. 132.

154 See Thurman, *The Holy Teaching of Vimalakīrti;* and Leighton, *Faces of Compassion*, pp. 275–304.

155 Bob Dylan, "It's Alright Ma (I'm Only Bleeding)" www.bobdylan.com/songs © 1965 by Warner Bros. Inc.; renewed 1993 by Special Rider Music.

156 Tanahashi, *Treasury of the True Dharma Eye*, vol. 1, p. 31.

157 Bob Dylan, "Dear Landlord" www.bobdylan.com/songs © 1968 by Dwarf Music; renewed 1996 by Dwarf Music.

158 Translated by Taigen Dan Leighton and Kazuaki Tanahashi, in *Udumbara* 3, no. 1 (1984), Minnesota Zen Meditation Center, pp. 27, 29.

159 See Joanna Macy, *World as Lover, World as Self* (Berkeley: Parallax Press, 1991); and Joanna Macy, *Widening Circles* (Gabriola Island B.C.: New Society Publishers, 2000).

160 For a clear refutation of recent calls for nuclear energy by Stewart Brand, see the article by Amory Lovins, "Stewart Brand's nuclear enthusiasm falls short on facts and logic," http://www.grist.org/article/2009–10–13-stewart-brands-nuclear-enthusiasm-falls-short-on-facts-and-logic.

161 From the *Philosophical Transactions of the Royal Society*, "Biological diversity in a changing world." See http://www.ecobuddhism.org/science/featured_articles1/stunning.

162 See Leighton with Wu, *Cultivating the Empty Field*, pp. 74–75, in which this phrase is rendered, "Do not pass your days and nights in vain."

163 James Green, trans., *The Recorded Sayings of Zen Master Joshu* (Boston: Shambhala, 1998), p. 21. For Dōgen's commentary see Leighton and Okumura, *Dōgen's Extensive Record*, pp. 242–243.

164 Thomas Cleary, trans., *The Flower Ornament Scripture* (Boston: Shambhala, 1984–1993), p. 1029.

165 See Tanahashi, *Treasury of the True Dharma Eye*, vol. 1, pp. 106–107; Waddell and Abe, *The Heart of Dōgen's Shōbōgenzō*, p. 51; Cleary, *Shōbōgenzō: Zen Essays by Dōgen*, p. 106.

166 Leighton with Wu, *Cultivating the Empty Field*, p. 49.

167 See Eihei Koso Hotsuganmon: http://www.ancientdragon.org/dharma/chants/#eihei_koso.

168 Reeves, *The Lotus Sutra*, pp. 279–281. For a detailed discussion of this story, including Dōgen's commentaries on it, see Leighton, *Visions of Awakening Space and Time*.

169 For a thorough academic treatment of this story and its historicity, see Albert Furtwangler, *Answering Chief Seattle* (Seattle: University of Washington Press, 1997).

170 Donald Rothberg, *The Engaged Spiritual Life: A Buddhist Approach to Transforming Ourselves and the World* (Boston: Beacon Press, 2006), p. 204.

171 See Garma C.C. Chang, *The Buddhist Teaching of Totality: The Philosophy of Hwa Yen Buddhism* (University Park, Pa.: The Pennsylvania State University Press, 1971), pp. 165–166; and Thomas Cleary, *Entry Into the Inconceivable: An Introduction to Hua-yen Buddhism* (Honolulu: University of Hawaii Press, 1983), pp. 37–38.

172 Stephanie Kaza, "To Save All Beings: Buddhist Environmental Activism," in Christopher Queen, ed., *Engaged Buddhism in the West* (Boston: Wisdom Publications, 2000), pp. 166–167.

173 Okumura and Leighton, *The Wholehearted Way*, pp. 22–23.

174 Donald Mitchell, *Buddhism: Introducing the Buddhist Experience*, 2nd ed. (New York, Oxford University Press, 2008), p. 325.

175 See the chapter "Ambedkar's Children" in Alan Senauke, *The Bodhisattva's Embrace: Dispatches from Engaged Buddhism's Front Lines* (Berkeley: Clear View Press, 2010), pp. 73–95.

176 See Joanna Macy, *Dharma and Development* (West Hartford, Conn.: Kumarian Press, 1983); and Macy, *World as Lover, World as Self*, pp. 125–152.

177 See www.ecobuddhism.org.

178 Naomi Klein, *The Shock Doctrine: The Rise of Disaster Capitalism* (New York: Metropolitan Books, 2007), pp. 406–422.

179 Snyder, *A Place in Space*, pp. 70–73.

180 Rothberg, *The Engaged Spiritual Life*, p. 204.

181 Walpola Rahula, *What the Buddha Taught*, rev. ed. (New York: Grove Press, 1974), p. 47.

182 Census studies from 2010 indicate the number of Americans in poverty is the highest in more than half a century, and the income gap between the rich and poor in the United States reached the greatest disparity ever in 2009. See http://www.voanews.com/english/news/US-Income-Disparity-Highest-Ever-105708773.html. As of 2007 the richest 1 percent received 24 percent of the nation's income. See http://www.slate.com/id/2266025/entry/2266026.

See also http://www.rdwolff.com/content/rising-income-inequality-us-divisive-depressing-and-dangerous.

183 See Scott Armstrong, "A Well-Grounded Air Force," *Buddhadharma* (Fall 2006), p. 88.

184 Public Papers of the Presidents, Dwight D. Eisenhower, 1960, pp. 1035–1040. See http://coursesa.matrix.msu.edu/~hst306/documents/indust.html.

185 As reported by the *Boston Globe* in January 2011, despite an apparent clear conflict of interest, from 2004 to 2008 eighty percent of retiring three or four star generals quickly took jobs as consultants or executives at weapons corporations. See http://www.boston.com/news/nation/washington/articles/2010/12/26/defense_firms_lure_retired_generals/.

Index

About the Author

TAIGEN DAN LEIGHTON is a Sōtō Zen priest and Dharma successor in the lineage of Shunryu Suzuki. Taigen first studied Buddhist art and culture in Japan in 1970, and he began formal everyday zazen and Sōtō practice in 1975 at the New York Zen Center with Kando Nakajima. Taigen then trained extensively for many years at the San Francisco Zen Center, and spent two years practicing in Japan with several Sōtō teachers. He was ordained in 1986 and received Dharma transmission in 2000 from Tenshin Reb Anderson.

Taigen is author of *Faces of Compassion: Classic Bodhisattva Archetypes and Their Modern Expression* and *Visions of Awakening Space and Time: Dōgen and the Lotus Sutra*. He is cotranslator and editor of several Zen texts, including *Dōgen's Extensive Record*; *Cultivating the Empty Field: The Silent Illumination of Zen Master Hongzhi*; *The Wholehearted Way: A Translation of Dōgen's "Bendowa" with Commentary*; and *Dōgen's Pure Standards for the Zen Community: A Translation of* Eihei Shingi. He has also contributed articles to many other books and journals.

Taigen is now resident Dharma teacher for Ancient Dragon Zen Gate in Chicago. He has long taught, and still does online, at the Graduate Theological Union in Berkeley, from where he has a Ph.D. He also currently teaches at universities in Chicago.

About Wisdom Publications

WISDOM PUBLICATIONS is dedicated to offering works relating to and inspired by Buddhist traditions.

To learn more about us or to explore our other books, please visit our website at www.wisdompubs.org.

You can subscribe to our e-newsletter or request our print catalog online, or by writing to:

Wisdom Publications
199 Elm Street
Somerville, Massachusetts 02144 USA

You can also contact us at 617-776-7416, or info@wisdompubs.org.

Wisdom is a nonprofit, charitable 501(c)(3) organization and donations in support of our mission are tax deductible.

Wisdom Publications is affiliated with the Foundation for the Preservation of the Mahayana Tradition (FPMT).